Programs to Reduce
Teen Dating Violence
and Sexual Assault

Programs to Reduce Teen Dating Violence and Sexual Assault

PERSPECTIVES ON WHAT WORKS

Arlene N. Weisz
and
Beverly M. Black

Columbia University Press   New York

Columbia University Press
Publishers Since 1893
New York   Chichester, West Sussex
Copyright © 2009 Columbia University Press
All rights reserved

Library of Congress Cataloging-in-Publication Data
Weisz, Arlene N.
Programs to reduce teen dating violence and sexual assault :
perspectives on what works / Arlene N. Weisz and Beverly M. Black.
p. cm.
Includes bibliographical references and index.
ISBN 978-0-231-13452-1 (hard cover : alk. paper)
ISBN 978-0-231-13453-8 (pbk. : alk. paper)
ISBN 978-0-231-50882-7 (ebook)
1. Dating violence—United States—Prevention. 2. Youth and violence—United States.
3. Teenage girls—Abuse of —United States. 4. Victims of dating violence—United States.
5. Child sexual abuse—United States—Prevention.
I. Black, Beverly M. II. Title.

HQ801.83.W45 2009
362.88083'0973—dc22   2008047972

Columbia University Press books are printed on permanent and durable acid-free paper.
This book is printed on paper with recycled content.
Printed in the United States of America

References to Internet Web sites (URLs) were accurate at the time of writing.
Neither the author nor Columbia University Press is responsible for URLs that may
have expired or changed since the manuscript was prepared.

To survivors of violence and those who work to prevent it.

A.N.W

In memory of my mother and Michael, and to all others who have worked and continue to work to end violence against women and dream of a world without violence.

B.M.B.

Contents

Contents

Acknowledgments

First and foremost we want to acknowledge and thank the prevention educators who participated in interviews for the book. Without their willingness to take valuable time from their busy schedules to share their knowledge and perspectives, this book would not have been possible. We are deeply grateful.

We want to thank the School of Social Work at Wayne State University for its support. Dean Phyllis Vroom initially supported our taking sabbaticals during the same semester despite the extra burden this created for her and the school. This time allowed us to work closely together throughout the semester. Dean Vroom also offered encouragement and repeatedly supported the project with use of the school's resources. The school's editor, Al Acker, provided helpful edits on the entire book. Our colleague Jerry Brandell read drafts of material and offered valuable advice; he also supported and encouraged us throughout the process. Additionally, numerous graduate students and our secretary assisted throughout this project: Ryan Hertz, Cheryl Collins, Rachel West, Rebecca Wiersma, and Marie Villanueva. We thank you for your help and comments. Our colleagues and friends, Peggy Brunhofer and Neva Nahan, listened to our many frustrations and supported our determination to continue on through to the completion of the book.

We want to thank Columbia University Press for believing in the project and especially John Michel, who saw such promise in the project during its early stages of development.

Lastly, we want to thank our families: Arlene thanks her friends and family for their support and enthusiasm about this project and her professional growth. Beverly thanks Robert for his support in all her work and especially with this long and intense project. He never complained about the many hours she devoted to the project and provided technical support for telephone gadgets and computers. Joshua and Nathan, I thank you for always asking how the book was coming along.

Programs to Reduce
Teen Dating Violence
and Sexual Assault

[1]

Introduction

Goals for the Book

This book describes the successful programs that experienced practitioners have implemented to prevent dating violence and sexual assault among adolescents. The authors, experienced researchers and prevention-program coordinators themselves, have observed that prevention practitioners seldom publish their experience or research and often are too busy to attend conferences to share their knowledge. We therefore undertook to write this book so our readers can learn from experienced presenters of teen dating violence and sexual assault prevention programs across the United States. As the book describes in detail, we interviewed experienced practitioners across the country. Our goal was to learn as much as possible about prevention programming. We also conducted an extensive review of published literature relevant to these programs, so that we can present both practice and published wisdom.

Our own work in youth dating violence and sexual assault prevention began more than ten years ago. We coordinated a prevention program for middle school youth in Detroit over a five-year period. We offered this program primarily in a charter school setting, with a brief change of venue to a youth program in a large church. Beverly Black went on to coordinate a prevention program in public middle schools in Detroit for another four years. We both have also worked with adolescents in other settings.

Working with prevention programs taught us a great deal but also raised many questions that were not answered in the literature or at conferences. Although prevention programs across the United States were doing excellent work with adolescents, only a few published their experiences or presented them at meetings. As a result, we developed a plan to interview prevention practitioners across the country. It was a privilege to talk with these hard-working, thoughtful people, and we are excited to share their thoughts and experiences with our readers.

In this chapter we discuss why practice wisdom, along with research studies, can make an important contribution to continuing and improving prevention programs. We also address the strengths and limitations of both empirical evaluations of prevention programs and the literature about practitioners' views on research.

Prevalence of Dating Violence and Sexual Assault among Adolescents

Before our first prevention program we talked with staff members of public schools in our city and learned that the teachers and counselors who worked closely with youth every day were well aware that many adolescents experience dating violence and sexual assault. Many people who work with adolescents often do not need research to tell them that this is a common and serious problem among their clients or students. At the same time research findings support practitioners' concerns that dating violence and sexual assault are serious societal problems.

Studies in the U.S. have found that between 11% and 59% of high school students have experienced dating violence (Bergman 1992; Center for Disease Control [CDC] 2003; Foshee et al. 1996; Malik, Sorenson, and Aneshensel 1997; Molidor and Tolman 1998; Silverman et al. 2001) and that dating violence impacts youths' physical and psychological well-being (Callahan, Tolman, and Saunders 2003; Silverman et al. 2001). Data also suggest that adolescent victims of abusive relationships may carry these abusive patterns into future relationships (Smith, White, and Holland 2003). Although definitions of sexual assault in published studies vary, these studies report that between 9% and 18% of female adolescents have been sexually victimized by a dating partner (Foshee et al. 1996; Molidor and Tolman 1998; O'Keefe and Treister 1998). The CDC's Youth Risk Behavior Screening Survey (YRBSS) (CDC 2008), which assesses risk behaviors among adolescents across the United States, revealed that over 7.8% of high school students reported that they had been physically forced to have sex when they did not want to.

Some literature on dating violence reports equal rates of perpetration by girls and boys (Halpern et al. 2001; Molidor and Tolman 1998). Several studies suggest, however, that dating violence is more frightening, and often more injurious, for girls than for boys (Bennett and Fineran 1998; Molidor and Tolman 1998). Foshee et al. (1996) found that 70% of girls and 52% of boys who were abused by a dating partner reported an injury from an abusive relationship. Literature on sexual assault continues to report that males are more likely than females to be the perpetrators (Foshee et al. 1996; Jezl, Molidor, and Wright 1996; Loh et al. 2005).

Importance of Primary Prevention

During the last fifteen to twenty years, youth dating violence and sexual assault prevention programs have been spreading across the United States. Currently the CDC's Injury Research Agenda, Healthy People 2010, places a high priority on the evaluation of programs that intervene before violence occurs, specifically mentioning the reduction of intimate partner and sexual violence. Other federal agencies, such as the National Institute of Justice, and private organizations, such as the Liz Claiborne Foundation and Robert Wood Johnson Foundation, have focused on adolescent dating violence and sexual assault. Prevention programs that target youths are hoping to engage in "primary prevention," reaching the target audience before any violence or sexual assault occurs (Wolfe and Jaffe 2003). This contrasts with "secondary prevention programs" that focus on selected high-risk groups, and "tertiary prevention programs" that attempt to minimize the deleterious effects of violence that has already occurred (Wolfe and Jaffe 2003). Focusing on youth for primary prevention efforts seems appropriate, as younger people are less likely to have been dating or to have already been victims of physical or sexual assaults associated with dating and male-female social interaction.

Strengths and Limitations of Empirical Program Evaluation

Empirical evaluation of youth dating violence and sexual assault prevention programming is essential, for, without such evaluations, there is a risk of spending a great deal of energy and money on programming that may well prove ineffective. Relying solely on practitioners' views about the effectiveness of their own work may, of course, lead to inaccurate assessments, as there are no "checks and balances" and "overgeneralization" may result (Padgett 2004). Because practitioners view certain techniques as effective, they may interpret all responses to those techniques as positive and overlook negative results. Nevertheless, quantitative evaluation approaches have limitations, as we summarize below, and so practitioners' narratives and views can contribute substantially to the continuing development of prevention programs.

Advantages of Disseminating Practice Wisdom

Writers vary somewhat in their definitions of "practice wisdom," but most agree that it encompasses reflection and learning based on accumulated

experience in practice (Dybicz 2004). Practice wisdom grasps the rich-
ness and variety of human situations that practitioners encounter, whereas
quantitative research is sometimes limited in its capacity to illuminate the
many complex variables that an ecological view (Bronfenbrenner 1977) of
human interactions should take into account:

> One cannot both measure some social event clearly and yet grasp its dy-
> namic complexity. It has been the tendency of empiricists to focus closely
> on specific client attributes without providing equivalent attention to the
> client and situation in totality. (Klein and Bloom 1995, 800)

According to Weick (1999), many practitioners feel that research does not
capture the "messiness" of actual practice.

Practice wisdom can provide knowledge that goes beyond pure guess-
work and bridges the gap between science and practice (Dybicz, 2004; Klein
and Bloom, 1995). Klein and Bloom (1995) discuss how workers formulate
and test tentative hypotheses based on their practice experience and the
available scientific knowledge. Their work, therefore, is not haphazard, and
their judgment and creativity include the coordination of positive unexpect-
ed events and enable them to react to crucial negative events that are difficult
to measure. Patton (1990) stresses that case studies can provide meaningful
depth and detail, including information about the context of a program.
"For example," in the words of Patton (1990, 54), "a great deal can often be
learned about how to improve a program by studying select dropouts, failure, or successes." Practice wisdom, therefore, can come from experienced
practitioners regardless of whether their programs are exemplary.

Some investigators argue that the interactions between service workers
and their clients may be valuable and meaningful in ways that are impossible to quantify (Imre 1982). For example, the personal warmth or cha-
risma, or the messages of some prevention program presenters, may have
unquantifiable influence on young people. The non-measurable aspects of
programs may have an impact long after researchers might have been able
to measure relatively long-term changes. Moreover, quantitative research
may be unable, thus far, to fully specify practitioners' interactions with
unique human beings (Klein and Bloom 1995). Padgett (2004, 9) notes
that qualitative methods are attractive, because they might grasp the "ever-
changing, messy world of practice." Weick (1999, 330) reminds us that
even a so-called hard science like physics, for example, now recognizes
the importance of "complexity and indeterminacy." Patton (1990) asserts
that researchers sometimes lose specificity and detail in quantitative data,

because these data group respondents together. Qualitative researchers, on the other hand, can gain rich details from interviews.

Surveys of social work students indicate that "learning derived from significant others" (Fook 2001, 126) was their most significant experiences in learning how to practice. Similarly, social workers report that they prefer consultation with expert colleagues to learning from published research (Mullen and Bacon 2004). Thus practice wisdom in literature potentially allows practitioners to learn from experienced individuals. By presenting wisdom from a variety of practitioners, we offer our readers an array of ideas that might increase the effectiveness of their practice. We are not claiming that one practitioner's approach is better than another, and so this book does not represent "authority-based claims" which have been criticized by some evidence-based practitioners (Gambrill 1999).

Klein and Bloom (1995, 804) describe how practice wisdom "is most fully developed" when practitioners' experiential learning can be "articulated in open communication with other professionals," and they believe that communicating to others is essential for knowledge to grow. Thus, some of those who participated in interviews for this book were helped in the process to articulate their practice wisdom. Most of the interviewees were enthusiastic and described the questions as "thought-provoking and thorough." Another benefit of interviewing is that it is a holistic approach (Patton 1990); although we divided interviewees' comments into sections in order to write about them, the answers reflect the interviewees' awareness of their holistic, interconnected experiences in prevention work.

Consistent with the idea that one does not have to choose between empirical and practice experience, this book includes both. At the same time that some practitioners use findings from quantitative research to improve their practice, they also respect the practice wisdom that their programs have accumulated.

Limitations of Prevention Programming Research in General

Although the literature suggests that prevention programs for adolescents can be effective (Durlak 1997; Nation et al. 2003), it is not easy to demonstrate these successes through empirical research. Some investigators note that few rigorously evaluated prevention projects have shown large effect sizes (making a noticeable difference regardless of statistical significance) (Tebes, Kaufman, and Connell 2003). There are multiple reasons for this difficulty, including lack of consistent standards for determining effectiveness, (Nation et al. 2003) as well as the difficulty of measuring behavioral changes.

A criticism of positivistic evaluation is that it is not always clear that statistically significant changes are truly meaningful (Edleson 1996). Researchers disagree as to which evidence proves that a program is worth adopting. Experts suggest that pre-post changes for a single sample are not necessarily good indicators and tend to "overestimate the effects of interventions" (Biglan et al. 2003, 435). The most rigorous prevention experts believe that programs should not be adopted without several randomized or time-series studies. In a randomized study, adolescents would be randomly assigned to intervention and non-intervention groups to avoid potential bias. Researchers also warn that publications about programs that were shown to be effective in one setting should include the caveat that they may not work in different settings or might even be harmful (Biglan et al. 2003). Evaluations should be done with numerous populations, various settings, and differing time frames. Moreover, it might require years to determine the parts of programs that would be effective under varying conditions.

Researchers consider randomized trials to be the gold standard of evaluation research (Biglan et al. 2003), but controlled scientific evaluations are difficult to replicate for several reasons. They are expensive (Nation et al. 2003), and the evaluations place a high priority on the consistent, measurable specification of concepts and processes that practitioners often find difficult to duplicate.

In recommending adoption of an empirically demonstrated prevention procedure, program developers often "fail to adequately take into account the local conditions of a given experiment" (Tebes, Kaufman, and Connell 2003, 45). Even when research shows that a program is effective, the published report may not give enough information to determine whether the program would work well with other populations. A program with empirically validated effectiveness "may have no beneficial effect or even a harmful effect when it is applied in a new setting, provided to a different population, or provided by a new type of provider" (Biglan et al. 2003, 6). Some investigators consider this to be a serious limitation in prevention programs, where "few propositions hold across all situations. To say that a program has been found to be 'effective' is to say very little unless one specifies what the program consisted of, for whom it made a difference, under what conditions" (Reid 1994, 470). Silverman (2003) asserts that prevention interventions addressing behavioral dysfunctions must include awareness that these behaviors are in a constant state of evolution as preventionists try to respond to changing transactional and ecological elements. So although replication is valuable for both practitioners and researchers, it becomes difficult to replicate and evaluate programs that respond to many changing elements.

Published outcome-focused empirical evaluations rarely describe the content of the programs in detail and almost never identify the most effective aspects of these programs. This drawback makes it hard for practitioners to learn from such evaluations. Rones and Hoagwood (2000, 238) note that studies leave many "unanswered questions about the active ingredients that lead to successful program implementation and dissemination."

Nation et al. (2003) suggest that practitioners are looking for practical information about what works, whereas funders are looking for evidence-based information. Although research-based programs are usually much too expensive for local programs to replicate, the general-effectiveness principles gained from research might help local programs distill and implement those elements that are cost-effective.

Strengths and Limitations of Evaluations of Adolescent Dating Violence and Sexual Assault Prevention Programs

Some well-executed evaluations of prevention programs have been published (Avery-Leaf et al. 1997; Foshee et al. 2004). However, reviewers have suggested limitations of even the most rigorous studies (Cornelius and Resseguie 2007; Meyer and Stein 2004), which itself indicates how difficult it is to design and empirically evaluate a good intervention. Acosta et al.'s (2001) review of literature about youth violence, covering articles from 1980 to 1999, found that prevention articles were less common than articles on assessment and treatment. In addition, only 5 of 154 articles on prevention were about preventing dating violence.

The literature contains only a few convincing empirical evaluations of dating violence and sexual assault prevention programs for adolescents. Most published evaluations of sexual assault prevention programs concern college students. Evaluated prevention programs for younger children and adolescents often cover sexual assault in the context of general violence prevention (Shapiro 1999). Because of developmental differences between college students and middle or high school students, much of the research on college prevention programs only suggests the approaches that might work with younger populations.

Although "most domestic violence programs in the United States have set prevention of domestic violence as a part of their missions" (Edleson 2000), these efforts are usually under-funded. Meyer and Stein (2004) reviewed school-based prevention programs across the United States and found that they "were not very effective at preventing relationship violence in the short term, and less effective in the long term" (198). Knowledge gains about dating violence were the most common improvements resulting from programs, but Meyer and Stein questioned "how knowledge about relationship violence translates into actual violent behavior and the likelihood that one will engage in such behavior" (ibid., 201).

Begun (2003, 643) also asserts, "Strong and convincing evidence does not currently exist to suggest that any particular strategies work as primary prevention of intimate partner violence." She reports that some studies have shown effects on knowledge and attitudes but have rarely demonstrated the persistence of these effects. Furthermore, studies have not addressed differences between girls and boys or between high school and middle school youths, and have also not shown that the programs change actual dating behaviors.

Another limitation of empirical evaluations of dating violence and sexual assault prevention programs is that programs usually attempt to change attitudes and knowledge rather than behaviors (Wolfe and Jaffe 2003). Controversy exists over whether changes in attitudes or knowledge lead to behavioral changes, which are clearly important but difficult to measure (Schewe and Bennett 2002). Of course, prevention programs have the additional problem of measuring the extent to which the target group avoided dangerous behaviors as a result of the intervention. A study would need to employ carefully matched comparison or control groups in order to estimate this outcome. A related important problem is that programs often only address prevention messages to young women, but potential victims have no control over potential perpetrators. Thus changes in potential victims' attitudes, knowledge, or behaviors may have little or no effects on rates of victimization. This makes it difficult to evaluate programs that are directed to both potential victims and potential perpetrators.

Although O'Brien (2001) asserts that the powerful short-term impact of school-based dating violence prevention programs is promising, few empirical evaluations have been able to use follow-up measures (Cornelius and Resseguie 2007). It is difficult, therefore, to determine whether improvements attributed to empirically validated prevention programs were sustained.

Few research projects have examined which program components contribute to effectiveness in youth dating violence prevention (Avery-Leaf and Cascardi 2002; Schewe 2003b; Whitaker et al. 2006). Schewe (2002) notes that journals rarely publish studies with negative outcomes. This is unfortunate, since even unsuccessful programs may reveal important issues. Some programs may be considered successful based on a very short questionnaire or may only be successful with females, whereas a program reporting a more comprehensive evaluation might appear unsuccessful.

Introduction

Practitioners' Views on Research

The literature suggests that some human-services practitioners are reluctant to use published research. The few publications that have documented practitioners' views on research (Fook 2001; Mouradian, Mechanic, and Williams 2001) note that practitioners believe that research is sometimes not "user friendly" and that researchers may fail to address practitioners' questions and concerns. The National Violence Against Women Prevention Research Center (Mouradian, Mechanic, and Williams 2001) conducted focus groups with 130 practitioners and concluded that "most evident was a strong emphasis on the need for research that will determine 'what works' to prevent and combat violence against women" (4). The practitioners also emphasized the need for research that is presented in a format that is "easy to read and understand; 'user-friendly' (a term used often in different focus groups); timely; concise; [and] easy to access" (6). Rehr et al. (1998) assert that practitioners often resist participating in evaluative research, because it seems to highlight their practice deficits. We note practitioners' concerns about research here to show how practice wisdom can add to the literature. However, as practitioners/researchers ourselves, we hope this book helps both researchers and practitioners to understand each other's perspectives and to further joint efforts to improve the effectiveness of prevention programming.

In later chapters we describe how we gathered practice wisdom largely by interviewing prevention practitioners. Then we proceed to share that wisdom, together with findings and ideas from the literature. We attempt to summarize practitioners' thoughts and solutions in each chapter, rather than attempting to evaluate their responses. Each chapter, therefore, presents various approaches to program implementation and responses to dilemmas in prevention practice. The book concludes with a discussion of the current state of prevention programming, the current tensions in the field, and how programs might develop in the future.

Project Design and Methodology

In gathering the information for this book, we did not evaluate the programs. However, our own practices and beliefs did affect the questions we asked the interviewees whose responses are a major portion of this book. Our personal views also influenced how we selected and organized the data from the interviews and the literature.

Why Combine Dating Violence and Sexual Assault?

The decision to combine wisdom from both dating violence and sexual assault prevention practitioners was partly the result of our strong interest in both areas of prevention. Moreover, many programs address both issues simultaneously, and even programs that attempt to treat each problem area separately may find an overlap in content. We are also aware that combining sexual assault and dating violence risks minimizing the importance of each and may lead to overlooking important differences, such as the frequent occurrence of sexual assault among adolescents not in a dating relationship.

Recruiting Practitioners to Interview

We sent letters to eighty statewide coalitions concerned with reducing domestic violence, sexual assault, or both, requesting the names of exemplary prevention programs for youth and staff members we might interview. Some states had two coalitions, and others had only one. We did not define "exemplary," deliberately allowing coalitions to define that term based on reputation, rather than scientifically derived criteria of excellence. This flexible concept of excellence was expected to help us achieve our goal of including programs that did not have the resources for extensive evaluation. Obviously this non-probability sample has inherent problems, but we believe that the knowledge gained will nevertheless be useful.

Appendix A lists the fifty-two programs that we contacted for interviews, representing twenty-two states and Washington, D.C. Of these, the program suggestions came from coalitions in eighteen states and Washington, D.C. In one state, programs were strictly self-nominated, and in another they were nominated by a coalition and by interviewees from that state. In still another state, both an expert colleague and a coalition nominated programs. In two states, only expert colleagues nominated programs. Our method of recruiting programs yielded a convenience sample, not a representative one. We have no data on the number of programs that existed in the United States or in the individual states in 2004, the year we conducted the interviews, so no statistics can be offered about the percentage of programs we were able to interview.

The coalitions' recommendations yielded seventy-three programs, and we added a few programs that nominated themselves or were nominated by expert colleagues. We then sent letters to the coordinators of seventy-seven programs and followed up with telephone calls to establish appointments for interviews. In a few cases, we did not contact programs nominated by coalitions, primarily because we received the nominations late and our sample had already grown much larger than we had initially planned. Judging from conversations and e-mail exchanges with several of the nominated programs, the primary reason some programs gave for their unwillingness to be interviewed was the educators' lack of time. The final sample of fifty-two programs includes almost all programs that agreed to interviews. Two programs that were willing to be interviewed were not included, as we already had a sufficient number of programs from that state or because interviews could not be arranged within our time constraints. We are extremely grateful to the interviewees for sharing their time and ideas with us.

Locations of the Programs

Fortunately we were able to include most of the regions of the U.S. in our sample. Of the fifty-two programs, the largest number, twenty-five, were located in urban areas (U.S. Census Bureau, 2005). Twelve programs were located in strictly suburban areas, with an additional five in areas defined as suburban and urban, and another two in areas described as suburban and rural. Finally, seven centers were located in strictly rural areas, with an additional one in an area designated as rural and urban. This distribution seems logical, because the areas with the highest population density are the most likely to have a need for and be able to support prevention programs.

The Interviews

With limited opportunities for travel, we expected to conduct most of the interviews by telephone. Distance or technology was not a significant obstacle, because we had previous experience doing telephone interviews. Whenever possible, we conducted interviews in person, because we thought the opportunity to meet the prevention educators and see their offices would be useful. We were able to conduct in-person interviews at eleven programs, including some in California, Texas, Louisiana, Illinois, and Michigan. Because our interviews represent a convenience sample and are not evaluative, we do not focus on possible differences between the in-person and telephone interviews. Most interviews lasted about an hour, with a few lasting only forty-five minutes and two or three extending up to one and a half hours.

Our semi-structured interview guide is shown in Appendix B. The questions were based on a review of the literature and our experiences creating and coordinating our own prevention programs for middle school youth and for our university community. We have cited all the literature reviewed before conducting the interviews elsewhere in this book.

We conducted the first interview together, in person, but did the rest separately in person or by phone, following the interview guide. We sometimes used different probes, but our interviewing styles did not differ substantially. Two research assistants reviewed four randomly selected interview transcripts to see how closely each of us adhered to the interview guide. Out of a potential 296 questions across all four interviews, we did not ask 21 (7 percent) of the questions. Our adherence rate actually may have been higher, as we sometimes did not want to waste interviewees' time by asking questions with obvious answers in the context of the interview. For example, if interviewees told us that they presented only in classrooms to all students, we did not ask them if they made special efforts to recruit youth already in violent relationships. We also stopped asking for nominations of other programs, as our sample had grown much larger than we had anticipated.

We asked all interviewees if they wished to review the interview guide before the interview, and we e-mailed the guide to those who wanted to see it. Most interviewees did want to see the guide in advance, but the amount of time interviewees had available to review it varied. We did not ask how much time they spent preparing for the interview, and we know that those who reviewed the guide thoroughly before the interview might have given different responses compared to those who did not review it. Again, because these interviews are not evaluative, we do not believe that differences in the level of preparation for the interviews affected the results appreciably.

Wayne State University's Human Investigation Committee approved this research, and we used a standard telephone consent form to inform the interviewees about the parameters of this research and their rights as "subjects." All interviews were tape-recorded and transcribed. Our only funding was a small grant from Wayne State University, and we used the grant to help cover transcription costs. To ensure that they accurately reflected participants' thoughts, we offered to e-mail respondents transcripts of their own interviews. Most of the interviewees took advantage of this offer, but few responded with corrections or further thoughts.

Interviewees

In most cases we received the names of agency directors or directors of prevention programming, and these individuals either participated in the interviews themselves or referred their most qualified staff members. All interviewees were prevention educators themselves or closely supervised the prevention educators. We usually interviewed one person from an agency, but in six interviews two staff members participated together, and in one agency three people were interviewed together, at their request. We conducted only one interview per agency.

Demographics of the Interviewees

All but two of the prevention programs we examined were part of larger agencies primarily designed to address violence against women with a variety of services. Some of the interviewed prevention educators performed other duties at their agencies, such as counseling or crisis intervention. Others were exclusively involved in prevention education. The number of paid prevention educators at the agencies varied from one to ten.

All but three of the sixty-one interviewees were female. They ranged in age from 22 to 65, with a mean age of 37.04 (SD = 12.23); the median age was 32. Twenty-eight interviewees had a bachelor's degree, and twenty-four had a master's degree. Three had JDs or other post master's education, and two had some college or technical training. The most common educational background among the interviewees was social work, sociology, psychology, and education. Most (80%) of the interviewees were European American, and several interviewees identified themselves as African American (5%); Mexican American or Latina (5%); Asian, Southeast Asian, or Pacific Islander (5%); bi-racial (3%); and Middle Eastern (1.6%).

Organization of the Data

We each coded our own interviews using the QSR-N6 software program to code the interview transcripts, according to the major program areas addressed in the interview. The software enabled us to code paragraphs and included the option of applying several different codes to the same paragraph. Our initial coding scheme followed the interview guide and divided the data into the chapters that were planned for the book. We each coded one of the other's randomly selected interviews and then had two graduate research assistants conduct a test of inter-rater reliability, which yielded a rate of 85% agreement between us.

Because paragraphs could contain multiple chapter topic codes, we were confident that each of us would have a good opportunity to view the data relevant to our chapters. Within chapters, we used a grounded theory (Strauss and Corbin 1990) approach to organize the data and minimize how much our preconceptions affected what we learned from the interviews. We each used spreadsheets to sub-code the content within our chapters according to themes and solutions for the specific issues and dilemmas addressed in the chapter. Finally, for stylistic consistency and another perspective, we contributed to each other's chapters.

Although we counted the number of programs that addressed each theme, our discussion includes percentages of programs that address particular topics, rather than reporting an exact count or stating which programs cover specific topics. We do not report exact counts, as interviewees might have forgotten to mention a particular topic or issue, even though it was important to their program. A space between the quotations throughout the book indicates that a new interviewee is speaking; ellipses in the quotations indicate deleted text. If we interviewed more than one person from the same program, their comments are included in a single quotation. The "unit of analysis," therefore, is programs, not individuals.

Limitations

We recognize that selecting programs by reputation may mean that some programs in our sample might not meet our own standards of excellence or the standards of scientific evaluation. Coalitions might have recommended programs based on their friendships with staff members or their approval of the philosophy of certain programs. Although we were unable to interview staff members from many exemplary programs functioning in the U.S., we believe that our approach allowed us to reach programs that may not have had resources for evaluation, as well as to include a broad selection of programs.

We do not attempt to evaluate whether the "quality" of interviewees' programs matched the interviewees' beliefs about the programs' effectiveness, as we observed only one of our interviewees' programs in action. To repeat the point: our goal was to inform readers about practitioners' ideas and experiences, not to determine the validity of the ideas in the programs. Readers can compensate for possible biases inherent in using one or two practitioners' descriptions of their own programs, because we include ideas from a substantial number of experienced prevention practitioners. The use of practice wisdom allowed us to obtain access to various ideas from a wide array of settings, which we believe will enable readers to find suggestions that might be useful in their own settings. Even though we have tried to describe rather than evaluate, our own biases inevitably influenced the selection and organization of the interview data.

[3]

Theoretical Considerations

The theoretical perspectives that guide violence prevention programs emphasize social learning and feminist theories. This chapter discusses how these perspectives influence program content and offers different views on the importance of theory-based prevention programming.

Theoretical frameworks have rarely guided research on dating violence and sexual assault (O'Keefe 1997) or the development and structure of programs to prevent these problems. Increasingly, however, researchers are calling for prevention programs to integrate theoretical foundations, as the most effective prevention programs may be those that articulate their beliefs about the causes of rape and base their programs on those beliefs (Schewe 2002). About 60% of the prevention programs whose staff members we interviewed identified a theory upon which their program was based.

Theoretical Perspectives

Wekerle and Wolfe (1999) state that social learning, attachment, and feminist theories are the three most influential theoretical perspectives on relationship violence research and intervention. Whitaker et al.'s (2006) review of the literature on primary prevention interventions for partner violence found that all eleven of the programs in their study used some combination of feminist theory and social learning theory. Although these theories may guide some research on violence interventions and model prevention programs, little is known about whether many community programs base their work on these theories. In fact, the prevention educators we interviewed agreed with the literature and identified the same two major theories—social learning and feminist theory—as guiding their programming. About half of the interviewees identified a social learning theory or its principles as key to guiding their programs; the other half identified feminist theory. Prevention educators also cited various other theories that guide their programs.

Social Learning Theory

Social learning theory, generally recognized as the predominant theory in relationship violence research, suggests that aggressive and violent behaviors are learned from prior experiences (Bandura 1977). The theory is an expectancy model that involves six components: expectancies, skill building, observational learning, modeling, self-efficacy, and reinforcement (Lanier et al. 1998). Rewards derived from the use of violence may include decreasing conflict-related aversiveness (e.g., feelings of tension, perceptions of neediness) (Jacobson et al. 1994) and increasing feelings of personal control (Dutton 1995). Children learn violence through direct behavioral conditioning or by observing and imitating the behaviors they witness (Lewis and Fremouw 2001). When children see others rewarded for violence, this vicarious reinforcement plays an important role. Social learning theory suggests that violence is often intergenerational, most likely comes from one's family of origin, and develops over the life course, beginning in childhood and adolescence (Anderson and Kras 2007; O'Leary 1988; Whitaker et al. 2006).

The literature on violence and its etiology generally supports the use of social learning theory (Cappella 2006; Jackson 1999). Researchers studying violence and aggressive behaviors often agree that violence is learned behavior (Anderson and Kras 2007; Weist and Cooley-Quille 2001). The early work of Bernard and Bernard (1983) indicated a direct mirroring of violence in that the exact types of aggression observed or experienced in the family were perpetrated in youths' dating relationships. Most researchers, however, also contend that violence is a complex learned behavior. Social learning theory clearly does not provide a complete explanation, given that not all children who observe aggression become perpetrators and some children who have not observed violence or experienced abuse nevertheless perpetrate sexual or physical violence in dating relationships, or both.

Numerous prevention programs discussed in the literature have been grounded in social learning theory. Gottfredson, Wilson, and Najaka's (2002) review of 178 school-based crime prevention studies found that the most effective interventions were cognitive-behaviorally based or targeted to social competency, using cognitive-behavioral methods. Whitaker et al.'s (2005) review of partner violence primary prevention programs that used quasi-experimental or randomization in some form also found that all the studies used social learning theory in some form as a basis for their intervention.

Dating violence and sexual assault prevention programs similarly identify social learning theory as the basis of their programs. For example, de Anda's (1999) ten-session cognitive behavioral violence prevention program in Los Angeles with Latino and African American youth taught students to reduce anger arousal by using relaxation exercises, changing their thoughts (self-talk) and beliefs, or with alternative nonviolent coping responses. The program, "Ending Violence: A Curriculum for Educating Teens on Domestic Violence and Law," is based on social leaning theory and targets Latino youths' attitudes about violence between intimates (Jaycox et al. 2006). Gidycz et al.'s (2001) one-hour rape prevention program, primarily based on social learning theory, found significantly less acceptance of rape myths in the intervention group compared to the comparison group.

Fifteen interviewees readily identified social learning theory as the basis of their programs. Others were less sure of the theory upon which they based their program, but they effectively described social learning theory despite being unable to identify it by name:

> Well, I would say our theory is that all bad behaviors are learned behaviors. Otherwise, we would have no hope for what we're doing . . . although a small percentage of abusers and rapists do have a mental illness problem or a chemical imbalance or something like that . . . [we believe] you still choose to do this stuff because you'd get away with it in our society.

> We do know that there's a tremendous amount of violence in the media. I know the kids are exposed to more violence; the video games have become more violent, more violence on TV. I think it is an environmental, situational thing. I'm not sure that's the specific cause of all of this, but I certainly think it contributes to the violence. We live in a very violent society now and the kids are very aware of that. They are surrounded by violence on an everyday basis. How they react to that becomes, I think, extremely important.

Feminist Theory

Feminist theory is also prominent in the research on violence against women. Many prevention programs are based on the feminist view that violence toward women is rooted in women's secondary roles and subjugated low status throughout history (de Beauvoir 1957). Feminist theory focuses on patriarchy, "the domination of the major political, economic, cultural and legal systems by men and stresses the need to identify the attitudes, expectations, language behaviors and social arrangements that have contributed to the oppression and marginalization of people" (Robbins, Chatterjee, and Canda 2006, 97). The feminist bell hooks (1984, 240) expands on the definition of feminism:

> Feminism is the struggle to end sexist oppression. Its aim is not to benefit solely any specific group of women, any particular race or class of women. It does not privilege women over men. It has the power to transform in a meaningful way all our lives. . . . Feminism as a movement to end sexist oppression directs our attention to systems of domination and the inter-relatedness of sex, race, and class oppression.

Feminist theory views violence against women as a social and political problem affecting all women, and it locates relationship violence within the pervading traditional power structures of male dominance and female subservience. All forms of abuse are about the power and control that is embedded in a patriarchal value system (Jackson 1999). Rape is viewed as a mode of systemic violence against women within the patriarchal structure and functions as a tool to dominate and control women. Briere and Malamuth's (1983) early writings describe rape as an extension of a male-dominated, competitive culture within a patriarchal society. A feminist analysis of rape would suggest that prevention efforts need to be directed at those who commit rape, not those who are raped. To prevent rape, we must change the patriarchal structures in society that permit rape to occur. Societal, not individual, changes must take place.

Many of the early dating violence prevention programs in the literature present themselves as grounded in feminism (Jaffe et al. 1992; Jones 1998; Krajewski et al. 1996). Sexual assault prevention programs were similarly feminist-based. Lonsway et al.'s (1998) rape prevention education program sought to challenge rape-supportive ideology by using a feminist framework. More recently, Salazar and Cook's (2006) gender-specific and culturally relevant "Violence Prevention Mentoring Program" for African American adolescent males is guided by feminist theory. Whitaker et al.'s (2006) review of programs on primary prevention of partner violence suggests that all programs emphasized feminist theory to some degree in that they discuss the nature of power and control issues in relationship violence.

The findings from our interviews support the literature's contention that feminist theory grounds many prevention programs. When asked to

identify the theory upon which they base their program, 30% of all interviewees mentioned feminism:

> I would say that at heart, our prevention effort is in line with the whole
> rape movement in terms of male privilege and the philosophy that a man
> has the right to have power over a woman or coercion is an acceptable
> thing. I think that that part of our prevention work, we're certainly in
> touch with debunking that, concentrating on the right of every person to
> be self-determining.

> I think it's feminist theory, radical feminist theory. We're challenging
> power structures. We're having kids step back and look at where they get
> their beliefs from and looking at who has power and who has control and
> how does this impact access to resources, how our laws are made, our
> political system, victimization and violence.

Empowerment Theory

Many interviewees described empowerment theory, which encompasses
many aspects of the feminist model and addresses the dynamics of discrimination and oppression, focusing on people's awareness of the exter-
nal and structural barriers that lead to injustice and inequality and prevent their well-being. This theory advocates greater access to resources
and power for disenfranchised individuals and groups. Gutierrez (1990,
2) states that empowerment is a "process of increasing personal, interpersonal or political power so that individuals, families and communities
can take action to improve their situations." Solomon (1987) also emphasizes people's need to identify the events and conditions that inhibit them
from developing the skills to be empowered. Some interviewees specifically identified empowerment theory; others talked about feminism and
empowerment simultaneously:

> We consider ourselves to be working under an empowerment model and
> the idea is to give our clients the benefit of our knowledge and experi-
> ence and our skills and information about all of the choices available to
> them and the potential consequences of one's actions. But we fully sup-
> port them in making their own decisions. We are very conscious at not
> pushing the idea of what is best on them or rushing clients to take action
> before they are ready or making judgments about clients who choose to
> do something that is not safe for them or good for them and letting them
> know that we . . . it is okay to make mistakes and even if they go back to

their abusers . . . they can always come back . . . it is really challenging taking that position with teens because there is such an impulse to rescue them, because we know better.

Our agency works on the theory of empowerment . . . everything that we do is done to give students a tool to do things and to give them options, resources and alternatives. I think the pro-feminist piece as well, just a nature of what we are doing with kids.

Other Theoretical Approaches

Some primary prevention programs are also founded on other theoretical models (Silverman 2003). Attachment theory, for example, is generally regarded as an influential perspective on research and intervention in relationship violence (Wekerle and Wolfe 1999). Attachment theory (Bowlby 1969, 1982) proposes that children form mental representations of relationships based on their history with significant caregivers. Healthy partnerships stem from secure attachment models, derived from consistent and responsive child rearing. Dysfunctional relationships stem from insecure working models, derived from inconsistent, aversive, intrusive, or unresponsive care giving (Wekerle and Wolfe 1999). Attachment theory suggests that programs should focus on relational changes from the perspective of the individual in an effort to develop healthier, more balanced models of relationships (Wekerle and Wolfe 1999). None of the interviewees identified attachment theory as the basis of their programs.

Ecological systems theory is another model that can be used to help understand the varied causes of violence and guide prevention programs. It recognizes that multiple factors and several systemic levels interact with one another to explain human behavior. The ecological approach identifies different facets of an environment (microsystem, mesosystem, macrosystem, and exosystem) that exert influences on all individuals. This approach also helps us understand human behavior (Bronfenbrenner 1977). The ecological systems model (Germain 1980) focuses on transactions between people and their environments at the various system levels.

An understanding of the various system levels involved in forming human behavior provides guidance for some prevention programming. Weist and Cooley-Quille (2001, 148) state that "multiple levels are involved in the etiology of youth-related violence and each must be the target of intervention to effectively reduce this public health problem." Effective violence prevention programs need to be holistic and address individual characteristics (e.g., antisocial behavior, psychological dysfunction), family variables (e.g., economic status, parental substance abuse, divorce, family abuse, parenting skills), and societal factors (e.g., access to weapons, media violence, inequitable educational and occupational opportunities) (Webber 1997). Foshee et al.'s (1996) dating violence prevention program used an ecological-systems to examine the etiology of dating violence. The researchers examined multiple domains of influence on adolescent behaviors, as opposed to only individual predictors of behaviors. Their program addressed factors at the social/environment level (peer environment, family environment, social norms) and at the individual level (personal competencies, involvement in problem behaviors, and demographic characteristics). Nadel et al.'s (1996) school-based violence prevention program, also grounded on systems theory, focused on three levels of intervention: individual, interpersonal relations, and social contexts. Only one of the interviewees explained how ecological systems assisted her program in understanding violence.

The literature identifies a few other theories as grounding violence prevention programs. Sheehan et al. (1996), for example, talk about the theory of planned behavior. This theory suggests that one's intention to perform, or not to perform, an act is the strongest predictor of one's future behavior (Ajzen and Madden 1986). None of our interviewees mentioned the theory of planned behavior. Heppner et al.'s (1995a) prevention program used the elaboration likelihood model (Petty and Cacioppo 1986) to guide their program designed to change students' attitudes and beliefs about rape. None of our interviewees identified this theory as the basis for their programs. This model suggests that people lacking motivation to change their attitudes are more likely to respond positively to a presentation if they find the presenter appealing. The transient nature of attitude change, when it is based on presenter characteristics versus personal motivation to change, presents challenges for prevention programs (Heppner et al. 1995).

Multiple Theories

Effective prevention programs may need to integrate more than one theoretical foundation. Of the interviewees who identified a theory, half identified more than one theory as the basis for their programs:

> The theory that I base all of my work is that we come from a position of "violence is about power and control. Violence comes from a place of oppression. And violence is learned, and, therefore, it can be unlearned." And so . . . most of my work comes from that.

It is based on a feminist theory, a humanistic approach, and absolutely with us having such a connection culturally with the work that, absolutely, the foundation is part of the civil rights movement. We try to take that approach in regards to nonviolence. I believe it is an empowerment [approach].

Most of what we do here . . . is based on an empowerment theory. We try to involve the youth in all the decision making about what the group is going to do and what direction they're going to go and let them take a lot of the lead on that, which I think is challenging because they are not used to that. But also some cognitive behavior aspects [are used] as well in terms of beliefs, skills, behaviors and responses.

No Theoretical Approach

Few articles on dating violence and sexual assault prevention programs discuss their theoretical orientations in detail (Whitaker et al., 2006). Forty percent of interviewees did not identify a theory underpinning their program. However, many described their beliefs and views about the causes of dating violence or sexual assault or both. Interviewees felt strongly that their programs were addressing the causes of violence. Thus, even though programs did not readily identify a theoretical foundation for their programs, they were, in effect, responding to many researchers' calls for them to base their programs on their beliefs about causes. Many of the people working in prevention programs believe that their experiences with young women and men tell them what causes violence. Their views and values about gender norms, interpersonal relationships, and power and control issues also appear to influence their perspectives on the causes of violence. Educators' experiences and value systems similarly inform them about what works with victims and how to develop programming to prevent violence. Some believe that a theory was not necessary:

I have some of my own individual theories that might work into that, but it is not like I picked a theory from any one place and said, "This is what we are going to do." I guess I wouldn't say it is theory-based.

It has been based on going into the classroom, six years ago, and doing what I did see from the previous educator . . . I added some more to it and I learned from the students. So no, I would say there is no particular theory.

It is just based on listening to teenagers, what they like, what they want . . . you know, we are a bunch of liberal feminists and we want to empower girls to speak up and boys to pay attention.

I think it is based on our general philosophy but not necessarily by any academic theory.

Summary of Theoretical Considerations

Dating violence and sexual assault prevention researchers and practitioners increasingly recognize the need to base programs on a theoretical framework. Prevention educators identified social learning theory and feminist theory most frequently as framing their programs. Many articulately expressed how violence is learned through the media and family; others described how power and control leads to male patriarchy. Other theories, such as empowerment theory and the ecological framework, were also identified as guiding forces for prevention programs. Some interviewees stated that their programs were based on multiple theories.

Many practitioners did not identify a theory upon which their programs were based. Some, however, described their own beliefs and views about the causes of dating violence and sexual assault, which formed the basis for their prevention programs. Even though, as academicians, we feel that programs benefit from being guided by a theoretical framework, we recognize the many successful programs that are not grounded in a formal theoretical framework.

[4]

Program Goals

The objectives of dating violence and sexual assault prevention programs may be categorized either as providing youths with knowledge, attitudes, and behavioral goals or as setting individual and societal goals. We begin the chapter with a discussion of the concept of prevention as a program goal and the controversy surrounding it.

"Prevention" Versus "Risk Reduction"

The concept of prevention is strongly advocated in many human service fields. Primary prevention works (Albee and Gullotta 1997). The prevention of violence of all forms of relationship and sexual violence is the ultimate goal of all programs. However, no matter how good prevention programs are, it is unlikely that violence will be totally prevented. Many of our interviewees discussed the concept of prevention with us; they echoed strong feelings about the meaning of the word "prevention" that are often expressed in the violence-against-women community. Some believed it was inappropriate to even use the word "prevention," because it implied that violence against women, especially sexual violence, can be prevented.

In the dialogue about prevention, a primary concern is that prevention often targets the victims of violence rather than the perpetrators; thus prevention can imply that victims are responsible. If women just acted correctly, dressed correctly, and made the correct decisions, violence against them can be prevented. Sending the message that a woman might have been able to prevent an assault may increase her sense of guilt. Moreover, although women's vigilance in staying safe may be helpful in "preventing" stranger assaults, it does not address the assaults committed by spouses, partners, and friends (Carmody and Carrington 2000). Bohmer and Parrot (1993) discuss this concern:

> Rape cannot stop until men stop raping. Telling women to avoid rape is insufficient to stop the problem. Unfortunately, the approach taken by most educators is to place the responsibility for avoiding rape primarily on the potential victims (for example, don't' go to a man's apartment, don't stay at a fraternity party after two in the morning, don't get drunk). This kind of advice not only blames the victim, it also gives women a false sense of security ("If I don't do these risky things, then I can't be raped"). Unfortunately, there is nothing a woman can do to guarantee that she will not be victimized; this is the reality of rape. (200)

Abbey's (2005) discussion on the lessons learned about sexual assault stresses that "far too many prevention programs focus on the victims of sexual assault rather than the perpetrators. Victims can benefit from risk reduction programs; however, primary prevention must focus on potential perpetrators" (41). Although many of our interviewees referred to their work as prevention, others explained that they avoid the use of the word "prevention" and instead speak of "risk reduction." Their reasoning was consonant with some of the concerns expressed in the literature about the use of the word "prevention":

> We try to shy away from "prevention" because to us, [we avoid] using the word prevention, because the only person that can prevent this is the person who is going to do it. The rest of us can reduce our risk. Does that make sense?

> I know that our agency, if you talk to the coalition in [our state], they probably told you that we got this huge grant from the CDC to re-do our community education programs to have more of an emphasis on primary prevention, rather than what we're doing. What we've traditionally done is . . . risk reduction, which they don't count that as being primary prevention. .

> I will start off with the premise that prevention work is really done with men and risk reduction is done with women.

Thus many practitioners clearly distinguish between risk reduction and prevention. Others separate outreach from prevention. One interviewee conceptualized outreach activities as often contributing to both primary and secondary prevention:

> We do outreach. So a lot of our outreach activities and presentations and trainings are prevention. However, the intent, for funding purposes, is to reach out to young people so that they know there are services if they are already in abusive relationships.

Avery-Leaf and Cascardi (2002) point out that, although many prevention programs strive for primary or universal prevention, youths may experience them as secondary prevention, as they have already experienced violence in their relationships (95). Universal or primary prevention programs usually focus on "dating violence awareness, conflict management skills, and addressing issues of gender stereotyping" (Close 2005, 5). Farrell and Meyer (1997) suggest that the phrase "violence prevention" is really more about the goals of the program than about outcome. Two prevention educators specifically discussed their programs in terms of primary and secondary prevention.

> I think programmatically, as we're looking at primary prevention, it's to learn how to engage more young men and adult men in creating an environment where men are saying, "It's not okay to abuse." Where coaches and youth providers are actively on message with that. At this point in time, they're not. And I just feel strongly if we're looking at primary prevention, that's what we have to do. We have to build that kind of peer environment. [We need to build] the leadership environment of men, saying "that this is not okay" and transmitting that to young boys.

> Our education program is aimed to be a prevention program, meaning we're reaching young people before they are experiencing abuse.

Knowledge, Attitudes, and Behavior

Although we differentiate between the objectives of providing goals based on knowledge, attitude, or behavioral, we recognize that the three objectives substantially overlap. Some interviewees described the content they presented and identified their goal as increasing knowledge, but other educators describing similar content indicated that their goal was to change attitudes. Many interviewees specified multiple program goals, including a combination of knowledge, attitudes, and behaviors.

In reality, how the goals of increasing knowledge, changing attitudes, and changing behaviors are related is not clear. Much of the literature emphasizes the importance of including program goals related to behaviors and skills, in addition to increasing knowledge and changing attitudes (Carlson 1999; Edleson 2000; O'Leary, Woodin, and Fritz 2006). Behavioral change is more difficult to achieve than changes in knowledge and attitude, and many of the more recent prominent prevention programs incorporated a behavioral or skill component in addition to knowledge (see, e.g., Foshee et al. 1998; Wolfe et al. 1996; and Rosenbluth and Garcia n.d.).

Knowledge

Many programs provide information to increase their participants' knowledge base. Schewe (2003b) suggests that a logical goal of prevention programs is to increase adolescents' knowledge about rape myths because research has shown that cognitive distortions commonly precede sexual assaults. However, Schewe (2003b) cautions that presentation of facts alone has not been found to be effective. Meyer and Stein (2004) found that the most common improvement in prevention programs was increased knowledge about dating violence, but they questioned how changes in knowledge relate to behavioral changes.

More than 70% of the interviewees stated that increasing knowledge or providing information was a goal of their program, and they stress the importance of providing knowledge:

> When we started our program, we knew we had to really, really educate both the kids and the faculty and the administration and other youth-serving organizations to recognize that there is such a thing [as dating violence or sexual assault] and know what to do when and if they see it.

> We are safety educators, which means that we want to equip them with the tools that they need to make good choices and to be safe. To be totally respectful of gender. We have slightly different goals because of the gender issue. What we want for the guys is maybe a little different than what we want for the girls. Our goals for the girls are really to help them to realize that their bodies are theirs and they can say, "no," and they can make the very best decision that they want to make for themselves and that that is absolutely to be respected. And for the boys, we're going to say to them the same thing, "The girls have an absolute right to make their decisions and to have power over themselves."

Awareness

Many interviewees talked about knowledge and information, particularly in terms of increasing youths' awareness. The distinction between increasing participants' knowledge and increasing their awareness of the topic is not clear. However, a quarter of the interviewees identified awareness as their program goal:

The goal was to be able to reach a lot of teens all at once to raise their awareness about these issues and the resources available to them and to sort of start more of a dialogue about these issues among teens. I don't believe we did that. We don't have a way of really measuring what happens when they go home. But there has been not very much attention . . . Prior to my program starting here, there really wasn't anything much in this community for teens around these issues. We were just trying to raise awareness at this point and that was one way of trying to reach a lot of teens all at once. The goal ultimately is obviously preventing teens from entering an abusive relationship and to educate others about how to get help for themselves or their friends if they are already involved in an abusive relationship. That is the broader goal—to increase awareness . . . help teens define what is an abusive relationship vs. a healthy one, what kind of warning signs do you look for and how do you look for help if you are already in a bad situation, what do you say to a friend.

I would say one of the major goals is just to build awareness of dating violence . . . A lot of times we go in and find that things are going on and they don't recognize them as dating abuse. We want them to be able to recognize warning signs in their own relationships as well as with their friends. We want to be able to offer them emergency and even follow-up assistance for things that are going on. And just kind of promote healthy relationships and nonviolent relationships in general, I would say.

I want them to be aware of what is sexual assault. How to define it. I want them to communicate with one another and I really would like them to communicate with their parents

Knowledge to Achieve Behavioral Change

Some interviewees identified their goal as increasing knowledge, but their comments actually revealed that increasing knowledge was, instead, a means toward achieving their ultimate objective of changing youths' attitudes. Others suggested that their aim was to increase knowledge, with the ultimate target of changing youths' behaviors:

[We] offer them some tools to break the cycle of violence in teen years. We want to expose them to information about healthy relationships and provide them with guidelines to working out problems without resorting to violence. Basically it is education and prevention. [The] main goals that we hope to accomplish with this program [are] to expose the youth to information regarding healthy relationships and unhealthy relationships. And provide them with guidelines to help them work out problems without resulting to violence . . . back on with the mission and some of the goals of our program . . . to educate people and empower them to lead a violence free life.

Because . . . and I'm pausing a lot because I think this is a really important question, because I think some people think the goal is to do 15 programs or see 250 people, and if you think like that, then you lose sight of the strategy of it. So, like what I said before, I think that the real goals about awareness and education are to know what populations are really dealing with this issue and to be in that population and we could call it "education awareness" and that might be the message that we are bringing, but I think what it is really about is being there, having a presence. So that a relationship is built, so that when people need us they know who to call, and they trust us. I see our education and awareness as much of a, I hate to say "marketing," but I do mean that in the sense of building the relationships with the sectors of the community, so the community knows how to get in contact with us when they need us.

One interviewee suggested that her goal was to increase knowledge with the ultimate objective of keeping youth safe:

I think to clarify the information for them. I think there are a lot of myths in regards to what sexual violence is and who creates it and all of those kind of things, who are the victims. I think to give them accurate information is probably our biggest goal. I think my goal as the director of a program is to create a path of equality in regards to . . . I think the kids deserve to have information that impacts their lives and not to make any assumptions about that and keep checking in with regards to what is happening in the culture and what's happening with them and to try and somehow balance that stuff out. I think that they deserve information in order to keep themselves safe.

Attitudes

The literature conveys considerable controversy about whether changes in attitude or knowledge lead to behavioral changes. This is true in the litera-ture of general social psychology (Terry, Hogg, and White 2000; Zimbardo and Ebbeson 1970) and that of dating violence and sexual assault (Schewe and Bennett 2002). However, general attitudes are usually poor predictors of specific individual behavior and better predictors of broad behavioral dispositions (Ajzen and Fishbein 2005). The correlation between attitudes and behavior is strongest when both are assessed at compatible levels of specificity or generality (Kraus 1995). Thus it may be most beneficial for prevention programs to target specific attitudes when the objective is to generate the desired specific behavioral changes. It is also important to be aware, however, that attitudes are just one of a range of factors influencing a person's behavioral responses in any given situation.

Although attitudes are often not related to behavior, the ease of measur-ing and demonstrating changes in attitude and belief relative to behavioral change has probably led many programs to center on these changes as indicators of successful programs. Avery-Leaf and Cascardi (2002) support an emphasis on attitudinal change in dating violence prevention programs, because a number of evaluated programs have successfully met this goal. The authors state that "social psychologists have long established that in the short term, attitude change is relatively easy to accomplish and can be done efficiently and effectively in a group setting such as a classroom" (100). Sochting, Fairbrother, and Koch (2004) criticize the fact that, given the absence of empirical support, most rape prevention programs continue to focus on changing beliefs and attitudes that, presumably, increase the likelihood of sexual violence. Approximately 12% of the interviewees stated that their program goal was to change attitudes:

> Primarily, we are focusing on trying to change attitudes about sexual as-sault. And part of changing those attitudes does require some amount of knowledge about the facts and the realities of the issue. But a lot of it is more, there is a lot of information that is more, it is opinion-based. It is people that either agree with you or don't agree with you. And there isn't, you know, a concrete right or wrong answer. There would be in my opinion . . . but so that's really the part that it is important to try and have a discussion back and forth with the students. To be able to have

the time to have an activity that draws out that kind of a dialogue and a debate or gets them to thinking about things in a different perspective. That you're not just standing up there saying, "This is the way it is and this is how you should believe, what you should think. Rape is never the victim's fault, no matter what." Well, I could say that to them, but if that's all I said and that's all I did, 75–85% of the kids in that room are going to disagree with me and they are not going to understand why. It is more important to have a dialogue back and forth about, "What do you think the victim's responsibility is and where do you draw the line and what is this and what is that?" So I think that is that attitude change part of it that we are trying to change people's attitudes and dispel some of the myths and the negative attitudes that our culture has about sexual assault.

. . . to reduce victim-blaming attitudes because it's amazing how much of that those kids get. It's amazing how pervasive the culture is that students, even with incredible disabilities, understand that if you're feminine and you're a boy, you're at the bottom of the totem pole and you deserve to be picked on. And if you're a girl and you're wearing a short skirt, you asked for it.

Behaviors and Skills

Because increasing youths' knowledge about a topic does not necessary transform into changed behaviors, many researchers are calling for the inclusion of skill training in prevention programs. Youths need time to practice new skills in an environment that encourages new behaviors (O'Brien 2001; Center for Disease Control 1993). Durlak (1997) states that programs must establish "mechanisms to support and reinforce behavioral change after it occurs" (17). Nation et al.'s (2003) review of prevention programs for youths, which focused on substance abuse, risky sexual behaviors, school failure, and delinquency, also concluded that effective programs needed an active, skills-based component.

A number of published reports indicate that few programs have different skill-building goals for males and females. In the Safe Dates Project (Foshee et al. 1998), boys and girls learn the same conflict management skills. In the dating violence prevention programs of Wolfe et al. (2003), boys and girls also learn the same relationship development skills. However, some research on sexual assault prevention programs for college students suggests that different content may be warranted for males and females. In fact, Anderson and Whiston's (2005) meta-analysis of sexual assault prevention programs concluded that programs targeting women are more likely to focus on risk reduction, whereas programs targeting men are more likely to focus on building empathy. If more programs move toward specifying different goals for males and females, gender separate programming will probably become the norm. (For more information on differentiating program content by gender, see chapter 8).

Many of the interviewees also discussed the importance of addressing behavioral change and skill building. Nearly 10% of interviewees stated that their programs target the behaviors of participants, even though behavioral changes are difficult to measure:

> We want people to be able to have the experience building skills on those issues in regard to power and trust, and so how do I really do that without sort of practicing it and seeing how it works?

> We focus on bystander education, meaning taking the initiative and noticing if a friend is in trouble . . . or if they need somebody to advise them about an unhealthy relationship they are in. We discuss safety planning. Like if a student is in an unhealthy situation, what they can do to stay safe, who they can access as outside resources to maintain their safety and eventually moving on from the relationship.

> Basically, our real goal is a whole social change . . . they need assistance in making that behavioral change, into changing their behavior from going along with these types of things versus stepping in and saying something.

Combination of Knowledge, Attitudes, and Behaviors

McCall (1993) observes that dating violence and sexual assault prevention programs must address multiple goals, as the causes of relationship violence and sexual assault are "complex and multi-factorial" (289). Current prevention programs recognize the need to be comprehensive and to address multiple risk factors across contexts. Wilson, Lipsey, and Derzon's (2003) examination of school-based programs to prevent aggressive behaviors found that many center on developing youths' understanding of conflict but also include significant skill-building components. Cappella and Weinstein's (2006) aggression prevention program focused on girls' knowledge, understanding of others, communication and social skills, and problem-solving abilities.

Dating violence and sexual assault prevention programs also target multiple domains. Evaluations often find that some program goals are achieved and others are not. Foshee et al.'s (1998) Safe Dates Project identified multiple primary and secondary prevention goals, including reducing the incidence of dating violence, increasing knowledge about community resources, changing attitudes that condone partner violence and promote gender stereotypes, and building conflict management skills. Although the evaluation found significant differences in the incidence of psychological and sexual violence among youth in the program compared to those in the control group, no differences were found in youths' help-seeking behaviors. The goals of Gidycz et al.'s (2006) program with college women were to increase women's knowledge about sexual assault and their assertive sexual-communication skills. Although program participants demonstrated more accurate knowledge about sexual assault over the six-month follow-up period compared to the control group, they reported no differences in their use of assertive communication skills. Foubert and Perry's (2007) evaluation of the Men's Program for college males targeted attitudes and behaviors of participants and found evidence that attitudinal and behavioral changes were still in place five months following the program.

About 65% of the prevention educators we interviewed discussed multiple goals for their programs that targeted knowledge, attitudes, and behaviors:

> The goal is to measure knowledge, attitudes that students have walking in the door about domestic and dating violence, sexual harassment, sexual assault, gender violence. And then obviously changing attitudes and knowledge that may perpetuate intimate violence. So that's our overall goal . . . What I tell them is that rape prevention isn't about changing what the victim is doing, it is about changing the belief systems, the attitudes and the knowledge of people who choose to use violence.

> First and foremost it is reaching out to the kids that are already affected. Second, it's changing attitudes, and, thirdly, I would say, for the future of the kids, know what to do and where to call and not be afraid to call the police or us.

> I think there is knowledge and attitude . . . knowledge such as consent, what consent is, what consent laws are in the state that they are living in . . . definitions of rape and sexual assault and sexual intercourse and all of that kind of stuff, so that way they have that knowledge. Then we will also address all of the rape myths that are out there, which is more kind of attitude and trying to tackle that and trying to get dialogue going and trying to have them think of things outside of the box and see how their attitudes might be affected and where are they getting their messages and all of that stuff. Then we will talk about things they can do to

reduce their [students] risk, so kind of building their skills that way, the attitudes with getting communication skills.

[Our program's] purpose is to educate youth and adults through[out] the county about violence and how to take action to prevent it by using teens who are positive, nonviolent role models. It says, "Our continued mission is to show others that violence is not okay, ever, through providing memorable presentations that people of all ages can relate to. We hope to make a difference through confronting misconceptions and educating one individual at a time to achieve violence prevention, as well as empowering victims and friends of victims to seek help from community resources."

Twenty percent of the interviewees talked about being able to help youth help themselves or a friend as a component of behavioral change:

We want kids to know how to respond to any sexual assault and any kind of sexual violence. And that could be whether they see it happen, whether they need to get help, whether they know their resources, how they respond even with themselves, being able to identify, "This is okay," or, "This is not okay with me." I think that's important. It can be, "My friend told me a story. What can I do or what can I say? How can I help this person?" So I think those are the main goals, to be able to provide some kind of awareness. And certainly true prevention would be to have the awareness before anything happens and know what to do. But certainly even if something has happened, to know what they can do now and that certainly they've got a choice of things.

Societal- and Individual-Level Goals

The literature does not address the importance of having either societal or individual goals for prevention programming. Some interviewees identified individual-level program goals, and others identified societal-level goals. Interviewees who identified the latter specified objectives for each program session that focused on individuals. However, because some programs must evaluate their effectiveness to satisfy funding agencies, establishing measurable goals is becoming increasingly important to them. One interviewee identified goals for the program necessary to bring about the ultimate objective of ending violence:

The goals are to increase awareness among the young people and the community regarding the issue and to provide resources and support services for young people. And to empower them so they can become advocates for themselves towards changing society and its views toward violence and the effect of violence on young people. That and wanting basically to eradicate violence, as lofty a goal as that seems, but to the extent that we can, that's a goal.

SOCIETAL-LEVEL GOALS

Almost one-third of the interviewees expressed societal-level goals for their programs:

> We are trying to change the way we raise our sons and daughters. We're trying to change the values of society.

> I think that one of the goals in the prevention end is to reduce the incidences of sexual violence, and I would love to say, end sexual violence.

Although some interviewees expressed the vast scope of their goals, or, as one stated, the "loftiness" of their goals, many had little trouble seeing the relationship between the activities they were performing and their ultimate goal of ending violence:

> We're targeting [violence] in general; it is a primary prevention. It is not looking for victims and perpetrators, because it is more about changing social norms and that kind of thing. We want to decrease the terrible incidence of rape and sexual assault, and we believe if we start young and we work with them to really understand this right of self-determination and freedom, that we can help to stop that.

> For long term, on the more sort of social change piece, that's what I'm looking for is the social change. And I think that we've seen some of that incrementally, like on a percentage basis already. But, I mean that's the whole focus of what I think domestic and social crisis centers should be doing in general, is looking at how do we put ourselves out of business in the next, next hundred years or so . . . and that's done very slowly and over a period of time.

> [Our goal is] that our audiences leave with more of an awareness about the issue, and that they feel like they can help in the reduction of rape, family violence in the community. And that it does take a whole community.

You know, if you can end domestic violence and not need a domestic violence prevention program, that, I guess, would be everybody's dream.

INDIVIDUAL-LEVEL GOALS

Some programs discussed in the literature identify very specific goals or
objectives for prevention programs. Farrell, Meyer, and Dahlberg (1996)
presented a sixteen–session, school-based, comprehensive violence prevention program to sixth graders that targeted environmental, intrapersonal, and behavioral factors. Specific environmental objectives included
developing norms and expectations for nonviolent means of conflict resolution; creating opportunities for conflict resolution and positive risk-
taking; and providing adult and peer models for conflict resolution and
positive risk taking. Intrapersonal objectives included providing knowledge to support the value of nonviolent conflict resolution and achievement; and developing values that sustain nonviolent conflict resolution
and achievement. Behavioral objectives included enlarging the skill rep-
ertoire for nonviolent conflict resolution and positive risk taking, providing opportunities for mentally rehearsing nonviolent means of conflict
resolution and achievement, and enabling participants to identify the
optimal violence-prevention strategy in a given situation with specific
personal skills.

Five of the prevention educators we interviewed identified specific goals
for their programs, as well as the content of specific sessions:

For example, session 1, we go over [our state's] sexual criminal conduct
law and we also go over culture, like what society or culture promotes or
encourages or tolerates disrespect between the genders? That's our initial session, "The law and why is this such a big problem?"

There are at least four main goals. One is to help the kids to heal from
past abuse. So that is definitely a goal. Many of the students, even the
ones who don't disclose at an intake, end up later disclosing previous
child abuse or sexual abuse or domestic violence, so that's number one.
Two, we're really trying to raise their expectations for respect in relationships, so make it the norm. So that they are more aware to lower levels of
disrespectful, abusive behavior and just have higher standards for what
they want, both from their partner and in their relationship with their
partner. And one that we have a goal of changing the school climate.
So we feel that our presence there is not only benefiting the kids in the
groups. We're educating some staff; we have newsletters that go home

quarterly . . . there's information about dating relationships . . . we're trying to improve the school climate and improve school safety.

Summary of Goals

Practitioners disagree over the use of the term "prevention" as a goal of
dating violence programs, especially programs that target sexual assault.
Some programs avoid referring to themselves as providing prevention programs or to their work as prevention work, whereas other programs clearly
identify with the concept of prevention. The importance of targeting males
in prevention work and targeting women for risk-reduction work appears
to be growing more widespread, but some prevention educators do not feel
the distinction is important. Language, however, has traditionally been important in the violence-against-women community because of the importance of the meanings conveyed through it. We predict that concerns about
the use of the word "prevention" will remain.

Interviewees' program goals varied somewhat. Many programs target
the knowledge and attitudes of adolescents, even though they recognize
that little is known about how changes in knowledge and attitude translate into behavioral changes. Nevertheless, programs increasingly focus on
behavioral change and skill development, while acknowledging that these,
though critical to success, are the most difficult changes to effect. Ultimately the practitioners were united in their goal of eradicating violence
against women and societal violence in general.

Recruitment Issues for
Prevention Programs

Gaining access to groups of adolescents is critical to successful prevention programming. All the prevention educators we interviewed gained access to youth through programs in the schools; about half the programs also involved youths in various other settings. This chapter examines the settings where dating violence and sexual assault prevention programs take place, focusing specifically on programs in schools. It includes descriptions of methods of recruiting school communities and other settings that participate in prevention programs. The benefits and drawbacks of various locations, including churches, social service agencies, and community centers, are discussed. The chapter also addresses the advantages and drawbacks of parental consent issues related to required versus voluntary youth participation and recruitment. We include interviewees' experiences in recruiting adolescents already engaged in violent dating relationships, those at risk of developing violent relationships because of their histories of abuse, and high-risk youths including pregnant teens and teens in the criminal justice system (Jankowski et al. 2007).

Recruitment of Schools and Other Program Settings

Dating violence and sexual assault literature rarely discusses how programs gain access to adolescents. Meyer and Stein's (2004) national survey of sexual assault and domestic violence organizations asked programs under what circumstances do they gain access to schools: over 91% of programs were invited to give a presentation; about 60% were brought in as a response to a crisis in the school; about 54% knew someone who provided access to the school; and almost 60% "pounded on the doors for years" to get into schools. When we asked interviewees how they gained access to schools or other settings, they indicated that they either had been invited to various settings or gained access through interpersonal relationships, and they related many of the challenges they experienced.

Invited

Similar to Meyer and Stein's (2004) findings, 30% of interviewees stated that they had been invited by schools, churches, and other organizations. Although many currently receive numerous invitations to present their programs, a substantial effort was needed initially to gain access to these settings:

> When I began the program in 1999, we sent out letters to every school, community centers, churches, other youth serving organizations letting them know about our services and . . . after we have done more and more, the word has gone out.

> We're very fortunate that [our agency] is very well known and has a prestigious opinion held by many educators and people in [our region]. We get a lot of phone calls from teachers and schools that would like us to come out with our program.

> The high school that I just did, this is their first year doing it. They saw it in a flier and they asked me to come out and talk about it. They had a late arrival day. So what I did, I came out there for 6 weeks in the morning, on their late arrival day during the period that they didn't have class.

Knowing Someone

Also similar to Meyer and Stein's (2004) findings, over 40% of interviewees indicated that relationships with people helped them gain access to various settings. One interviewee described how she was able to enlist influential people to assist in gaining entry:

> Every year I try to pick three new people at the schools that I haven't met or talked to and send them a letter to tell them what our services are and a poster of the different topics that we can present, then offer for them to hang that up in their break room or something, where they can have other teachers see it. I always send, at the beginning of the year, to

teachers whose classes I have been in, in the last year. I will send them a letter saying, "Hope you had a nice summer; thank you for having us in your class. Hope we can do it again. Also included is a poster for you to share with any other teachers you might think are interested." Then if ever there is a new principal, administrator or guidance counselor, I will meet with them at the beginning of the school year to let them know what we have been doing in the school in the past, what we could be doing in their school if they wanted to do more and what our services are. Then every evaluation that I have, that I would give to a teacher or whoever asked for the presentation, there is a spot on there too for them to put, "Please list any other place that you think might be interested in the presentation." So sometimes they will list other teachers or community groups.

Clearly building relationships with school personnel and others was a long process:

We've worked really hard in building the relationship with the school board and with the counselors and that type of thing. It took many years before I ever came along here. Many years of relationship building in order for us to get our foot in the door and have our curricula approved by the school board. It was a very long process. And even once you get that approval, that does not, that's not a mandate that the teachers call and include you in their classes.

We had to prove to the school district that it was something that they needed to accept. We went into the student services department in the district and developed an ally in that department. Showed our curriculum, talked about the curriculum with her and brought her on board in terms of accepting that this was a program that was needed. She helped us to select certain schools that would probably be more willing to accept this curriculum . . . Then we had to go to the schools and convince them that what we had was what they needed. But it was basically one on one with teachers and principals and now we have a blanket approval with the school district because we have been so well accepted to go in, and we actually are part of their life skills program.

Contract

Several programs specifically stated that they had a contract or agreement with the school system to do prevention programming, but many others only implied that they had such agreements. For these programs, gaining access was no longer an issue:

> We have a list of agreements that we ask the school to agree to before we begin our program and our contact person has to get the Principal to sign off on the agreements before we offer to put the program in.

> We have a contract with our local school district in the area of sexual abuse and sexual harassment and we're in every middle school in our district.

How to Promote Interest in Programs in Schools and Potential Participants

Many of the programs have consistent recruitment efforts that eventually enable them to be invited to present programs or establish relationships with key organizational personnel. Some prevention educators recalled their initial recruitment efforts:

> We have strong relationships with the school counselors, and at the beginning of the year, we do training for the school staff, so that they know what the program is about and who to refer into it. That way, we have the adults on campus having a resource to send kids to. We have posters, not very fancy, very simple that we hang up for students to see themselves and inquire about the group if they're interested. And in the classroom presentations, the speakers will mention, "There is a group at your school."

> The group worker goes out and markets the program. Usually, she meets with all of the students and tells them about the program and what the goals are and how long it will last. Then she sends a sheet around and asks who is interested. From that list, she takes it to the guidance [counselor] and they go over and decide which ones [students] that are most in need of hearing this information, based on what guidance staff has heard.

Letters, fliers, and mailings play a prominent role in recruiting for many programs. Although many mailings receive no response, interviewees often cited their mailings as the source of access to settings. Follow-up is also very important:

I send them [letters] to the guidance counselors, and this past year, I sent one letter to the guidance [counselor], one letter to the principal . . . For the principal letter, I focus on doing in-service for the teachers. If I have a connection with another teacher or a health teacher, I will send a letter to them as well . . . I sent out two letters to each of the schools and I sent a flyer asking them to post it in their teacher's lounge. I got a lot of speaking offers from that. And then after I speak at a school, I send them a letter thanking them, with an evaluation form, asking them to return it back to me, and in the evaluation form it asks if they know of anyone who might be interested in a presentation. Then I make sure that person also gets a letter.

I have fliers to put up at a church, just trying to get the word out because people . . . the houses are so far apart, and most of the time, the parents they don't . . . they aren't really involved with the children at school. So even if it was something that I was trying to send out through the schools to send information, they are not really involved in the schools. It has just been difficult for me to get out into the rural area.

Some programs determined that it was most effective to send mailings, letters, and fliers at certain times of the year:

At the end of the school year, we send out a letter asking them to think about us for next year, "let us know what you are thinking." In the fall we would send a letter to ask what they wanted to do for programming and how we could plan that out.

We do a mass mailing twice a year. In the summertime, right before the school year starts and then at the middle to end, to affirm to the schools who haven't signed up that we're a service that's available. And we mail out to the vice principals as well. Vice principals because they do a lot of the discipline stuff. And to the health/peer ed teachers.

Recruitment Challenges

A few interviewees pointed out that recruitment can be difficult and described the many challenges they endured to gain entry into schools. A school's failure to acknowledge the issues of dating violence and sexual assault can make it difficult to gain access, and going through a school approval process can be time-consuming and difficult:

In a more rural community, a social worker was "gung ho" to have us come out and talk about dating violence. The principal shot it down. He said, "I don't really think our community could benefit from that message. But thank you."

It is a lot more difficult for me to get into see the children even in our public schools. Just because of the subject matter, they are a lot more cautious. They want me to write up the curriculum, which I haven't done yet and they said they would like to go over it and see what they would like submitted and what I can talk about and what I can't talk about.

It was a long process to have the program approved in the school district . . . the coordinator who was here at that time, they had to present it at the school board, they had to take suggestions, they had to bring it back, adjust it. And it was a long process to be approved.

Rejection

A few educators described how they had been rejected by some of the personnel at the sites they tried to recruit:

A lot of them just say, "No, we don't want to talk about that in our schools. Some of them will be honest enough to say we don't want to [upset] parents . . . Sometimes it is strictly the individual teacher who for some reason, they do not want us.

We tried approaching the principals directly and in high school the principals who have spoken to us say, "Oh, we don't [present] that stuff. We let the teachers do that."

One prevention educator knew she would not be invited to return to a site after talking with a school official prior to her first presentation:

[I said,] "I don't know what you mean, 'talk about sex' and I really don't understand, but this is what I am going to say." She went on to say, "These children, they don't do this, that and the other and we don't want da, da, da." And I kind of pointed across the gym because there was a group huddled up and they were dancing very, very inappropriately and seductively and I said, "Oh, that's what you are concerned about." And she said, "Oh." I went on and I gave the presentation and I told them everything I wanted them to know, and it just so happens she thanked me and rushed me out of the building. I knew I wasn't going back there.

Very Limited Recruiting Necessary

A few programs also noted that they actually do very little recruiting. They have been successful in taking the program to the point that recruitment is no longer necessary. They are sought after and fully booked. Some programs cannot fulfill all the requests they have:

> We are on such a roll that people just start calling us. We have a lot of previous customers . . . Within a school district, they will start talking to each other and we work with SRO's, School Resource Officers, as well. They will implement a lot of our programming or get the ball rolling on getting us into their schools.

> We get a lot of calls from them at this point, from the schools. A lot of repeat visits. From year to year, a lot of repeat visits. When semesters change, different cadres of kids come into the same teacher's classroom.

Advantages and Drawbacks of Various Presentation Settings

Although prevention programs are presented in various settings, much of the focus in the literature, and in discussions with prevention educators, is on school settings.

School Settings

Most violence prevention programs and specifically dating violence and sexual assault prevention programs discussed in the literature are presented in schools (Botvin, Griffin, and Nichols 2006; Foshee, Bauman, and Greene 2000; Jaycox et al. 2006; Weisz and Black 2001), and schools are often cited as the preferred setting for violence prevention programs (National Center for Health Statistics 1995). All the interviewees conducted programs in school settings at least some of the time.

ADVANTAGES OF SCHOOL SETTINGS

Schools present an ideal opportunity for offering prevention programs. They provide universal education (prior to the legal drop-out age) and opportunities for repeated contact with youth (Jaffe et al. 2004), and they have a positive effect on many early and pre-adolescents before they might become violent (Whitaker et al. 2006). School-based programs target all youths and are known as universal programs (Carlson 1999; Harned 2002; Pittman, Wolfe, and Wekerle 2000). Presenting programs to all adolescents rather than those considered vulnerable or at risk decreases the stigma of attending the program (Durlak 1997). Youth might be more receptive to messages that are received under less stigmatizing conditions. Another argument favoring programs at schools is that sexual violence and dating violence frequently occur in and around schools (Astor and Meyer 1999). Wekerle and Wolfe (1999) suggest that in-school programs have practical benefits including adequate space, access to youth, available transportation, staffing support, possible administrative support for research, and communication with parents. Programs delivered within the school community also can reach adults, such as teachers and administrators. Further, programs can be conducted in natural contexts, such as health classes or other mandatory classes that reach a cross-section of the student body.

In discussing the advantages of presenting programs within the school setting, about 15% of the educators cited the value of having a universal "captive" audience already present:

I prefer the school setting in that we get a cross section of kids. You know, a lot of times when you do a church youth group or a Girl Scout troop, you're ruling out a lot of, you're getting a lot of kids that are very similar to each other. When you do school, you're getting a little bit of everything, which I think is nice, and to me, that keeps it the most interesting.

Obviously, being in a school makes sense, because that's where they are, and they're a captive audience. Likewise, being in a classroom setting is actually . . . I found it somewhat helpful because, again, we have a captive audience and there are some implicit expectations of how they're going to behave.

But for us, the schools are really the best way to get that consistent, large group of students. We've tried community organizations before and you just get smaller groups and inconsistent attendance and things like that.

We prefer schools. And the reason why we do is because from the very beginning, we have believed that the message that we have is for every child and we believe that the school is the optimal setting for reaching every child. And once you move away from that, you begin to move away from the opportunity to reach numbers of kids. And when we're looking at reaching about 20,000 kids a year, with our total programming, we really feel that it's critically important to continue to reach higher numbers. And so schools are the best place to do that.

Another important reason identified by both the literature and our interviewees for placing programs in schools is that it provides an opportunity for schools and prevention programs to partner in the effort to reduce violence. Further, schools have the opportunity to integrate dating violence and sexual assault content into the school curriculum (Durlak 1997; O'Brien 2001; Rones and Hoagwood 2000). Meyer and Stein's (2004) study of programs across the country found that 43.8% of respondents believed that schools wanted to add violence prevention material to their general curriculum. Prevention presenters also felt that topics needed to be infused into all courses in schools in order to connect the issue of gender violence to more traditional school subjects, such as history. Dating violence and sexual assault content should be incorporated into classroom curricula over a long period for any significant changes in behavior to occur. Meyer and Stein (2004) suggest that schools will be more receptive to violence prevention if the issue is integrated into traditional subject areas, because schools are under so much pressure to raise test scores.

Some researchers advocate that the teachers present the programs (Gamache and Snapp 1995). Others suggest that teachers and prevention educators form a partnership and work together. Avery-Leaf and Cascardi (2002) discuss the advantages of having a teacher rather than an outside person present programs. They point out that a teacher "is likely to be a skilled educator with polished pedagogical as well as classroom management skills" (98) and also to have ongoing relationships with his or her students. Teachers can continue the program in their classes year after year at no additional cost to the school, and school personnel have multiple opportunities to communicate and reinforce the program's messages to students, and not just during "program time." Schewe (2003b) suggests that dating violence and sexual assault curricula should meet state guidelines for health education, so that the content will receive more time and sessions in health education classes.

Durlak (1997), in contrast, cautions about having teachers present programs, because he believes that if teachers present the curriculum, they may make their own decisions about what parts of the program to present. Avery Leaf and Cascardi (2002) acknowledge that teachers do not always communicate well with their students and that independent educators of dating violence are probably more knowledgeable about the subject, may be more sensitive in handling disclosures, and may have more knowledge about community resources. Moreover, research suggests that adolescents rarely view teachers as viable options for help with their problems or dating violence (Ashley and Foshee 2005; Black et al. 2008; Tishby et al. 2001). O'Brien (2001) suggests that the combination of violence prevention experts and teaching experts creates "a wonderful role model and sets a high standard for students" (411).

A few interviewees pointed out that locating programs in the school offers the opportunity to partner with classroom teachers. Teachers can reinforce the message and assist students in practicing the desired behaviors:

> I really feel that school really does provide a wonderful venue for a prevention program in the sense that students spend so much time of their lives in school, and it is often the first place where students get the opportunity to really practice any type of learned behaviors.

> If you create a culture within this school where you have messages of anti-violence that is surrounding them, you are better . . . that whole reinforcement and consistence and ongoing reinforcement of those messages is quite effective. Whereas if you go to a church and you hit that church one time for an hour, those kids get an hour's worth of message, but then that's it.

> We have just found that our relationships with the schools have been really good, and the health teachers are very cooperative and really wanting to incorporate some of this prevention in their work.

Limitations of School Settings

The literature indicates that an important limitation of school programs is that a critical group of teens is excluded when the programs are presented in schools. Older teens who have graduated, or those who are truant or have dropped out of school, cannot participate (Cornelius and Resseguie 2006; Seimer 2004). Begun (2003) states that "an important caution to reliance on school-based efforts is [that] many of the students 'at risk' for becoming perpetrators of IPV [intimate partner violence] have poor school attendance and may not respond well to interventions delivered by educational authorities" (646). Schissel (2000) notes that, "the problem with classroom based programs is that they may teach and preach, but they do little to create a real-life atmosphere in which males and females gain empathy for one another" (979–80). Another limitation with school settings is that they may place restrictions on program content. Meyer and Stein's (2004) survey of prevention programs found that over 60% of programs had restrictions placed on their curricula by the school system and that over 8% required that the school board or administration approve the curriculum or the presentation.

In discussing the drawbacks of presenting programs in the school system, some interviewees pointed out that limited time and the structure of the school classrooms created problems:

> The problem we have with schools, certainly some schools—but it is really the biggest problem, is time. Schools don't want to give up time. Now if you could fit into their 42 minute class period, but you can't do an effective workshop in 42 minutes.

> I think schools, during the school day are very problematic. And the reason being is, there are a couple of places where it works out well and let me qualify that. If the school says, "We're going to have this time to be for groups," for example. Everybody's sort of in a group, or they're in homeroom, or they're in study hall, or something like that. But when we start pulling kids out of class, it is really complicated and the teachers get a little bit grouchy about it. Or if they say, "Okay, we'll let you pull kids out of class, but you always have to be doing a different class each week." So the same kid isn't getting pulled out of the same class each week. So it might [be] Monday at first period, and then the next week it's Monday or Tuesday at second period and that just ends up being so chaotic that even the kids don't even know. So we've done it and will probably continue to do it if that's the only way to get it done. But I don't think it works out well.

A few interviewees also described their frustration with the restrictions that parents and schools placed on their program content:

> It's kind of harder to get into schools because there are a lot of other things, like parents not wanting their children to hear information on dating violence or violence in general. I guess a lot of parents are unsure of what the curriculum contains, and so we try to offer our curriculum so they can look at it themselves.

> I think in a school setting it would be limited as to what I could say, and I know videos are even more difficult to get instituted.

Other Settings

Although dating violence and sexual assault programs and curricula can be presented in non-school settings including churches, community centers, mentoring programs, the juvenile justice system, teen pregnancy programs, and health education programs (Seimer 2004), few programs discussed in the literature have been conducted outside educational settings. Wolfe et al. (2003) conducted a rare community-based program. Cornelius and Resseguie (2006) suggest that it is important to examine the efficacy of prevention programs with older adolescents who may not be equally represented in school settings. Howard and Wang (2003) emphasize that we should locate programs in settings that target youth with risk profiles for victimization. As noted at the beginning of this chapter, about half the programs included in our interviews also presented to youths in settings outside schools. These included alternative schools, community centers, detention centers, courts, churches, scout organizations, pregnancy programs, and hospitals. The interviewees discussed some of the advantages of presenting programs outside the school system and in the community:

> One of the other benefits I think about doing it through existing youth organizations is . . . first of all, if you don't want to have mixed sex groups, in a classroom you are going to. In other settings you can choose to do it a different way.

> Usually, when I get a request from a community setting, they are very open about how much time and things like that, where at school it is very restricted to a 50 minute block of time and limited to how many sessions and working around the schedules.

> Environments like the after-school environment tends to work best in the sense that . . . and it's really varied, but like the school setting . . . the 45- or 50- or 90-minute setting and the general kinds of stuff that go on in schools, like the hierarchy that happens . . . the whole culture of high school just does not seem conducive to raising these issues.

Other interviewees noted that community settings provide greater flexibility and create greater commitment on the part of participants:

> My favorite place is either like a church or a community center or a youth service bureau where you really don't have those same kinds of require-

ments. Like kids are just coming for that specific thing. I think you need a place where you've got some privacy because, you know, I've also had that, too, "Oh, you can have this end of the gym."

The other benefits of working outside the schools, something about being in class makes teens may or may not want to really engage with the materials. You tend to have larger groups, which mean the conversation is not as intimate.

I prefer community groups over schools . . . I feel we have a lot more freedom in the community organizations, and the people who usually coordinate the presentations, they are usually a bit more involved. Not just with education or tutoring or something, but they're hearing the stories that happen at home, and they might live in the community with the students. And the setting is usually a bit more informal. There aren't the rules that exist in the school, things like that. So it's not as rigid and I like that.

Although no interviewees noted specific disadvantages of presenting programs in the community, many reported that they lacked the resources to do the needed programming in community settings in addition to the school settings where they could reach more youths. Avery-Leaf and Cascardi (2002) suggest that it is unwise to debate whether school- or community-based settings are superior, but rather "it may be more fruitful to focus on how best to combine prevention strategies in the two arenas" (99). Indeed, several of the prevention educators pointed out that programs in the schools and in the community are both needed:

In school settings it [the program] is very structured. It is something that could be integrated into their health curriculum for instance. Whereas a community center or local center, it might kind of be a hit and miss kind of thing. In terms of how presentations go themselves, I don't see a difference. I enjoy them both and I think there are benefits. I wouldn't say it works better in one or the other, except that we can have the ability to reach larger numbers of young people through the schools.

Schools work when the people who are bringing you in have an understanding, or schools don't work when teachers are making comments like "if you want to see domestic violence, you better sit down." Any setting will work for us as long as the people who are bringing us in have a tone that is set.

Targeting Special Populations

Already Violent and High-Risk Populations

Because few programs target youths who have already displayed dating and sexual violence, we do not know how effective programming may be with this population. A noteworthy program, however, is the Violence Prevention Mentoring Program (VPMP), which is specifically designed for adjudicated adolescents. Salazar and Cook's (2006) evaluation of the program with adjudicated, African American adolescent males found that program participants were more knowledgeable about intimate partner violence and less patriarchal in their attitudes than a control group. Differences were maintained at three-month follow-up. The authors concluded that the program was effective despite participants' high rates of violence against women.

Research results are somewhat mixed concerning how effective programs are for those already victimized by physical and sexual violence (Anderson and Whiston 2005). Hanson and Gidycz (1993) reported that college women who were survivors of sexual victimization reported no change following their participation in a prevention program compared to women without a history of sexual victimization. However, subsequent studies of modified versions of their program reported varying results. A program directed at women with histories of victimization reported having no impact on women with or without histories of victimization (Breitenbecher and Gidycz 1998), but another program that added role-playing and discussion found significantly reduced rates of victimization among those who had already been moderately (slapped, punched, shoved) but not severely (beaten, shot, stabbed) victimized (Gidycz et al. 2001). Marx et al. (2001) conducted an intense two-session program targeting college women with histories of sexual victimization and reported that participants had reduced rates of sexual victimization in the two months following the program compared to the control group.

Programs that specifically target youths previously involved in violent dating relationships are clearly needed (Carlson 1999). Programming needs differ for those who have experienced violence versus those who have not yet been victims or perpetrators (Eckhardt and Jaminson 2002; Yeater and O'Donohue 2002). Lonsway (1996) suggests that traditional programs of only one to two hours may not be effective for previously victimized participants, but longer programs would give participants time to overcome initial emotional obstacles and manage their victimization experiences in a meaningful way. Yeater and O'Donohue (2002) found that women who have been repeatedly victimized were better able to discriminate risk in date rape situations than women with a single victimization incident. Thus the authors suggest that prevention programs should target women with a single incident of victimization and assist them in learning to identify and respond to risks in social settings.

Few of the interviewed practitioners stated that they conducted programs specifically for youths who had already perpetrated violence or had been victimized in a violent relationship. On the other hand, many spoke of working with youths who had experienced violence in their families, some of whom may already have been involved in violent relationships or victimized by sexual assault:

> I don't really target that population, but I can say that in the alternative schools that we facilitate, I couldn't tell you an exact percentage of how many students have experienced this, but a very large percentage of them have experienced either sexual abuse as a child, maybe sexual assault or domestic violence, maybe currently or in the past where they have witnessed or been a victim of physical, emotional or sexual abuse within the home. But I also see that working with probationary youth, a lot of them have also experienced ... it is not the only reason why they would be involved in the program if they have had that, but I know that the probation officer would say, "Okay this family could definitely benefit from the student participating."

Many researchers discuss the need for prevention programming among high-risk youth, including those who have been exposed to violence in the home (Carlson 1999; Wolfe et al. 2003). Johnson-Reid and Bivens (1999) advocated for programs targeting foster youth. They found that although youths in foster care experienced similar levels of dating violence as youths in the general population, those in foster care had greater difficulty ending abusive relationships and thus may be at "greater risk for injury and later adult involvement in domestic violence" (1260).

Despite the need for programs for high-risk youth, only a few dating violence and sexual assault prevention programs specifically target at-risk youth. Wolfe et al.'s (2003) program was specifically designed for adolescents thought to be at risk of developing abusive relationships because of their documented histories of maltreatment. Over a two-year period, participants in the program perpetrated fewer incidents of physical and emotional abuse toward their dating partners and were less frequently victimized by physical and emotional abuse than youths not participating in the program.

Several researchers offer suggestions for prevention programs targeting at-risk youth. Durlak (1997) states that programs for only high-risk people need to determine, first of all, who is at high risk. Although we cannot predict exactly which adolescents are most likely to have problems in the absence of interventions, the appearance of problems at early ages does place children at risk for later difficulties. Interventions must be tailored to meet the needs of high-risk youth and be based on a solid theoretical framework (Whitaker et al. 2006). Weiler's (1999) review of successful programs for at-risk young women offered three suggestions: (1) provide a comprehensive counseling component addressing multiple problems, including sexual abuse and violence; (2) provide educational and occupational support; and (3) address the needs of young women who are unable to remain with their families to access caring adults or organized community activities.

The prevention educators we interviewed discussed several high-risk populations that they targeted for programming, including teen parents or pregnant teens, teens in foster care and detention centers, and teens referred by the court system. A quarter of the prevention educators stated that they specifically targeted youth in high-risk settings, including teen parents, and youth in psychiatric facilities, residential and group homes, homeless shelters, and alternative schools. Many of those presenting programs to high-risk groups, and about 20% of all programs, reported that they provided programming specifically to young people in detention centers and the court system:

> [We're] implementing [a program] for [our] county family court. I met with their core administrator and the juvenile probation officers and discussed the program with the family court judge and told him that I thought it may be something beneficial . . . for kids that are on probation through their department and they were really interested in that and so we kind of set up . . . It is done a little bit different in that the students are required to participate as part of their probation. So in order for them to complete their probation, they have to finish the program . . .

Two interviewees stated that they provided specific programs to youth in foster care. A few programs also targeted teen parents because they found that teen mothers are at especially high risk of being abused:

> We do certain specialized, targeted outreach to certain groups that we have found to be more at-risk. One example is pregnant and parenting teens. We do a lot of work with pregnant and parenting teens . . . often . . .

because [the] clients [of] our legal services program are teen moms who are being abused by the father of their child.

There is a teen parenting program in the school that invites us to work with their teens. I feel like when I am talking to these girls, the studies say what 26% maybe have [experienced dating violence] . . . I feel like I am talking to 100% a lot of the time. So the incidence and the intensity of it are greater and the stakes are higher in some ways after having a child.

Mandatory Versus Voluntary Programs

Few dating violence and sexual assault prevention programs reported in the literature specifically state that they are mandatory, whereas about one-third of our interviewees stated that their programs were required. Natural-ly, when programs are presented in a class during the school day, students are expected to attend. Several interviewees reflected on the benefits and limitations of having required programming versus voluntary program-ming. All but one stated that it was the school that required the program, and not the presenters:

We have three implementation sites right now that actually made [our project] mandatory for all their incoming freshmen and new students. And in those cases, a lot of times those teachers will teach the classes themselves.

Our youth advisory group has lobbied the board of [the local school dis-trict] for compulsory sexual assault education. So I feel like they would say "You have to go." Just as a practitioner, I feel like if you don't do it that way, the perception is that the kids that do go have some sort of a problem.

One interviewee discussed how parents sometimes require their children to participate in the school's prevention program once the par-ents learn the value of the program. Other interviewees discussed how sometimes school personnel can make strong recommendations, but not require, specific youth to participate in a program. Several preven-tion educators discussed why prevention programs need to be required of all youth:

When it's voluntary, you often end up preaching to the choir. And, well, that's still certainly good and sometimes nice to have a nice group going in that you know is going to be receptive. This stuff is so important and it's the people who wouldn't normally voluntarily go to hear about this information are the ones that need to hear it the most. So I do like the captive audience plan.

I think they're only good from a required standpoint if the school will stand by it. Or that youth service agency, or whoever's requiring it. What I notice all too often is that . . . using schools as the example, they say, "We've got a problem with sexual harassment, or respect, or bullying, or whatever the situation is in the school. Let's just get everybody to go through this mandatory training or this mandatory presentation or this mandatory assembly on this topic and now they'll know that this is not okay and they'll cut it out and won't do it." And the truth is, is that's not how it works; plus the school is not taking the responsibility to deal with the disclosure piece of it.

Required programs are generally short-term programs or one-hour presentations. Youth in ongoing or group prevention programming most often self-select. Prevention educators generally feel it is important to have voluntary youth participating in ongoing programs:

The kids self-select to come. Of course, I advertise it every time I go to any health class or anything. But these kids come on their own. It's everywhere from 7th grade to 12th grade, but usually it's 7th to 9th graders because once they get their licenses and jobs and stuff, they just don't have time to come anymore.

What I do tell all the schools is that they cannot force a student to participate, so even if a student is referred, it is still up to the student whether or not they want to participate in it.

Most programs, even one-time presentations, often provide the option of not participating. One prevention expert explained why it is important to allow this option:

I think from the school standpoint they would want to mandate it, because it is considered part of their class or what not. We did have actually a situation this fall with the prevention program where we showed the play and right in the beginning of the play, a female audience member became really anxious and asked to leave. She said she couldn't sit through that. She had a very understanding teacher, who let me know and I said, "Oh please, let her go, obviously this is touching on something for her." So I guess it would be a case by case basis. I guess I would always advocate for respecting the student's feelings and for some reason they are that uncomfortable with the subject matter that there is a reason for it.

Parental Consent

Literature most often fails to mention the use of parental consents for youth. We found that few programs use parental consents when presenting to large audiences or for only one-time presentations. However, longer prevention programs and peer-education programs do require parental consent. In pointing out that they did not use parental consent, many interviewees explained that they viewed parental consent as the responsibility of the school or other particular setting:

We leave that up to the facility that we are working in, and so we tell the facility what we are offering and we leave it up to them to decide whether or not they need to inform parents about our presentation or not or how they are going to do that.

Since our curriculum is approved by the Health Advisory Council of the school board, if it's good enough for the school board to allow in the school, then we don't have to have a parental consent form.

One of the original schools that started with us did send out parental consent the first semester and found out that there were some kids that were not allowed to participate by their parents. And these families had histories of violence . . . And so they just made a decision. I mean, I have to admire them. Administration went out on a limb.

That varies school to school. A lot of the middle schools have asked me more for a permission form which I have devised. I make it available to use at their discretion. It's not a policy that we set that every student who participates in our program has to sign a permission form. It just depends on the school and whether they feel like they need to have it or not.

Parents are often given the option to deny their child permission to participate in dating violence or sexual assault prevention programs, but few parents actually choose to do so. One interviewee estimated that less than 1 percent of parents refused to allow their adolescents to attend her prevention program. A few interviewees noted that they use passive consent. They send information to parents and presume consent if they do not receive information to the contrary.

[Local city] schools, well, private schools can do anything they want but basically how they do it is passive consent. They send out a thing saying, "This is what is going to be covered in health class and if you want your kid to be exempted send it back."

No, it was incorporated into their classrooms. They do send letters saying, "This is the program that we are going to be having in your child's classroom, if you have any issues with that, let us know" . . . if a parent says no, then they would find something else for their child to do.

We do. I know some schools . . . when we go into a new school some of them have it and some of them say, "Well, I don't think that's really necessary, but we insist on it." And it's up to them if they have the informed consent. We have a form letter they can use that they can add something to. But we think it's important . . . The form letter states the topics we're going to be talking about with the kids and that grades three on up have a pre- and post-questionnaire and they need to be aware of that. Even though it's anonymous, they need to know that it's . . . We tell the parents there's a date they can come in and talk with us. And we always schedule a parent program before we start with the students. First of all, it's our way to try to educate them. But also to inform them of what we're going to be talking about, if they have any questions or concerns about the program, to let them know that if they want to come in and observe a program, that it's absolutely okay . . . And if they have any concerns but can't make the meeting, they can certainly call us . . . Couple [of] schools do that. Most schools don't. On the consent form it says, "If you do not want your child to participate, please contact your teacher, or this person." And some parents do. There's not a whole lot, but every so often you get one or two students that, for whatever reason, the parent may choose to not have their child participate.

Parental consents were consistently used by peer education programs, support groups, special projects, and multi-session programs. Interviewees discussed their use of parental consent in these situations, especially permission to leave the school for training, presenting, or special projects:

For the peer educators, as part of the application, there is an attached sheet that has to have their parents sign it. I put a letter in there from me that says, "Your son or daughter is interested in this program; this is what we do. To do presentations; they will miss school. Please sign the consent form for them to be in here. They will be considered a volunteer and then they have to return that with their application." If we do a student group at school, the schools that I mainly do a group at, they will send one home with the kids, saying that, "Your son or daughter is interested in being in this group. This is the type of things that we are going to discuss. If you approve of them being in the group, then please sign and return the form to the school."

As soon as they've come, and before I can definitely have them in my car, because we do offer transportation, which is a huge bonus. And then I have a release form, so after they've come to at least one, I need this release form signed . . . it just releases me of responsibility when they're in the car. But it also kind of tells the parents, "I realize that subjects covered in skills learned in group may include but will not be limited to violence prevention, communication skills, self-defense techniques, mental and physical skills will be practiced, and healthy relationships."

For our programs, however, we do have to have obviously parental consent, for [one project] and the other youth programs. Not the mentor programs, but the other programs where we're taking them on field trips and so forth. We do want to have them complete; it's . . . it's almost like a contract but, various forms and approve obviously of their child participating in those programs.

Summary of Recruitment Issues for Prevention Programs

Most prevention work discussed by our interviewees was conducted in schools, which often present many challenges in gaining entrance. Prevention educators often worked hard over a long period to gain access by writing letters, sending fliers, and making phone calls. Personal relationships with someone at a setting provided a helpful avenue to gain entry. Gradually building a trusting relationship with someone from a school is important. Some of the programs that have built a strong relationship with schools and community settings have established themselves as a strong and sought-after community resource.

Schools present both strengths and limitations as a program setting. The ability to reach many adolescents is a major strength of schools, and universal programming also reduces the stigma of attendance for special populations. However, programs developed in other settings generally face fewer constraints in terms of program content and time. Some programs are involved in efforts to reach high-risk youth who are often not participants in school settings, and other programs want to do more to reach high-risk youth. Many interviewees felt comfortable mandating prevention programs for youth, while allowing those youth who are clearly upset by the presentations to be excused. Most programs leave the responsibility of parental consent to the host setting.

We feel that prevention work in the schools is absolutely essential if dating and sexual violence is to be addressed in our society. We are aware, from our own experiences, that developing and maintaining collaborative relationships with schools is a slow and very difficult task, but we believe it is necessary in most communities.

[6]

Membership

This chapter addresses issues concerning the participants in prevention programs, especially the matter of gender composition, as educators often disagree about whether it is best to have both girls and boys in a group or to separate groups by gender. The chapter also addresses program leaders' views on optimal group size and the ideal age-range of participants. Also included is a discussion of leaders' perspectives on the advantages and disadvantages of their current approaches to group composition.

Same- and Mixed-Gender Programming

Empirical evidence is scarce on gender composition, but, drawing on the literature regarding educational and therapeutic groups, we know that homogeneity leads to group cohesion and the sharing of experiences (Corey 2004). Heterogeneity offers its participants "a microcosm of the social structure that exists in the everyday world and an opportunity to get feedback from many diverse sources" (Corey 2004, 84). Findings from prevention programs for adolescents focusing on other areas report benefits of both mixed-gender and same-sex groups but often note that girls gain additional benefits from participating in an all-girls group (Chaplin et al. 2006). Although much of the literature on dating violence and sexual assault prevention programs in college (Anderson and Whiston 2005; Gidycz et al. 2006) and in high school (Foshee et al. 2001) suggests that separating genders is useful, many programs discussed in the literature, (Wolfe et al. 2003) and the majority of programs presented across the country, use mixed-gender groups (Meyer and Stein 2004).

Mixed-Gender Groups

The literature rarely advocates including both genders in prevention programs, but many programs have that arrangement (Fay and Medway 2006; Foshee et al. 2001; Wolfe et al. 2003). Meyer and Stein (2004) surveyed sexual assault and domestic violence organizations across the country and found that 81.7% of the programs had mixed-gender groups. Satisfaction among youth participating in mixed-gender groups appears high. Anderson and Whiston's (2005) examination of sexual assault prevention programs for college students found stronger effects on women's rape attitudes in mixed-gender groups than in all-female groups. However, they found no evidence that men in mixed-gender groups benefited any more from the program than those in same-gender groups. Black (2005) found higher satisfaction among boys in mixed-gender groups than among those in same-gender groups, and no difference for girls among middle school youth.

Over 50% of the interviewed prevention educators reported that they used mixed-gender programs. Some groups were mixed-gender simply because of the classroom setup in the schools. Others strongly advocated keeping the boys and girls together during their program, as they placed much value on the ability of males and females to listen to one another in mixed-gender groups:

> In life in general, they're not really going to be segregated, boys or girls, and they need to have that open conversation from the time when they're young . . . So there has to be that communication. And they're not really inhibited by the other gender being in that classroom.

> I'm really open to, at some point, exploring that idea more with people, because I think there is value to doing it [presenting programs] in mixed groups, because you can model the kind of respect that you want them [girls and boys] to show each other. You can have the young men hearing what girls think about . . . [and] . . . you can engage them both.

> Part of my goal is to get them talking. If I can get them talking about anything about sex in a classroom . . . then I feel the chances of them continuing that dialogue or being able to have a dialogue with any sexual partner. Certainly we have done separate groups, but I just feel very strongly about the other way.

> With mixed groups, the guys hear how the girls feel, and vice versa . . . and it's important . . . for them to hear it. And if I'm just talking to the

girls, it does become more of a "girls beware" kind of thing. And they're not hearing any ... they don't get any feedback from their responses. And that's what I really want. I want the responses from the guys to have feedback and for them to go back and forth.

Targeting One Gender

No interviewees specifically targeted only one gender in their programming. Although some may offer a specific program for girls, they were clear that programming had to involve both boys and girls. One interviewee's agency refused to offer a program just for girls:

Usually they are asking us to come in and talk just with the girls. That doesn't fit in with our philosophy of risk reduction or prevention so we won't do that.

One person we spoke with saw that even separating the genders caused girls to feel that they were unfairly targeted:

I think that sometimes there are those tensions that come up when you separate the groups. The girls feel like, "Well, you're only talking to us. We're not the ones causing the problems."

Same-Gender Groups

Although some programs prefer to work with mixed-gender groups, the focus, goals, and strategies for reaching males and females may need to differ (Arriaga and Foshee 2004; Gidycz et al. 2006). Much of the literature relating to group work, as well as research on prevention efforts with adolescents in other areas, also suggests that women in same-gender groups experience greater benefits, including an environment that is more conducive to change (Capuzzi, Gross, and Stauffer 2006; Chaplin et al. 2006). Weiler (1999) contends that, to serve young women effectively, programs must consider that girls' problems are often gender-related (sexual abuse, male violence, the role in the family, early motherhood, occupational inequality) and thus require gender-specific approaches. Foshee et al. (2001) found that risk factors for dating violence differ for males and females, and they concluded that intervention strategies may also need to vary. For example, dating violence against females may be predicted by having friends who are victims of dating violence, using alcohol, and belonging to a racial minority, whereas dating violence by males may be predicted simply from the males' attitude that dating violence is acceptable. Anderson and Whiston (2005) found that studies assessing college women's changes in behavioral intentions following sexual assault education may have better outcomes in all-female rather than in mixed-gender programs. Brecklin and Forde (2001) also found that separate programs for men were more effective than programs with mixed-gender groups.

Twenty-five percent of interviewed prevention educators separated boys and girls in their prevention programs. Even though many of them saw benefits in mixed-gender groups, they generally felt that separating the genders was more beneficial than keeping them together. Many programs consciously attempted to target males and females separately, and many of the interviewees expressed strong feelings about the importance of separating the genders:

It is very clear that you have an entirely different conversation when you have boys in the room, rather than just the girls. I felt like, given my limited resources, I wanted to focus on working with the girls. There was a lot more candor, a lot more honesty, and a lot less defensiveness on both sides. You didn't have the same kind of posturing and you could actually be real and talk about honest experiences and what is going on, rather than when they are all together.

Both the girls and the boys, especially, are more willing to speak up and speak out and ask more intimate questions that might be intimidating if the girls are in the class. When you think about it, what if you are a girl in a class that is mixed, and in that class, her boyfriend is there and is an abuser. And we are giving a talk about dating violence. What is she going to be able to do and say?

I have been to certain schools where there is so much of a problem on campus with sexism or gender roles. You really have to split people up, because the girls really weren't going to talk in front of boys. They were completely silent.

When I see the genders split out, you really have an opportunity, for example, to talk a lot more in depth about what is power, what is trust, what does vulnerability really look like, because I think when I'm just with a group of guys, for example, and I don't know, because I'm not male, but what I've noticed in those discussions, is there's a little bit more willing-ness to say, "Well, here's the part that really confuses me."

Separate and Then Mixed-Gender Groups

A few practitioners described the value of initially separating boys and girls and later bringing them together, thus reaping the benefits of both separate and mixed-gender groups:

> . . . through reading different research studies and also attending dif-ferent conferences, [I] have learned about the value of having separate programs to begin with and then bringing them together at the end to have a combined program. But I think that most of the time those are really only effective when you have a male educator, a male facilitator, to deliver, either be the sole facilitator or at least co-facilitate the program to the male group.

> I think if it was an ongoing support group, I think it should be offered to all girls and all boys, but I think it would be nice to have it mixed at the end. If I could have two ongoing groups and then have a couple weeks where they intervene with each other, I think it would be nice.

Using Both Same- and Mixed-Gender Groups

Meyer and Stein (2004) surveyed organizations across the country dealing with sexual assault and domestic violence and found that almost 17% of the programs reported using both mixed- and same-gender groups. Thirty percent of the people we talked with used both mixed- and same-gender groups. Schools ask that programs be flexible, but many educators dem-onstrated that many factors were considered before ultimately deciding whether to separate the genders, including a specific request from a school, the topic and specific population that is addressed, and the availability of time, space, and male facilitators.

> Depending on the amount of time we're given, we keep the group to-gether, boys and girls. If we've negotiated for or been allowed more time, we divide the boys and girls.

> It just depends on the schools. If they ask us to . . . they say, "You know we are really having a problem, and we would like to have the boys and

girls split up." We would be more than happy to do what we can to accommodate that.

For some programs, the topic determines whether males and females are mixed or separated. The prevention educators interviewed believed that, for some subjects, males and females might benefit from listening to each other, whereas other subjects might engender too much discomfort in a mixed group:

It depends on the topic. With talking about healthy boundaries, it is kind of nice as a female to have a group of females to talk to about this. They might open up a little bit more. It seems that when kids are together, they still have to put on that front for the opposite sex or whatever the case. I like it when I have a group where I can create some dialogue among the females. With sexual harassment and some other things, it is good to have the guys and girls together, because they get to hear each other's perspective.

Some of the issues that this group [girls] talks about right now, they flat out told me that they weren't going to be comfortable having boys in the group, so it also depends on what you are going to do in the group.

Some interviewees noted that, instead of the topic determining the group composition, the composition sometimes influenced the choice of topic. The type of audience or group also played a role in the decision of whether to separate the genders:

If it is not possible to have it divided by men and women, then we have a different presentation that we will do for a mixed-gender audience, so we kind of have different presentations. If we have mixed gender, we do kind of more an educational informational program . . . We have a couple of role-plays that we use that the students do, so they will do inter-action with each other.

The only time that we are speaking to single-sex groups, in general, is when we go to juvenile detention facilities. Generally, they are separated by gender, as are programs for pregnant and parenting teens, who, gen-erally, are just girls.

The school was having a real major problem with sexual harassment, and I refused to do boys and girls together.

The availability of time, space, and male facilitators also determine whether males and females are mixed or separated for many programs:

> At a particular program we did divide up the males and females and talked about gender issues and then we came back together to kind of continue the conversation. But the issue for us has been resources. There just aren't people in our community who have been able to [volunteer] . . . It would really benefit our program to have that male voice, and I think it is really important for kids to see male and female co-facilitators presenting a program and talking about these issues and that they are not just women's issues.

> It's often just not possible because the schools don't have the facilities. They would need another teacher to supervise the second group and all of that.

Black (2005) found that gender composition may not make a difference, as youth reported high levels of satisfaction with both programming formats. One of the educators we interviewed said that it did not seem to matter to the adolescents:

> And what we found in our evaluations, ironically, is that it didn't make a bit of difference [if the genders were mixed or not]. The kids didn't seem to learn any differently in the co-ed groups than when we separated for gender. . . . When it all came out in the wash in the evaluation, we didn't get a difference in our evaluation.

Of the educators we interviewed, one-third were conflicted about the gender makeup of groups, as they found benefits in both gender-separate and gender-mixed groups:

> I have mixed feelings about it. I think there's value in boys and girls hearing each other, because we don't do that very much. So for boys and girls to hear, "Oh, I didn't know it was like that for you," is very valuable. At the same time, when we're talking about sexual violence, the issues are somewhat different, depending on which group we're talking about.

> I think both are necessary really. I think the conversation, as far as changing the culture in the school and getting the issues out on the table and talked about comfortably amongst the boys and girls, it is definitely necessary. And at the same time, I think there is great benefit to having dialogue separately.

Girls seem to shy away from these topics in front of boys when speaking about them, and because you really can only teach somebody as much as they are willing to learn, but that also means that if they don't ask the questions, they may not get the information . . . Boys I think, in front of girls, just want to do a lot of showing off, so I think it would be great to separate them. On the other hand, I think discussing it together, I think it is important. Also, to let them know that these things can be talked about, especially in opposite sex relationships. They need to be discussed within their relationships themselves.

A few educators we interviewed were unsure of which type of programming was most effective. One person mentioned that those involved with her program had considered asking the youths themselves their views on same-gender versus mixed-gender groups. Another interviewee said that her group planned to conduct programs in both formats and then compare the results. Still another program staff person mentioned that her organization was in the process of experimenting with using a different gender configuration:

> For date rape we have always had them together. Our skits portray a party where a couple of rapes occur. We are finding that very difficult for them. The resistance and the victim blaming is, it seems like, the girls are silenced by the boys' reaction, in our experience, which is very frustrating. So we are actually considering for the first time splitting them up.

Age Range in Programs

Little research has centered on the optimal age at which prevention programs should target youth, but many violence researchers, including dating violence researchers, agree that pre-adolescence and adolescence is the ideal time to reach young people (Finkelhor and Asidigian 1996; Fredland 2005). Meyer and Stein's (2004) national study of prevention programs found that most programs targeted ninth through twelfth graders (ninth grade, 62.1%; tenth grade, 64.8%; eleventh grade, 61.4%; twelfth grade, 59.5). Some researchers believe that prevention programs should target pre-adolescents and early adolescents in middle school, because violence in relationships begins early. Kreiter et al. (1999) found that 7% of seventh graders and 11% of eighth graders reported dating abuse. Close (2005) states that "interventions for middle school adolescents can help youth preemptively manage relationship problems before dangerous interpersonal habits become established" (7). Meyer and Stein (2004) found that about one-third of the dating violence and sexual assault programs around the country reported programs for both seventh- and eighth-grade students. Sixty percent of the interviewed prevention educators concentrated their programs in high schools, but about one-fourth said that they present at least some programs in middle schools. Some of the prevention educators in our study contended that eight- or ninth-grade students were the optimal age for these programs:

> A primary target is ninth-grade classrooms . . . because ninth grade is sort of a critical year in terms of . . . developmentally for young people starting to date and all of that. Also, you catch a lot of young people in ninth grade who, by the time you get to eleventh or twelfth grade, are either too cynical at that point to really be open to the information, or often have dropped out.

> So we decided that we had sort of hit on it, a good age group to start the teen violence prevention thing as, at least a test project, because it seemed like eighth grade was a transitional year. They went from being little kids to big kids and . . . and teenagers . . . A lot of kids had not been necessarily seriously dating at that point, or having to think about these issues in concrete form. But yet certainly by the time they were at the end of the eighth grade, they were really needing to have this basic information to be able to make solid decisions about their own life choices.

Homogeneity of Age in Groups

Literature regarding age suggests that the age span for adolescent participants must be kept relatively small, as maturity and interests can vary greatly (Zastrow 1993). Some of our prevention educators clearly saw the importance of including youth of similar ages in their programs. Those that have programs for adolescents of varying ages cite the inherent challenges:

> I have done some girls [groups] with the Girl Scouts recently, where the age range has been middle school all the way through high school seniors. . . . I think I would prefer them to be around the same age, only because high school seniors definitely have more experience. They are more perceptive about things than the middle school kids. So some of the things I have said will go over their head, but some of them, the middle school kids, weren't there developmentally. So I definitely think there is a benefit because you can really focus the presentation and everything on where the kids are developmentally, whether they are older adolescents or younger.

> Usually we don't have them ask for anything else. I have been at classes where I have had freshmen through juniors in a classroom. I find that

they will act differently . . . like the juniors will act like the big dogs or the freshmen are going to try to speak up to seem cool to the older kids.

Researchers (Rones and Hoagwood 2000) and practitioners agree that the program content and presentation clearly must be age-appropriate:

We generally have not done a sexual assault presentation under a high school level. We might talk a little bit about it, but not a full-out presentation. . . . In the middle school, they want a more general dating violence presentation, not just focusing on sexual assault, but on all the aspects of dating violence.

It depends on the subject. We prefer to do date rape for eleventh or twelfth, particularly twelfth in the spring, just because college freshmen are at such high risk [for date rape].

Usually, with the sixth, seventh, and eighth grade school systems, they won't let us do sexual assault, so we substitute gender images instead, which is okay, because that's addressing, you know, the myths that support an abusive society. But it usually winds up that when we get to the question and answer period, they ask all the sexual assault questions anyway.

Group Size

From the literature on groups, we know that group size strongly influences member satisfaction, level of interaction, and group cohesion (Zastrow 1993). Although little empirical evidence exists to guide violence prevention educators in planning group size, many programs are for classroom-size groups (Foshee 2004; Jaycox et al. 2006). Wolfe et al.'s (2003) Youth Relationship Project limited groups to six to ten participants. Meyer and Stein's (2004) survey of sexual assault and domestic violence prevention programs across the country found that over 96% of the programs reported that they made presentations in regularly scheduled classes; over 70% of the classrooms had between twenty-one and thirty participants; less than 20% of programs made presentations to groups of more than fifty students; and 45% reported that they gave presentations to school assemblies.

We asked the interviewees about the typical size of groups to which they present. We also asked about their preferences regarding group size. Some preferred classroom-sized groups of about twenty-five to thirty students in order to engender discussion; others preferred even smaller groups to ensure a dialogue that was important in the group. Two respondents felt, however, that when groups are too small, achieving purposeful interaction and discussion is challenging:

> And sometimes they'll do a group of five kids and it's hard, in that sense, to get as much discussion and get as much kind of class involvement when you have five people, so I would say, 30 as well would be ideal.

> When it's too small, you don't get a lot of different . . . well, I guess you could get different perspectives but it's just kind of . . . I don't actually know. The girls actually like about ten to fifteen and I don't really know why. I think it's just better when you have more people involved and you can do more activities. You can break them up into groups better and it just kind of works better with the workshop structure.

Advantages of Small Groups

Small groups offer many advantages but, according to the prevention educators we interviewed, the most important and obvious one is the opportunity for interaction and discussion:

> I think that the more you can be interactive and get people to come up with some of the information on their own, that they may buy into it a little more, that they'll get it [into] more active learning. We did a couple of assemblies and you could tell that people were chatting with their friends next to them and they weren't all listening.

> If you have 20 to 15, the smaller groups, they tend to, the individuals will speak more instead of it just being dominated by a few confident and talkative kids and it's easier to draw them out 'cause then you have, you don't have as many kids. So you have the time during a particular, that, whatever session you're doing, to encourage interaction, to ask direct questions and say, "What is your opinion?" or call on them for something without embarrassing the kid, and in . . . in drawing them into the level of participation in the group.

A few people we surveyed mentioned that specific topics might make smaller groups especially critical:

> I think the bigger the group gets, the more it can be really hard to talk about the issue, because then you have got all of those dynamics in there.

You have the power and control of the group going on with the kids themselves, so you might have a voice that has a lot of power in the room saying, basically, "this is dumb and we don't want to hear it" and then you are really nowhere.

Disadvantages of Assembly Presentations

Most prevention educators try to avoid addressing assemblies (Hilton et al. 1998), as large groups pose the potential of ridicule or discomfort and do not ensure confidentiality or opportunities to reveal personal beliefs safely and openly (Werkele and Wolfe 1999). About 40% of our interviewees said that they tried to avoid presenting to large groups, especially school assemblies:

I don't particularly like assemblies because there's less interaction. So you really are just lecturing to them. And if someone does have a question or wants to bring up some points, it's hard, maybe, for everyone to hear them . . . you lose the effectiveness of the smaller groups because there is less interaction. . . . it might seem a little boring to them or it might just seem like another class to them because I really can't, you know, get into one-on-one's and group discussions. I can't get into group discussions like we usually do. So I really don't like assemblies too much.

Because it causes a lot of chaos. A lot of people talking all at once, especially with the kids.

Three interviewees refused to participate in school assemblies, because experience has taught them that large group presentations are ineffective:

I made a decision about 12 years ago that we would not do assembly-style work for a lot of different reasons. One, because the sensitive nature of the information and making direct contact with kids or not being able to have that ability. And not knowing if we made an impact on the students and kind of leaving them hanging. I felt it was ethically not appropriate in regards to sexual assault issues. So we do not do assembly-style work.

Accommodating Group Size

Our respondents often reported that, despite their preferences for smaller groups, they often need to present to audiences of varying sizes. They also try to accommodate the requests of their host settings:

We do change, if there is a huge group . . . So like the assemblies, we'll do more arts-based stuff. We change it that way because you can't facilitate a discussion for all those people.

We try to have no more than 30. However, I have done one-shot presentations with an assembly, but we try to shy away from those if we can. But if that's all the school will do or can do, then we will definitely try to accommodate them.

Summary of Membership

Program administrators differ in their views as to whether separating or combining girls and boys in program groups is more effective. The literature offers little guidance for programs regarding this issue. Many prevention educators recognize the benefits of both mixed-gender and same-gender groups, and sometimes they try to use both arrangements in different phases of their programs. The great majority of educators favor smaller groups in order to create more interaction and engagement among youth. Practitioners' strong negative reaction to school assemblies parallels reports in the literature that question their effectiveness. However, many programs find it necessary to accommodate the needs and requests of their host setting regarding both gender mix and group size.

[7]

Structure

The prevention professionals we contacted took various approaches to structuring their programs. We begin this chapter with a discussion of varying program lengths and session spacing, which are strongly influenced by the schedules in different school systems. We then describe the presentation techniques that educators use, including videos, role-playing, and discussions versus lectures. Finally, we address educators' views about their experiences with classroom teachers and about assigning homework in prevention programming.

Program Length and Session Spacing

Little empirical evidence exists for the optimal length of dating violence and sexual assault prevention programs. Thus, even though one-hour programs covering information on dating violence and sexual assault are common in colleges, high schools, and middle schools, their effectiveness is questionable. A review of sexual assault prevention programs (National Institute of Justice 2004) called for research on differences between single-session and multiple-session programming. As with the length of the programs, evidence is scarce for the relative effectiveness of various patterns of session spacing. This section summarizes existing literature and presents comments that we gathered from prevention experts about the length and spacing of program sessions.

Length of Programs

The number of sessions presented in programs varies greatly; most programs include between one and twenty sessions of varying lengths. Although researchers concur that a single one-hour presentation has little lasting impact on attendees (Foshee et al. 2000; Schewe 2003b), we do not know the optimal number of sessions for dating violence or sexual assault prevention programs, and research has not substantiated that multi-session programming is more effective than a single-session. In a survey of the literature of batterers' intervention programs, Gordon and Moriarty (2003) report that the greater the number of treatment sessions that batterers attend, the lower the recidivism rate, while others support having more frequent sessions at the beginning of the intervention to increase the intensity (Gondolf 2002). In school intervention programs, multiple sessions are presumed and standard (DiGiovanni 2006; Hopson 2006).

The varying length of dating violence and sexual assault prevention programs is demonstrated in the literature. Foubert, Tatum, and Donahue (2006) used a one-hour program that included a video and presentations by four undergraduate peer educators. Avery-Leaf and Cascardi (1995) and Macgowan (1997) used a five-session dating violence prevention program with adolescents. Weisz and Black (2001) held twelve one-and-a-half-hour sessions in their program on dating violence and sexual assault, and presented the program in two configurations: once weekly for twelve weeks, and twice weekly for six weeks. Wolfe et al. (2003) conducted one of the longer prevention programs discussed in the literature: their eighteen two-hour sessions were delivered in a community setting, targeting at-risk teens.

Meyer and Stein's (2004) survey of sexual assault and domestic violence programs across the country found that 96.6% of respondents presented programs during regularly scheduled classes. Because the majority of classes are between fifty and ninety minutes, presentation time is limited to those durations. Several authors suggest that time constraints imposed by schools might constitute the primary factor limiting the effectiveness of prevention programs (Lonsway 1996), and that multi-session programs are more effective than single-session programs (Anderson and Whiston 2005). It is probably unreasonable to expect attitudes, and, even more so, behaviors, to change following a brief program, when those attitudes developed over many years. O'Leary, Woodin, and Fritz (2006) suggest that, although no data support the claim that longer programs are needed to change behaviors (and attitudes) our general experience with efforts to change behavior suggests that longer programs are probably more effective.

The effectiveness of multi-session programs is also reinforced in the experience of general violence prevention programming (Conduct Problems Prevention Research Group 2002; Nadel et al. 1996), as well as programs on dating violence and sexual assault prevention. Anderson and Whiston (2005) found that "longer interventions are more effective than brief interventions in altering both rape attitudes and rape-related attitudes" (374). Lonsway et al. (1998) contend that programs of longer duration allow greater time for youth and leaders to establish trusting relationships in which youth may feel more willing to openly discuss and challenge their stereotypical attitudes and behaviors. Time may be an essential element needed to generate open communication in prevention programs. Close (2005) also advocates for programs to be of "sufficient length to enable teaching of a full curriculum using various teaching strategies, including role-playing, interactive games, and art-related projects that engage various interest levels of age groups while delivering important information" (7).

Single-Session Presentations

In spite of their concerns about the limitations of one-time presentations, 35% of our interviewees said that they often presented only a single session. Most often, schools limit the presenters to one class period. Thus educators frequently had a forty-five-minute to one-hour presentation prepared. One educator referred to her one-hour presentation as "Dating Violence 101 for Healthy Relationships."

Multi-session Presentations

In contrast, or in addition to the one-time presentations, many programs offer a multi-session alternative for youths. Some of these programs are two sessions long; others range from sixteen to twenty sessions. Longer-session programs often involve a group of adolescents who have chosen to participate. These include support groups and curriculum-based programs.

> Every ninth grader sees this performance at the beginning of their health class rotation and then weekly throughout their half-year health class . . . I go in and do workshops on dating violence prevention.

> We're only going into two local high schools with that right now. We've been doing it for over two years and we see the same groups of kids like

every ten school days or so, on their rotational calendars. So that's an ongoing group, which is really great.

We also have like an ongoing program at one of the high schools . . . that does differ somewhat from our middle school and high school presentation and this is more of an ongoing, once a week type thing that goes for about 12 consecutive weeks.

Flexibility in Session Numbers and Session Spacing

Despite the program presenters' strong preference for greater numbers of program sessions, many reported that they were willing to be flexible in order to meet the demands of the school schedules:

[The programs] range from a one-time presentation on sexual harassment, all the way to an eight-week, multi-session group that focuses on sexual violence and issues connected to it.

We leave it up to the teacher or the program coordinator or whatever. We want to work with their schedule. We don't like to do a one-hour session, because there is just so much information that needs to be conveyed. That is almost impossible to do adequately. But if they say they want a one-hour workshop, then we'll do a condensed version of our curriculum.

[We tailor the program] very much to how the school perceives their need. We would prefer to do multiple sessions and we do some multiple sessions in some of our high schools. A great many of our middle school ones are one-time presentations.

The program presenters we interviewed also recognized the need for flexibility in the spacing of program sessions. To accommodate their schools' schedules, they would offer back-to-back sessions, one weekly session, or sessions on alternating days.

To our knowledge, no empirical studies have examined the spacing of program sessions. The Heppner et al. (1995b) study of college students suggested the need for frequent, short-term interventions. Krajewski et al. (1996) held ten consecutive classes over a two-week period taught by a health education teacher and a counselor from the local battered women's shelter. Practitioners differed in their perspectives on benefits to various spacing of program sessions. Some practitioners prefer consecutive sessions to increase consistency and continuity, as they believe that consecutive sessions lead to greater trust among students and between students and the presenter. Those who stressed the importance of consecutive programming said:

> Well, you know, there's real benefit to coming back multiple days in a row. There's a trust that is built between the speaker and the students. And we find a very dramatic difference between the students' openness and responsiveness [from] day one [to] day three.

> If they have questions in the first day, they are not going to remember it a week later. And you can say "Please write it down so you don't forget," but they will lose the paper or they will forget what you said. So I prefer that [consecutive programming], because I think I get a lot more questions from the students.

> It is really better if you can do seven straight days. Or at least five straight days. If we can do five sessions, that's kind of like the ideal. And you just go in for an hour or an hour and a half, however long the class is, five straight days. That way the kids don't forget everything they've learned, you know, last week.

Other practitioners preferred some time between sessions, even for programs of short duration, to allow students time to process information and formulate additional questions:

> We encourage [sessions to be] about a week apart, so the kids can process the information a little more . . . and then kids talk about the information, so we feel like they might even use some of those things . . . if we're in and out, it just happens too quickly, I think.

> Eight weeks, once a week. It gives [students] the opportunity to do some processing. I think that that's helpful. I wouldn't want to go more than a week. And maybe even if, for example, that group met twice a week, that might even be a little bit more ideal . . . If you [students] had that opportunity to process for at least a couple of days in between sessions, I think that would be really useful.

One person felt that a break between sessions allowed time for teachers to reinforce the content with students:

> We like to go in once a week and the reason why is, when we go in once a week, and we've got these good relationships with the teaching staff,

they're reinforcing throughout the week the things that we've been talking about . . . [the teachers] reinforce and carry the conversation and keep it going and bring up the issues that we were talking about.

An all-day format for programming was rare. Only one educator mentioned that her program held an all-day workshop. This program offered a large plenary session in the morning, with break-out sessions in the afternoon. Another educator mentioned the desire to develop an all day workshop for the community. The lack of resources appears to limit the ability to offer all-day programs.

Presentation Techniques

The literature scarcely touches on how various presentation techniques affect outcomes. Many publications discuss various techniques, but they do not compare the effectiveness of these approaches. Interaction seems to be the key factor in many current youth prevention programs. Wekerle and Wolfe's (1999) review of six prevention programs found that both didactic and interactive programs brought about positive changes in attitude, at least in the short run. Wolfe et al.'s (1996) Youth Relationship Project was interactive in nature but used various learning strategies, including guest speakers, videos, behavioral rehearsal, visits to community agencies, and a social action project. O'Leary, Woodin, and Fritz's (2006) review of the literature on adolescent dating violence and sexual assault prevention programs found that the programs had many similarities, including the importance of participant interaction.

Although little has been written about which presentation formats are effective, some evidence appears to indicate that confrontational methods are ineffective. Lonsway (1996) found that the confrontational format decreases the likelihood of success in rape prevention programs, and may even lead to a backlash. While prevention necessitates challenging participants about the myths surrounding dating violence and sexual assault, leaders and facilitators should probably avoid personal confrontation. None of our prevention experts discussed the use of confrontation as their primary presentation format.

In the following section, we discuss the presentation techniques of videos, role-playing, and discussions versus lectures.

Use of Videos

Of the many presentation techniques program presenters employ, videos are used the most. Wolfe et al.'s (1996) eighteen-session, coeducational intervention groups used videos, in addition to other strategies, de Anda's (1999) ten-session, cognitive/behavioral violence prevention program in Los Angeles targeted for Latino and African American youth included video depictions, along with discussions and other various techniques. Lonsway et al. (1998) used videos as part of the evaluation of their prevention program. Despite this widespread use of videos, empirical evaluation does not necessarily support their use (Schewe 2003b). Johansson-Love and Geer (2003) found that the presentation of the movie *Campus Rape* was successful in reducing rape-myth attitudes among male college students, but Heppner et al. (1995b), using the same movie, found a rebound effect after five weeks. Despite these findings, judicious use of short videos can attract youths' attention and raise important issues for discussion.

One-fourth of our sample of prevention educators confirmed that they used videos as part of their program presentation and as a mechanism for initiating discussion among the youth. Many of the videos are relatively brief (three to five minutes), supporting educators' comments that they use the videos primarily to attract attention and generate discussion.

> I have them identify the bystander in the video and what were the things that were effective? "What are barriers to people confronting friends about abusive relationships?" And we often take up quite a bit of discussion on that.

> We show videos for all of these programs. We have really good visuals for them. They respond very, very quickly to those visuals.

> We also use some videos that are pretty effective. Kids like visuals, and like interactive kinds of stuff. We use the videos, and then we break up into groups and we have the groups go over the issues that happened within the video.

> The video is maybe like 25 minutes, and in between the segments I will stop it, because they have little questions that pop up after certain segments, so then we will discuss them.

Our interviewees frequently mentioned youths' interest in videos. But even more frequently they discussed the challenges of using video. Some noted the continual struggle of seeking school approval to show videos:

> That's a constant thing. If a colleague sees a video or if I see a video that we think is fantastic and it complements well, we can't introduce

that into the classroom until we set an appointment to go to the Health Advisory Council.

Other interviewees explained the difficulty of making sure videos are not outdated, to ensure the receptiveness and interest of youth:

Kids are very sensitive and receptive to the fact that, when you get a video that was done in the 80s, the kids are like "Oh, man." And they are laughing and hysterical the whole time. Talking about how weird the hairdos are and the clothing. We have to really be careful that we keep our material up-to-date.

[We look for videos showing] people who are urban, African American or Chicano, who are young, who are from 2004 . . . and who can use some of the terms that the students use, and just believable and who don't have . . . who might have accents.

Several of the interviewees noted that it was a challenge to find videos with ethnically diverse characters:

Now a lot of times the teachers will ask us when we are showing a video, "Well, do you have a more diverse video that you can show?" We do have a couple of them. Like we have one called "Dating in the Hood" and it is predominantly for the African American and Hispanic population, deals more with kids of a lower socioeconomic background, you know, and it gives a general idea of what it might be like to go to school in the inner city as opposed to a cushy suburb. And so we like to show that sometimes in [urban] schools.

I do not use it [the video] in every school, because culturally it isn't balanced. In some schools the kids like it and, it works really well. And there are some areas that I cannot use it.

A few educators we interviewed commented that they do not use videos because of the many challenges they present, and four survey participants said that they had dealt with the many challenges by simply making their own video:

My colleague and I got a grant to do a date-rape video, and we are just filming the first one. The first two short videos [are], like 15 or 20 minutes. The first one is a story about a rape that occurred. The second one is going to be more of a documentary of people talking about their experience, or guys talking about why guys should care.

I have a video that the agency had done a couple of years ago which . . . it's like the twenty-minute video with teens from when they talk to teens about dating violence and I put together a study guide, so I give each classroom teacher a free copy of the video and study guide.

Role-playing

As with other educational approaches in this field, little empirical research has been done on role-playing. However, experts have recommended role-playing, theatrical presentations, and other media events to change attitudes and develop youths' skills (Gidycz et al. 2001, Schewe 2003b). Many programs use modeling and role-playing as mechanisms to build participants' sense of self-efficacy (Cappella and Weinstein 2006; Walsh and Foshee 1998). However, the prevention programs discussed in the literature view role-playing as just one of several techniques that should be used to engage students (Ferrell, Meyer, and Dahlberg 1996; Pittman, Wolfe, and C. Wekerle 2000).

Seventy percent of the prevention educators in our study stated that they used role-playing in their programs:

> We do role-playing in the class, where they will have a certain scenario that they have been given, maybe a sexual harassment scenario, and they would play it out, and we would have to show what is an assertive way of responding and a non-assertive way, or what may be an aggressive way of responding, and why is it more beneficial to use an assertive response, and then the people who are not in the role-playing, the rest of the group, their job is to be the observers and point out ways that they [the actors and actresses] could have done things differently

Many educators discussed how much the youth like role-playing. Seldom do they find that anyone is reluctant to participate:

> I actually have some different scenarios that are already prepared. I can kind of pull out at anytime . . . Or if we have a group that is kind of shy, we have some scenarios on paper where they can work in very small groups to discuss and come up with how they would respond in this situation or what the impact might be or various things like that. Generally the role-plays are very effective. It is very rare where students haven't wanted to do them.

Structure

I love to [have them] do as much role-playing [as possible], especially with the special-needs kids, because they don't . . . people don't think of doing that stuff with them that much. And they get right into it, and it's really helpful to help them understand fantasy from reality if we can do these little skits.

Sometimes it can be a challenge to find students for role-playing, but most of the time it's not. Most of the time we can find a student, a guy and a girl that are comfortable.

Other interviewees noted that they were not able to use this technique because of time constraints. A few people surveyed remarked that role-plays simply do not work with certain groups of youth:

I found that role-playing did not work in the situations where we tried it, because they [the students] were too timid, embarrassed, or too cool . . . It didn't work very well. It is the middle school kids who generally don't want to get out of their seats. They don't want to get up in front of anybody; they are very self-conscious.

So discussions just work a whole lot better than picking a couple people out to role-play something out. I mean, we've tried the role-playing; it just doesn't work.

I have a group of kids that feel pretty comfortable with each other, they seem to be okay with that . . . I typically find that it works better with our girls groups than our boys groups. Our boys groups tend to want to do more worksheets.

For kids that are less chatty, we might do an art project or role-playing to get them talking . . . each topic area has a number of different choices depending on the culture of that specific group.

When we asked about the use of role-playing, practitioners most often discussed using them as a means to an end. Some said they used role-playing to generate discussion, interest, and involvement:

We want discussion. We want debate. We want role-playing. We want to hear opinions and look at the continuum of how people look at things.

I try and do something active with the students, whether it is role-playing or just a quick little activity, so that they're . . . not only is it that they're learning through hearing, they're learning through seeing.

The majority of our skits are set up to end at a climatic [*sic*] point, when you are not sure what the character is going to do next, so that you can start a discussion about it and then they can ask the character as well.

One educator we interviewed described how role-playing demystifies the judicial process:

Part of the reason why we do the court role-play . . . to demystify the court process and to give them the opportunity to recognize that it's not as intimidating [as they think].

However, most of our survey participants used role-playing as a means to building youths' skills. They wanted youth to have an opportunity to practice the behavioral skills they were learning from their programs:

The other curriculum is talking to friends in an abusive relationship and that's a role- playing activity where the educators role-play a situation that shows the wrong way to talk to a friend . . . and they get suggestions from the audience about what they could do better . . . then they role-play the same situation but in a healthy way to talk to a friend. Then after that, they break up the audience into several groups, and they do their own role-playing activity to kind of practice how they would address the situation.

We'll do a role-play with two educators and then have them pick it apart and analyze it, you know, and prep them that way.

Prevention educators, of course, plan the length of role-playing to fit the time available for a presentation:

If it's a 45-minute presentation in the middle school, I would think it's pretty much 20 minutes; 20 minutes because I'm giving them, you know, 10 minutes to prepare the role-play and 10 minutes for everybody to present them.

I would say probably 40% is giving out information and then maybe the rest of it is about discussion and role-play.

I would say 50% is education and then the other 50% is a combination of them asking questions and discussion and maybe doing a role-play.

Some educators write out scripts for participants. Others ask participants to generate their own script. However, many students appear to readily take on their roles:

> Their script is already written for them. . . . The survivor says to them, "Teacher, I'm being abused, can you help me?" And their response is already written on the back of the card and they say, "I am really glad you told me, I just wish you had told me sooner." And they turn their back on them. So everybody gets a speaking part and plays a role, but they don't have to act and they get really into that; they like that.

Finally, a few of those we interviewed suggest caution when using role-playing. They warn against forcing adolescents to participate against their will. They also note the importance of being aware of the classroom dynamics:

> I think a lot of adults assume when they walk into a classroom that you have a cohesive group there; that is not a cohesive group. You have got a ton of power dynamics in that classroom. You could have a rapist and a victim right there in front of you who haven't told a soul. The classroom has so many issues going on inside of it. I don't know if I would feel safe.

> Kids don't want to be forced into acting something out that they feel funny about.

Discussion Versus Didactics

Once again, little empirical research has been done on discussion versus didactics in prevention programs. But as we stated, experts recommend interactive discussion time (Lonsway 1998; Schewe 2003b). Walsh and Foshee (1998) advocate discussion as an important step in building participants' sense of self-efficacy. Yeater and O'Donohue (2002) also contend that "presentation programs that are more discussion focused and interactive may be more ecologically valid and effective at changing relevant behavior" (1143). At-risk students may also respond better to interventions involving discourse than didactics delivered by educational authorities (Begun 2003). Gidycz et al. (2001) suggested that the way to increase prevention programming saliency and the processing of information is to promote greater discussion and provide information in a personalized manner. Discussion of issues that students raise seems to attract their attention and helps make the content relevant. It may also be useful to distribute discussion guidelines at the beginning of the program. As with video presentations and role-playing, prevention literature often underscores the importance of using discussion in combination with other activities (de Anda 1999; Proto-Campise, Belknap, and Wooldredge 1998; Wolfe et al. 2003).

We asked the prevention educators whom we interviewed to describe their use of discussion and lecture while presenting program content. Only two stated that they use the lecture format as the primary technique:

> Typically we tell the students at the very beginning that any time they feel that they want to discuss something, then we're totally open for that. But the majority of our presentation is giving information.

Thus, almost all the interviewees reported that interaction and discussion formed the basis of their program. Most believe that youth learn better through active participation. A few noted that discussion helps participants learn more about their lives:

> We know that it [discussion] is more effective. That is the way that you can pulse whether they are taking in the information or not. If you lecture them and give them statistics and do all the chatting . . . how do you know whether or not the kids are taking in the information?

> I like to speak for about eighteen minutes . . . class is typically fifty minutes . . . [I spend] a few minutes more, I guess, on the discussion. I actually think that's the best. We might be able to capture them with the stories, but I think the best learning process is through their questions and us trying to answer them.

> My style is very interactive; it is more conversational than lecture format. Even when I am presenting the information on what abuse is. Most of the information that I am presenting . . . it is actually asking them questions and having them give me the answers or pulling it out of them.

> The more they participate, the rowdier the classes, the more chatting that is going on, the more questions that they ask, the more hungry they are, gives me some kind of indication that okay, we did our job.

> What happens is they start talking more about the topic. They really do. Sometimes once you get them going, sometimes it's hard to say, "Well,

gee, we'd better wind down now. Remember we have question time, so we can continue talking."

I would say 50% or more is, if you want to talk about discussion versus lecture/didactic, at least 50% is discussion where they are answering questions, giving input . . . we have increasingly made our middle school presentation interactive, because early on that was one of the complaints from the teachers, is that they, and that is certainly what I've learned about middle school students. They cannot sit for 45 minutes and be talked at.

You really want to engage, and not to say that they have to be verbal to be engaged, but you want as much participation from them as possible so that, so they have a chance to air their thoughts and their feelings. It is their lives we are talking about, so they have a right, and should speak about their feelings and their thoughts. And we also learn from them, too. That is part of it, too. We are not experts on everything. We walk in, and we have information and we have experiences, but so do they.

Variety of Presentation Techniques

Over 40% of the prevention experts discussed the importance of using a variety of presentation techniques in programming with youth:

We really try and make it a mix. No one wants to be talked at for an hour. So we really want to have some discussion and to get them engaged by asking them questions. We also know that it's much more valuable to give them a chance to . . . to not just give them the information but give them the tools they need to apply the information, and then to give them a chance to start applying the information.

I usually do a lecture and then I'll do some sort of experiential type of activity with the whole group. Like, I don't know if you've ever done the string exercise, something like that to kind of get them to think about what it would be like to be somebody who is in a violent dating situation.

Throughout the lecture, there are overheads that we put up, and actually right now we are going to be revising that into a Power Point presentation, and we are actually going to be using video with that.

We've been using a lot of music lately in regard to, like, we will play the music and everybody is like snapping their fingers and shaking their booties and doing all that stuff. Then I turn the music off and then we go through the lyrics. So that we can kind of get a clear understanding about being called a "bitch and a whore" . . . what that all looks like. "When I rub your nipples, they get hard" and all these lyrics that are misogynistic. Insulting to women.

Although most of the interviewees engaged in discussion with youth most of the time, we were interested to learn their estimates of how much time was devoted to discussion versus lecture. Responses indicated that the majority spend at least 50% of their time in discussion. Several said that the amount of time spent lecturing versus discussing depends on various factors, including the specific topic being addressed. The time of day seems to influence the degree of class interaction. They were able to be flexible in their presentation depending on the nature of the situation:

There are certainly some times when my program is limited to 45 minutes, which makes it really, really difficult. And then there are times where I have like a block-scheduled class, where you've got an hour and 20 minutes so you can do more things and have more activities and interaction.

Occasionally I get a class that, it's 7:30 in the morning and they aren't really awake yet, so trying to get them to interact is a real challenge.

We kind of do all of that; it depends on the topic. Topics like date and acquaintance rape, that seems to generate a discussion. We welcome at the beginning of the class, we say . . . If you have comments, if you disagree with something that I say . . . this is an open environment and you are not going to shock me and positive participation is great." So with date and acquaintance rape, it just happens.

Of course, you know the smaller amount of time we have to deliver the program makes that more and more difficult to have that [discussion], because although those activities and things can be very beneficial for capturing the students' attention and also probably for them absorbing information, they take a considerable amount more time than just me as the facilitator delivering information to them.

Classroom Teachers and Homework

The literature reveals little about either the role of the classroom teacher as a partner in prevention programming or how the classroom teachers' participation relates to the effectiveness of prevention programming. Research also rarely addresses the effectiveness of assigning homework to prevention program participants.

Role of Classroom Teachers

Classroom teachers apparently play a highly variable role in sexual assault and dating violence prevention programs. In a few programs teachers actually present the material (Avery-Leaf and Cascardi 2002), and in others teachers and prevention educators work together. Jaffe et al. (1992) had teachers co-facilitate discussions with community nonviolence leaders following the large group presentation. Krajewski et al.'s (1996) prevention program had a classroom health education teacher and a counselor from the local domestic violence program present their prevention program together. Both attended a day-long training session offered by the director of the shelter. However, few of the more recent programs have relied on classroom teachers as presenters. Some teachers probably feel uncomfortable with the dating violence and sexual assault material, and others may feel unqualified. Gottfredson and Gottfredson (2002) found that critical to the success of prevention programs is that the programs are delivered by individuals who are adequately trained and knowledgeable about the subject. A potential problem is that teachers who are asked to take on this new task may view it as an extra burden on top of an already heavy workload.

Prevention educators commonly collaborate with classroom teachers to varying degrees. Meyer and Stein (2004) found that 72% of program presenters said they collaborated with the classroom teacher prior to the presentation, and that 35.5% of the teachers reviewed the material to be presented. Meyer and Stein (1997) also found during 87.4% of the classroom presentations that classroom teachers stayed in the room during the presentation of the program, and 7.4% of the programs reported that teachers were important for resolving disciplinary problems in the classroom.

Only one of our prevention educators reported that classroom teachers actually presented the program. In that program, teachers have been trained in the content area of dating violence and sexual assault, and they offer an elective class for students who wish to learn how to present the information to their peers. Students from that class then have the opportunity to present the content to other classrooms in the school.

In some cases, classroom teachers can act as co-facilitators during the prevention program presentation. One prevention educator described how the classroom teacher took on a character in a role-play and assisted in processing the discussion that followed. Another educator mentioned the importance of the teacher's introduction of the educators in setting a positive and productive tone for the presentation:

> He [the teacher] kind of preps the students; he sees these kids every day. And this is an ongoing conversation with them before and after we come in, so they are already excited about this . . . It's not as if they don't know who you are or what we're here for. He has already kind of set up this culture in the classroom "this is an important thing you need to talk about and this is a treat that we're having these people come in" and that changes the entire presentation.

As opposed to the strong commitment and involvement of some teachers, other educators described how a few teachers would sit in the back of the room and grade papers during the presentation. One educator described how a teacher's presence can even be counterproductive to the goals of the program:

> I was at school, and I go to one classroom and I give the pre-test. A kid is sitting next to the teacher. He says, "What does this mean?" [The teacher says] "Don't ask me; this isn't my idea to bring these people here. If anybody touched me, I'll just take down my 45, shoot them and keep on going."

Almost 20% of the prevention educators talked about their meeting with teachers ahead of time to discuss the program and the teachers' expectations. Some presenters ask that teachers distribute pre-tests before the presentation to allow more time for the session itself. This process seems to work well for many:

> We meet with the teacher. We discuss the program with them; we discuss the expectations that they are our partners in this process and that they would still be the primary person to control the class as far as discipline issues and we need them to be in the room with us when we are facilitating, just so that those kinds of things can be handled like they normally would be in their classroom. We give them a teacher's guide

for implementing the program, so they have all of the homework assignments that the kids do. They have all of the activities; it is very clear what they should be doing with the students when the facilitators are not there.

The most common situation we encountered among the prevention educators we interviewed was that they presented the program and teachers served as support persons in the classroom. About 40% of the educators reported that they encouraged classroom teachers to remain in the classroom throughout the presentation:

We strongly encourage them [teachers] to stay. It kind of ticks me off, actually, when the teachers don't stay in the room.

[Teachers] they're legally required to stay. I don't know if this is universal nationwide, but, in general, our experience has been that there are requirements of having a teacher of record in the classroom who is officially designated by the school. A lot of teachers want to leave the classroom. They think of it as a free period for them. It's something that we really emphasize with the teachers that it's important on two levels . . . on a discipline level and from a liability level. But also, from the perspective of continuing education and allowing them to be able to learn from the topic as well and to be able to continue discussion about these types of issues . . . after we're gone.

Some teachers just don't care anymore [chuckles] and they leave. And the younger teachers stay. I mean, this is just my experience . . . There are many teachers who have been there a long time who do care to stay and they are the ones who invite us back year after year.

Sometimes prevention educators even refuse to do presentations if teachers are not in the classroom:

It's only the teachers who have such a good control over their class and they know who they are—will leave to go to the bathroom or maybe go to the front office and do something . . . with teachers now, they will call me if they are not going to be there and I said "let's reschedule."

When asked why they preferred to have teachers remain in the classroom, most responders cited discipline issues. Others mentioned the benefits of having teachers do follow-up after the presentation:

Some kids pay attention better with a speaker; some kids take advantage of the fact that the teacher is not in the room and talk with each other.

It is also important to have the teacher in the classroom for any kind of follow-up. If the teacher has no clue of what we talked about, and the kid asks about it, and they weren't there, then they can't follow up with that student or anything.

Even though I'm certified and even though our staff is certified, a teacher there certainly hears everything in context, so if anything was repeated out of context, there would be staff there. And the other important thing is, it tells the students that the teacher is interested in this. We tell the teacher they can be active or sit in the back if they want. We can't tell them not do to their book or their grades, you know.

They know their students . . . and we're pretty observant to see how kids react to this information. If we see that someone seems like they're getting a little upset or having a difficult time, we can try to work with them or talk with them ahead of time. They might notice it before we do because they know the children better. And with two people in the classroom, if one person can very subtly make an excuse for a person to be able to leave without any "to do" about it. That's very effective.

Although many prevention educators were insistent that teachers remain in the classroom, a few actually preferred that the teacher leave, citing concern for the students' comfort levels. They worried that the students may not be as open to the discussion with the teacher in the classroom:

I will say that I feel frequently that students feel more free to ask questions. It always seems like an extension of Mom and Dad. "They see you every day; you have control of them for those [hours] every day." I'm not. I'm much safer for them to open up to.

If an adult is present, sometimes teenagers tend not to express their feelings as much and so . . . And we try to create a safe environment for the audience to be able to talk freely and openly.

I've worked with [teachers] for five years now, they know that sometimes the kids will ask a lot more questions or disclose a lot more if the teacher isn't there in the room.

Homework

We were unable to find any empirical evidence regarding the effectiveness of assigning homework to program participants. However, the rationale for assigning homework in prevention programs appears to be similar to that for assigning school homework in general: it reinforces the content and the message taught. A common prevention-program assignment is to ask youth to notice and report back on gender stereotypes that they observe in the media:

> There is follow up curriculum that we give to the teachers. There are worksheets that they can do that they can go home and look at the issues of sexualized violence in the media. Come back and report on those to the teachers and the larger group.

> [The homework is] "Collect some media images of sexualized violence or how women are portrayed in the media."

> We will ask them to pay attention when they go home and watch the TV ads and/or look through a magazine, pay attention to the advertising and let us know tomorrow if you've caught anything.

A few of the educators who spoke with us mentioned giving homework assignments but acknowledged that the assignments are limited:

> We have one particular portion of our curriculum where we discuss a story, an actual story, that a young woman wrote that kind of details her experience of dating violence. It starts off with dating violence. . . . She was 12 years old and she dates this guy, marries him, and she is with him until she is 21. She's got 9 years of domestic violence with this guy. And we ask the students to finish the story as a homework assignment.

> We try [to give homework], not hugely, it really depends on the class. I mean if the teacher, some teachers are like "yeah, give them homework." And then they get homework. Sometimes the homework is not like really hard. But, "think of a song that has . . . in it. . Bring it in," something like that or whatever.

Most prevention experts do not assign homework to participants in ongoing programs, because they have learned that few students actually complete it:

We've tried to do homework assignments; it hasn't typically worked. They don't bring them back or it's "I left it in my locker, can I go get it?" Yeah, so we typically haven't been very successful.

Not usually, because of the makeup and the nature of those students and where they are coming from. It just wouldn't be successful. They probably would not; they would not be able to complete the assignments.

A few interviewees mentioned the need to provide an incentive for completing homework assignments, even though the assignments were not difficult:

Rarely. I rarely give them. Sometimes I will give them worksheets that I want them to look at and fill out and usually, if I do that, I give them an incentive to bring it back.

One person we interviewed believed that using homework would be effective, and wanted to begin incorporating homework into the program:

That's been a weakness of ours and it's been shown to be really effective to ask them to do homework. We really haven't. It's something that we may take a look at again and see whether or not it's possible.

Summary of Structure

Like researchers, the large majority of those we interviewed believe that one-hour or one-time presentations are rarely effective. Longer programs provide more time for attitudes to change and skills to be developed. Despite the strong preference for programs of longer duration, one-time program presentations are a reality for many prevention educators. The structural limitations of school schedules often make multiple-session programs impracticable or impossible. Most prevention educators are flexible and provide programs of varying lengths and variable session spacing to best meet the needs of their host settings. Although prevention educators may not have a great deal of control over the length of programs they can present in school settings, more research is needed on optimal program length to use limited resources most effectively. Most important, research is needed on the optimal length of programs to achieve skill development and behavioral change.

Prevention educators concur with the studies cited in the literature and emphasize the use of multiple presentation techniques, including videos, role-playing, or other creative techniques to stimulate discussion among adolescents. Although educators find the use of videos and role-playing effective to varying degrees, they generally agree that these techniques are best used as a way to generate discussion. Despite the strong preference for interaction and discussion, time limits or other constraints sometimes make it necessary on occasion for educators to lecture with limited discussion. Views varied on the desirability of having teachers present in the classroom during the presentation, yet most thought that teachers played an important role in reinforcing the messages conveyed to students. Finally, few educators use homework assignments, primarily because students simply do not respond.

[8]

Program Content

This chapter centers on the topics prevention educators include in their presentations to adolescents, and cites relevant studies in the literature relating to each topic. Although the topics a program covers are closely related to its goals, prevention educators differ on which goals relate to specific topics, and so we confine our discussion in this chapter to topics alone, without assigning them to specific aspirations. (For our discussion of program goals, see chapter 4.) Each program, of course, may not cover the full range of topics examined here in every presentation or even in a series of presentations. Some programs do a variety of presentations to the same group within a single year or over several consecutive years, whereas others may give a presentation only once to a particular group. Several programs discuss certain topics with middle school youth and examine other subjects with high school students, but not all prevention educators agree on which topics are appropriate for which age group. Our discussion, therefore, includes all topics the interviewees mentioned, citing the audiences for which they might be relevant.

We begin the chapter with a discussion of whether programs combine or separate presentations about dating violence and sexual assault. We then report on specific subjects that interviewees discussed, starting with those applicable to both dating violence and sexual assault presentations, and then turning to topics specifically related to dating violence or sexual assault. Finally, we look at topics that fit within neither of the two broad categories.

Do Presentations Combine Dating Violence and Sexual Assault?

We found no research addressing the wisdom of separating or combining the topics of dating violence and sexual assault in one presentation. We know from conversations with other prevention practitioners that they worry that combining the two areas may result in minimizing or overlooking important content in one of the areas. Viewing sexual assault as an element of dating violence, for instance, may play down or eliminate content on acquaintance rape.

The requirements of funding sources may determine whether programs address dating violence or sexual assault or take on both topics. Some states have separate state-sponsored funding streams for programs dealing with each of these social problems. Foundations may also fund programs with a single focus. Our interview data indicate that two-thirds of prevention programs focus on both areas equally or nearly equally, whereas 10% center more on one area than the other. An example of the latter is one that addresses date rape as a type of dating violence but does not discuss sexual assault in general. About 10% of programs focused full attention on sexual assault, and 6% on dating violence. Eight percent had a single focus but collaborated closely with an agency covering the other area. One or two agencies had prevention educators who each addressed either dating violence or sexual assault. The data we present here may not reflect national trends in separating or combining dating violence and sexual assault presentations.

Topics Relevant to Dating Violence and Sexual Assault

Definitions, Warning Signs, Risky Situations, and Safety Plans

About half of the interviewees reported that their programs contain content on definitions, dynamics, and types of dating violence. Similarly, about half specified that they present content on definitions and dynamics of sexual assault.

Schewe's (2002) review of rape prevention programs suggests that "factual information such as legal definitions of rape, descriptions of victims and offenders, description of rape trauma syndrome, and information about local resources for survivors" (108) have not demonstrated effects on students' attitudes. Some literature supports the inclusion of content on unhealthy behaviors and warning signs. For example, the Safe Dates program (Foshee et al. 1998) uses the Health Beliefs model of the importance of perceived susceptibility and severity as cues for adolescents to get help. O'Brien (2001) notes the importance of defining specific behaviors as abuse, as research shows that adolescents often do not view physical or sexual aggression as abusive. Literature on college sexual violence prevention supports the inclusion of definitions (Heppner et al. 1995b) and rape myths (Schewe 2002).

Investigators suggest that the warning signs for sexual assault should not be discussed in any way that appears to hold potential victims responsible for preventing assaults (Casey and Nurius 2006b), but presenting information about high-risk situations is effective (Casey and Nurius 2006b; Schewe 2002). Bachar and Koss (2001) note that most college sexual assault prevention programs focus on rape myths, attitudes, and knowledge. Schewe (2002) writes that teaching women to avoid high-risk situations is possibly an effective prevention strategy but should not be presented to male or mixed-gender audiences, because potentially it could help would-be perpetrators circumvent women's self-protection strategies.

About a third of the interviewees specifically mentioned covering warning signs, risky situations, and safety planning in their programs:

We do a handout of just questions, you know, that, "If you find yourself . . ." you know, "if you're currently in a relationship or have had a relationship and he doesn't . . ." like one example might be: he doesn't agree with who your friends are. Or he's telling you like what you're supposed to be wearing . . . And then, "How you feel?" You know, "Do you feel like no one else can like you or love you like he does?" . . . And if they answer "yes" to any of the questions or think "maybe yeah" then there's a potential that their relationship might [be dangerous]. Like "does he criticize or humiliate you in front of other people?" "Are you scared of disagreeing with him or her? Do you feel pressured by them when it comes to sex?" . . . And we're not saying that if you answer "yes" to these questions that you are in an abusive relationship. It maybe has the potential to be.

We're letting the kids know what date rape drugs are all about, what warning signs are, you know, don't leave your drink alone, you know some of the basic kind of messages. Get to know the person that you're with. Don't let yourself get isolated. You know, try to be careful of your surroundings and your environment.

So they present them with a potentially dangerous situation in regards to sexual violence and sexual harassment and dating violence. Then they kind of back into it with asking them questions about how do they feel they could best facilitate it differently. Or do it differently. So [we] take ideas. And then that way, kind of broaden their ideas to a greater knowledge of "here is how you really, truly can keep yourself safe and absolutely right." It is validating; it is empowering, giving them the opportunity to participate on that level and then giving them a little bit more accurate information.

Twelve percent of the interviewees mentioned the Power and Control Wheel, which has segments labeling types of dating violence, with examples in each segment. In the teen power and control wheel that is commonly used (http://www.ncdsv.org/images/Teen_PC_wheel_NCDSV.pdf), the rim of the wheel shows that dating violence can be physical, psychological, and sexual. The segments include peer pressure, anger/emotional abuse, using social status, intimidation, minimize/deny/blame, threats, sexual coercion, and isolation/exclusion. Presenters who use the wheel described how they help adolescents review the segments of the wheel so that the audience will be able to identify specific types of violence and relate the information to their own experiences and observations.

Presentations about specific survivors' or victims' stories can be part of a discussion on dynamics and warning signs. Three interviewees spoke of including these elements in presentations:

We want kids to recognize the warning signs. We want them to recognize the difference between love and jealousy and controlling . . . and, too, we want them to know about our shelter, in and of itself, because the four counties that we serve are the counties that our shelter serves as well. So we want them to know what we do.

Practitioners stressed the importance of not blaming victims or holding them responsible for prevention when teaching about warning signs. One participant noted that teaching self-defense skills may not be a realistic way for potential victims to help themselves:

There is some degree that [safety planning] can be accomplished, but I don't know how much of muscle memory, is that really going to be cognitively absorbed and be able to applied in a situation. I don't know. I don't know that if someone attacked me right now, that I would be able to apply anything. At least that's the kind of person that I am. I would probably freak. I would probably go, "ugh." I don't know how realistic it is for kids to be able to do it.

Some of the interviewees had specific ideas about safety for those in high-risks situations:

It also talks about safety at home . . ." If the person came over that you were in a relationship with and you didn't feel comfortable, is there someone you could call to come over or who could you call for help?" Just like "if you had to escape through the house, where could you leave? If you feel threatened and the person keeps calling, what can you do, can you screen your calls, change phone numbers?" Logging the incidents, letting the parents know what is going on, if it is harassment and we talk about stalking and talk to them again in the safety plan. "If you have a boyfriend that is stalking you and he is following you around, what can you do about that and how can you keep yourself safe?" Another thing I touch upon with them is safety in the home: if you are living in a home with domestic violence . . . I also kind of talk to them about safety in the home for those who may have parents who are abusive or may have domestic violence in the home.

One person's comments demonstrated the connection between safety planning, bystander intervention, and seeking help:

We cover various topics, but primarily we help the students learn to identify the various types of abuse that can happen in a relationship. What does a healthy relationship look like versus an unhealthy relationship? . . . We discuss safety planning. Like if a student is in an unhealthy situation, what they can do to stay safe, who they can access as outside resources to maintain their safety and eventually moving on from the relationship. Basically, our real goal is a whole social-change idea: that we've seen just through our pre-tests that we conduct for the program, that the students know what the five types of abuse are: mental, emotional, sexual, physical, verbal. But the problem lies with the students acting on that knowledge. They can put on paper that it's wrong and identify it, but they need assistance in making that behavioral change, into changing their behavior from going along with these types of things versus stepping in and saying something.

And I proceed to connect it with the whole . . . how when you go to the grocery store you always check the eggs . . . And how a lot of times people are more careful and conscientious with their eggs than they are their own relationships. They really get that connection. Then . . . I make the kids spread out like a clock face with that toilet paper roll in the center of the circle and they each have their signs on that say, "I am emotional abuse," or whatever. And I tell them that we are going to balance this egg. I place the raw egg in the toilet paper tube and step back. I say, "What's important to remember is in a healthy relationship, it's all about being equal. If all of you stay at an equal distance and none of you push or pull your string too hard or nobody walks too fast, this egg is going to be safe and keep intact. But the second you guys don't communicate and don't understand that we all have to work together, it's going to fall and break." So they love the challenge of keeping this egg safe. Well, once they have gotten to a point where they are holding the egg up with the tube, I tell them that I'm going to tell them a story about a high school couple and what happened in their relationship. But while I'm telling it, they have to walk clockwise in a circle while maintaining the balance of that egg, because like a relationship is constantly evolving and changing, we can't just stay still . . . I tell this story and at certain key points, I ask the eight people to stop and I have the students who aren't among the eight identify what type of abusive behavior is happening right now? Which one? So the students will identify, "Oh that sounds like he's using isolation," or, "She's being verbally abusive." So I validate them that, "Yes, you are correct. That is an example of this type of abuse." And whomever is wearing that type of abuse around their neck has to drop their piece of string from the activity. So now we've lost one of the supports in the relationship and they're left with seven members to try and balance the egg. So they have to start walking faster to keep up and they have to figure out how to space themselves out and accommodate the change in the relationship. And they go through this all the way until I usually get three people trying to balance the egg and everybody's on the edge of their seats waiting for it to hit the floor and, "What's going to happen?" and, "What's happening in the relationship?" And it's really powerful. It's funny that something as cheap as a roll of toilet paper and an egg and yarn get such an impact from the students and the teachers, because they're becoming involved and are making that connection that this is a fragile thing.

The amount of sexual content to include in specifying definitions of abuse and assault can be a delicate issue, especially within the subject of sexual assault. Some states and school districts have strict criteria limiting what presenters can say. However, one presenter, who is able to be specific, notes some important advantages of being explicit:

We talk about sodomy and oral sex and that's where it gets dicey. Where people don't want to talk about it or people are like, the substitutes [teachers] are like, "Wow, I didn't know that you were going to say something like that." If someone asks, "What's oral sex?" I'm going to tell them. Our thing is—I don't want anyone sitting there thinking on any level that "whatever has happened to me is so awful and weird that even the rape lady won't talk about it."

Discussions of the dynamics of relationships sometimes include obstacles to getting out of a violent relationship. This interviewee connects these obstacles to gender roles and societal values:

One of the things we'll talk about is . . . growing up in a traditional environment with traditional understanding of gender roles and oppression of women. Those are more complicated words than we would use in the classroom, but that those impact someone's ability to get out of an abusive relationship or to recognize that they deserve better than that, or that this isn't just the way it is in relationships. And so things like cultural acceptance of violence or of male dominance or things like that could impact somebody's ability to recognize and get out of an abusive situation. And also influence somebody's perpetration of abuse . . . While we don't address the societal [issue] of gang violence, we do talk about how gang involvement can complicate somebody's ability to get out of an abusive situation.

Healthy Relationships/Respect

Nearly half the educators we contacted said that their programs address healthy relationships, including the importance of equality. One-quarter of the programs cover communication in relationships, and an equal number address the related topics of assertiveness and setting boundaries.

There is little empirical research evaluating the effectiveness of discussing healthy relationships in youth prevention programs, but experts support the inclusion of the subject. Bloom and Gullotta (2003), discussing prevention in general, state that "there may be situations in which it is insufficient merely to prevent some problems from occurring; one must simultaneously attempt to bring some desired state into existence in place of that predictable problem" (14). This suggests that programs should teach concepts and skills for healthy relationships. Similarly, Durlak (1997) writes about the importance of emphasizing protective factors and the need for training in positive skills, rather than merely warning youths about potential problems. O'Brien (2001) supports a discussion of rights and responsibilities within healthy dating relationships as part of all youth violence prevention programs. Jaffe, Baker, and Cunningham (2004) support an emphasis on healthy relationships, because they believe that this approach is less likely to alienate or discourage an audience than focusing on abuse, power, and control. Schewe (2002, 117) notes that parents of younger students may be more amenable to prevention presentations when they know the emphasis is on healthy relationships rather than a "frank" discussion about sex. He also notes the importance of addressing communication skills—the literature suggests that rapists misinterpret women's behaviors—although no research has directly evaluated communication skills for these programs. Nagayama and Barongan (1997) believe that "schools should move beyond the sole emphasis on academic skills and train students to value interpersonal relationships, which have traditionally been emphasized by feminist and ethnic minority communities" (11).

Our participants stressed the need to sketch out for youths the characteristics of a healthy relationship, including equality, respect, and the need to communicate one's needs and boundaries. Various practitioners noted the lack of role models for healthy relationships in our society. Some reported that their presentations use the concept of assertiveness, and others talked about boundaries and limits. Still others mentioned self esteem:

> We start off looking at the self and self-esteem and get into boundary setting and then we talk about skills for setting boundaries, which are using assertiveness skills. We do role-playing in the class, where they will have a certain scenario that they have been given, maybe a sexual harassment scenario, and they would play it out and we would have to show what is an assertive way of responding and a non-assertive way or what may be an aggressive way of responding and why it is more beneficial to use an assertive response. And then the people who are not in the role-play, the rest of the group, their job is to be the observers and point out ways that they could have done things differently or things that they could have said that were more assertive and talking about why that is important to use assertiveness over aggressiveness or non-assertion.

In some communities, presentations stressing healthy relationships may be more acceptable than those centering on violence or sexual issues:

> There's a lot of conservatism in the counties surrounding us, and so they really . . . We would have to do a heavy concentration on healthy relationships and boundaries more than talking about, you know, sex . . . So, we have to approach it differently. We wouldn't go in and probably talk about drinking because that would not be acceptable. Because they don't believe the kids would be doing it.

Some respondents pointed out that discussions of assertiveness and communication give students empowering tools:

> I am hoping to give them skills to have the courage to speak up about what their boundaries are and how their boundaries change—to discuss that with the person in their relationship.

> We had responses from the students that they don't really know what to do after they learn all this information. They might feel a little disempowered, so we can get to focus on: "Okay, what would you say? Specifically what would you not say? How would you say it?"

One of our program educators made a strong connection between the need for programs that offer role models, as well as communication and conflict-resolution skills. She described how some youths are honest and frustrated about their limited skills and options in handling conflict:

> Boys come up to me and say, "I tried to walk away but what am I supposed to do?" They really know [that violence is wrong], but they just do not have the skills. And when I bring up things to them like, "Well, if you are unhappy in the relationship why don't you just end the relationship?" "What?" The choice is beat her up or break up with her? "You don't have to beat her up?" And they had never thought about that. That kind of thing. They feel like they have been pushed into a corner where they have no other option. But they will admit that . . . They are like, "Yeah, I did that and I feel awful and I don't know why I did it but I really tried and this is what I tried and none of it worked."

Myths and Blaming the Victim

Nearly half the interviewees mentioned myths and blaming the victim as important subjects in their presentations. We treat them here together, because most myths imply that the victim is responsible for the assault. In connection with definitions and the dynamics of dating violence, programs often include a discussion of victim blaming and explore why victims stay in abusive dating relationships.

The acceptance of rape myths is commonly discussed in rape prevention programming (Schewe 2002), and Seimer (2004) recommends that programs include discussions about myths regarding dating violence. Schewe (2002) suggests that rape myths are a logical target, because research has shown that cognitive distortions commonly precede sexual assaults. Presentations on dating violence also stress negative attitudes or cognitive distortions related to victim blaming. For example, Cascardi, O'Brien, and Avery-Leaf (1997) focused their intervention partially on justifications of aggression, and they found improvement on scales that measure this construct.

One interviewee asserted that the discussion of myths is a major task of prevention programs, because "that's what primary prevention is—to get out there and do those big myths and stereotypes and the values that support abuse." Another interviewee suggested that debunking myths might seem "simple" for an experienced presenter, but, in fact, myths are often deeply entrenched within youth culture:

When I say "tried and true and simple," I'm talking about like date rape myths, for instance. What are the things that people think about rape that are just not true? One of the gender bias ideas that may be held out there that simply aren't true. And debunking those. I mean pretty straightforward, to me, kind of stuff. It's not real tricky. It's not real complicated. It's pretty simple. You know, it's just getting those messages out there and being willing to sit and talk them through. They're simple from the standpoint of messages but when you've got some beliefs that are pretty solid against that, when I say the message is simple, getting it through may not be. And you just have to [be patient]. I've got a lot of patience.

Another educator discussed myths and cultural groups:

A lot of, especially the young ladies, will still blame [the victim]. They will blame the females for staying in a relationship. They blame the females for getting assaulted. They will say, "Well, if she wasn't in that location, that bar, or wearing that short skirt or whatever it is, that low cut thing, she wouldn't have been sexually assaulted." And we try to get them to understand that anybody can be sexually assaulted, at any time, even if you take those precautions.

One very experienced presenter described how she engages adolescents in debates about these myths and seems to elicit their honest views:

And the guys want to talk about the girls. This one guy said . . . "they have their little hoochie mama clothes on and it's hanging out all there." And the girls say "we can wear what we want to wear." . . . So yeah, I tell them that, "Sure, what people wear, I wouldn't wear into the cupboard, some of them, but that's a person's right and it doesn't give anybody permission to touch them." And try to help them understand, why people are raped. Because [teens say the reason for rape is] "because they are horny and they want [sex]." . . . You may have a couple of males that has it [understand the presenter's message] and they aren't afraid to say it. "Oh, no, I don't agree with that. Man, how can you say that?"

As discussed in the previous chapter, when presenters have time, they often have participants practice healthy relationship skills.

Gender Roles and Stereotypes

More than a third of the program educators we spoke with indicated that they covered the subjects of gender roles and stereotypes related to adolescents' self-definitions, awareness, and skill repertoires for healthy and unhealthy relationships.

The literature suggests that few programs for adolescents have "an emphasis on gender analysis" (O'Brien 2001, 399), nor is there much evaluation of gender analysis content. Avery-Leaf and Cascardi (2002) report that researchers found a strong connection between attitudes that dating violence is acceptable and actual aggressive behavior, but they add that research does not yet exist to support targeting sex-role socialization. In writing about programs for college students, Sochting, Fairbrother, and Koch (2004) have observed that addressing stereotypical sex-role behaviors is a promising direction for programming, although no research had demonstrated its effectiveness.

Several participants in our study reported that they do an exercise where they ask adolescents to specify social norms and sanctions for appropriate male and female behavior. This exercise, called "the box" in our interviews, was apparently based on one developed by Kivel (1998):

I think it's impossible to separate socialization from abuse . . . the kids have to look at what are the messages they get as a young man that makes them feel that . . . where they have to prove their masculinity in a variety of ways, by either putting down other boys who they deem as feminine. We also point out through the box exercise, they look at everything, um, that they deem as not okay or not, um . . . the whole dynamic of: "Don't act like a girl. Don't throw like a girl. Don't be like a girl." We surface that. And the fact that it's a male who is saying that, saying, "Look, this is a code that we've learned as boys, and look what this code has done, you know. It hasn't allowed us to really communicate adequately with young women. At one point early in our lives we're told not to act like them.

And then if and when we become interested in dating them, how are we supposed to date someone that we're told not to act like?" It's this double message, double standard.

We do a bit of work about how boys are kind of boxed in, in terms of how they are supposed to view themselves as men. That means they have to be tough and strong and they can't cry, show emotion and how that reinforces the notion that they are supposed to [be] domineering and forceful and so forth. And girls, conversely, are supposed to be docile and submissive and so forth and that perpetuates the notion that they are supposed to accept whatever comes to them because that is their lot in life, so to speak.

Interviewees also talked about male privilege and the types and use of power:

Mostly the larger societal value issues that we would talk about when we do our presentations really have to do with improper use of power. We really look at that. We really look at what may be the male privilege, okay, and how that has prevailed and try to debunk that. That would be usually the primary thing that we're looking at when we're going in with them. Because we have so much to cover in such a short period of time, unfortunately, but that's something that we feel is very important and that is the improper use of power and controlling other people, the importance of utilizing power over only yourself and your own behaviors and then male privilege and how that has entered in and really biased relationships.

Redefining male roles relates to material on bystander intervention and also to redefining social norms, as in approaches to substance abuse prevention (Reis, Trockel, and Williams 2003). An educator described some of this work:

We're doing more of that redefinition of masculinity. I think that's very exciting work to awaken the silent majority of males who are being held hostage by this minority who are the abusers and the rapists. And so to do that redefinition work that women did 30 years ago, well that's what guys are doing right now.

[We] talk about ranges of interventions. You know, everybody doesn't have to be confrontational. What are the different ways that you can intervene and help or counter some value or something? So that's all very interesting social norming work, which they've applied to alcohol up until now. But more and more, they're doing it for these other issues. And so there's not a proven way of doing that yet. I mean, they have done it on some, like James Madison Campus, they have applied social norming to sexual assault . . . But it's very exciting. It's completely new ways of looking at stuff. It makes you want to stay in the field. Just when you think you know everything, news comes out, a new way of approaching it that just makes it all exciting all over again.

Laws

About one-third of the participants present some material on laws, which can include legal remedies or resources for victims, as well as information on the legal repercussions of committing a crime. They noted that adolescents are often unaware of which behaviors are criminal. A common topic was "age of consent" for sexual relations.

Schewe (2002) reports that research is scarce on programs that remind men of the potentially negative consequences of rape, but two of three programs that were evaluated showed positive effects. However, Schewe primarily reviewed literature about programs for college men.

Although some practitioners include a discussion of rights and responsibilities within presentations on equality and healthy relationships, others indicated that their rights and responsibilities discussions stress legal rights:

And then on the second and third days we talk about the law, what the various legal systems are, what legal remedies are available to young people who are experiencing abuse and what potential legal consequences are [there] for abusive behavior. . . . It's very interactive. We follow through a scenario of two young people who are in an abusive relationship and walk through what the young woman who has been the victim of abuse, what her options are and ways that she can go through the legal system as well as otherwise what she can do to protect herself, and also what the potential consequences are to her abuser, her boyfriend. It's a very interactive program with games and role-play and a mock hearing for a domestic violence restraining order.

Some interviewees pointed out that adolescents are extremely interested in learning about the age of consent for sex, but others brought up potential problems with the subject of legal consequences. One educator noted that she does not want to frighten adolescents by discussing legal consequences:

We don't want to traumatize people or anything but sometimes like [showing] the rape kit [to teens], just talking specifically about that kind of thing, people forget the issue and they are focused on certain things that people tell them . . . Six years ago we talked a lot about laws in the harassment portion of our curriculum. The evaluations came back that people were learning "sexual harassment is against the law and you'll get in trouble." And our philosophy was more like, our curriculum looks at building empathy skills and pro-social skills, which is not like scaring people that they are going to get in trouble. So that is why we don't focus on it. My feeling going in is they are all nice people and you want the people in your relationships to like you and not be afraid of you . . . you know, not like, "You are a batterer." 'Cause I think teenage batterers are completely different or teenagers who use violence in their relationships are different than adult batterers. They are not so ingrained in a lot of [behaviors].

So we're going to be giving out some of those very same messages . . . doing a big thing with the guys on coercion. You know that "no" means "no." It doesn't matter if the girl's under the influence. That's rape. "Yes" under the influence is not a real "yes." We're going to be giving some pretty clear messages.

I think a lot of times the boys impede discussion and I think that people get really hung up on the age of consent in classes.

Age of consent being 16 put us in a very interesting position because philosophically, to tell people they are criminals if they are in sexual activity at 16 years old is a problem for me personally. Because I don't think it is realistic. I think it is not a good idea to be sexually active when you are only 14. I don't think it is a great thing, but it is a realistic thing. So, for us to criminalize the heck out of it in these presentations, we really have to walk a fine line. We are not sex educators, so we are saying things like "the age of consent is 16 years old and [state] law is designed to protect you." We are saying it is really hard to make that decision before you are 16. Not that you don't have good capacity and maturity and information but it is designed to protect you because there are so many older people victimizing younger ones. . . . You should see the 12th grade boys cringe when you tell them that "you can [rape] your girlfriend [according to the legal definition]. You are sexually assaulting them."

Media and Music

Adolescents receive many messages about gender roles and how relationships function from visual media and music. More than one-third of those we interviewed specifically mentioned including media or music in their presentations.

Interviewees mentioned connecting media and music to gender roles and asking youth, "Where do you think abusers learn this kind of violence?" Sometimes they show videos or use magazine images to stimulate discussions:

> Then we also do a program that is specific to sexualized violence in the media. So giving them a little bit more information about how the media operates, manipulates, kind of looking at video games, looking at music, those kinds of things.

> And we do a lot, like I said, with pop culture. We really encourage them to think about things. So, for example, when we're doing gender roles we have a piece where we encourage students to watch commercials and deconstruct them. And so we know that forever changes watching TV for students and that they, you know, will come and say, "Oh, I saw this commercial and that commercial." So we're really changing their thought process in a lot of ways.

Several educators in our survey believe that youth were dramatically impacted by discussions about media:

> It is more of a nonviolent critiquing [of] the culture: where does it come from, what about words, what about media, that kind of stuff. And how does it connect to racism and how does it connect to homophobia. All those things. And to be able to have that dialogue, the kids love it. When she [a colleague] showed me that media thing I'm like, "Are they going to get it, with all these ads?" And of course they are horrific, you've seen them. . . . Most of the kids got it. "Oh yeah, wow. If you do look at that for more than 5 seconds, it really is disturbing. Yeah what a message, why is she on her knees and oh, that looks like she's . . ." You know really, and having some very frank discussions and us being able to do that with them without getting calls from parents."

If I had to pick out key things that have made our program successful . . . the use of media literacy. The kids are really interested in that. It really sparks their attention and gets kids that the rest of the time sit there and don't say a word. When you start looking at a BET video or looking at a clip from professional wrestling, it gets most of the kids.

Societal Violence and Values

Presentations on music and media often refer to general societal values. When we asked interviewees if they specifically addressed general societal violence, one-third said they did.

The published literature makes no specific recommendations for content on societal values, but some authors have views on whether dating violence and sexual assault should be included in programs that address other types of societal or youth violence. Durlak (1997) recommends that different prevention programs join into integrated programs. Researchers suggest that, because there are common risk factors for multiple adolescent problems, it is sensible to have comprehensive prevention programs addressing more than one problem area (Nation et al. 2003; O'Leary, Woodin, and Fritz 2005). Johnson, Farquhar, and Sussman (1996) think that schools like to combine a narrowly targeted prevention program with other, broadening topics, but they question whether this is effective for all issues. Some researchers found a broader focus effective for smoking prevention but not drug and alcohol prevention. O'Brien (2001) focuses on global violence prevention, a subject that he thinks can decrease male defensiveness.

Although several programs evaluated in the literature included content on general societal violence, the effectiveness of that topic was not specifically examined. Macgowan's research (1997) showed positive effects on adolescents' knowledge, using a program that began with a discussion of general societal violence. Grasley, Wolfe, and Wekerle (1999) reported that the third section of their program for high school youth discussed society's encouragement of violence, including considerations of sexism. Gamache and Snapp (1995), in designing their program, did not want to use materials on violence in general, because they wanted to specifically counter social messages supporting violence against women.

Some interviewees start their programs with broad discussions about violence and oppression, because they believe it is important to place dating violence and sexual assault within the context of the oppression of women and minorities:

We start off the first day, we are starting off broadly about what violence is. Students are really, at that point, brainstorming what violence is, what could it be, where does it happen? Then we kind of branch off into, we talk about Martin Luther King. We bring him into the curriculum quite often about what his definition of violence is and we talk about that. The second day, that is when we do the dating; we focus on ways teens hurt each other in their relationships at school.

I think it is very difficult to talk about the issue of sexual violence without talking about oppression. And we have worked really, really hard in the program to incorporate that information. . . . There are some programs where we don't, are not afforded the time to be able to do that, but specifically like within the sexual harassment presentation, it is a perfect opportunity because we are able to give them a definition of the Title IX program in regard to discrimination and look at the whole kind of historical piece. So we use every opportunity to talk about homophobia within our programs. . . . Around who perpetrators are, in regards to who victims are, those kinds of things and then, of course, always sexism and always racism.

Many seventh graders aren't dating yet, but they are on the brink of thinking about it and moving toward it. If we were to go in and do a whole thing on just dating, we would have parental uproar. So we really needed to find a way to . . . to still bring it up but appeal to the broader range of violence, which certainly ties into teen dating and "passing on the pain" and all the concepts that we talk about, without making all four days about that. So, this was part of working with the school district, finding out what they wanted. They really wanted [us to cover] sexual harassment, because they see it so much. They really wanted us to touch on homophobia but . . . as a domestic violence agency, so we need to keep within our parameters as well. . . . So, we are trying to really broaden the middle school students' concept of what violence is. That it is not just about hitting.

The educators we spoke with try to connect the subject of dating violence and sexual assault to adolescents' experiences of violence in other contexts. An interviewee who works in a city with a high rate of community violence talked about how it would not be meaningful to ignore other types of violence in adolescents' lives:

But we do talk about what is going on around us. Again, we live in a very violent city. Most of the kids that we teach in this area, in this city, are from areas that are poor, so a lot of these kids, most of these kids, see drugs, see violence, know people that have been killed either in their family or friends. Many of them have seen people killed on the street. This is community violence, not necessarily domestic violence or intimate partner violence, so we talk about that a lot.

How to Help a Friend

One-third of our participants said they present material on how to help a friend who has been a victim of dating violence or sexual assault. This topic connects to content on where to find help and on bystander intervention.

Most research does not address the effectiveness of including prevention material on how to help a friend, except as a way to minimize male defensiveness. Multiple studies suggest that adolescent victims of dating violence are more likely to tell an adolescent friend about their experience than they are to tell an adult (Black et al. 2008; Molidor and Tolman 1998; Ocampo, Shelley, and Jaycox 2007; Watson et al. 2001). Other research indicates that adolescents are often uncertain about, or very limited in, their ability to help a friend who has been victimized (Ocampo, Shelley, and Jaycox 2007; Weisz and Black 2008). Authors of these studies therefore encourage prevention programmers to prepare adolescents to help one another in the aftermath of victimization. Similarly, writers on sexual assault among adolescents also stress the importance of peers' supportive responses to disclosures (Casey and Nurius 2006a).

Some program staffers we spoke with talked about the need to achieve a balance between empowering adolescents and recognizing behavior that is developmentally appropriate for adolescents when discussing how they might help a victimized friend. They want to encourage teens' initiative and self-efficacy and acknowledge their need for independence, while also recognizing that many have no idea how to respond to a friend who has been victimized:

We also cover things like how to help a friend and not just telling them, "This is what you do." It is kind of giving them the tools and the resources and even the language, right down to "this is what you can say," so they know what to do.

I talk to them a little bit about if they know someone who is in the situation, don't judge them. Let them know that they are not alone, and that there are resources available. I will give them some literature. Just having the knowledge, you never know who you will be able to pass on the resources to. So, I give them different phone numbers and things like that.

If they react in a supportive way, great, but also know that, "it's likely you're not a counselor and you should not feel that you, just because you were supportive the very first time, does not mean that you're now suddenly a counselor. Because it's very hard to, if you don't have the training, and you want to help this person, because they are your very close friend. You want to help them, but what they're telling you scares you and what they're telling you makes you nervous. And you're suddenly finding yourself not being as trustful and this is affecting you as well." And so kind of letting them know that this is a good way to respond, but you shouldn't also feel that you are somehow, because you responded that way, now you're the only one that can help this person. No. This is great that you were supportive, but know that you can pass it on to a professional, and these are the resources.

And also giving them skills to help a friend out. Because typically a young person is going to confide in a friend before they confide in an adult . . . and then encouraging them to confide in an adult after they have confided in their friend. And, as a good friend, offer to go along with them and continue to support them.

Where to Find Help

About one-third of those we interviewed address the topic of where adolescents can find help for themselves or their friends if they are victims of dating violence or sexual assault. Other interviewees pointed out that the mere presence of representatives of domestic violence or sexual assault programs alerted youth to the availability of outside agencies that offer help. Most of the presenters give adolescents information about how to contact them (see chapter 14). A noteworthy aspect of presenting information about resources that can provide help is that it places these prevention programs beyond the category of primary prevention, because it assumes that some youth in the targeted audience or their friends have been or will be victimized and will need help.

Literature rarely addresses the efficacy of presenting information on agencies offering help. Schewe's (2000) evaluation of a ten-session program supports the inclusion of content on seeking help. Other programs present material on definitions and attitudes that relate to seeking help, because youth will not seek help unless they define behaviors as assaultive or abusive (O'Brien 2001).

Grasley, Wolfe, and Wekerle (1999) describe a unique approach to presenting material on where to get help, with the goal of decreasing anxiety about seeking help. The program staff assigns pairs of participants to interview staff at agencies that help domestic violence victims. The prevention program sets up the interview for them, and the group helps the youths rehearse for the interview. The youths then share their findings with the group, so that all members become more familiar with resources in their community. The researchers report significant improvement one and a half years later in the intervention group's knowledge of formal agencies offering help.

Many practitioners believe victimized teens have trouble knowing where to go, so it is important to provide information about resources:

> And just also with identifying resources, there is a need. I think a lot of teens are unsure of where to go and through our evaluation, we can see that that's still a need because of the percentages we get [on pre-tests]. . . . we distribute a lot of resources, because just getting the information out there, I think, is a really good tool.

A few interviewees mentioned geographic and social-environmental factors that interfere with seeking help. Rural environments might contain few confidential resources, and in urban settings gang membership can be a major obstacle to seeking help. A small number of interviewees also mentioned that content on seeking help includes help for those who realize that they have been abusive or assaultive.

Bystander Intervention

One quarter of the educators said that they address bystander intervention, a subject that was initially investigated in Latane and Darley's classic article (1968) and is now receiving increasing attention among prevention coordinators at both the college and adolescent levels (Banyard, Plante, and Moynihan 2004). This concept generally refers to the idea of intervening in the midst of threatening or violent situation (Berkowitz 2002; Latane and Darley 1968), but it can also include confronting people who create a sexist or threatening atmosphere verbally, with jokes or comments.

Some research exists on college prevention programs that consider bystander intervention, but very little targets middle school and high school programs (Weisz and Black 2008). The results of two years of evaluation of the Mentors in Violence Prevention program, which stresses bystander intervention, were posted on the program's Web site (http://www.sportinsociety.org/vpd/mvp.php [accessed July 26, 2008]). In the second year, they used a quasi-experimental design (comparison groups without random assignment) and reported that the intervention group showed statistically significant improvements in knowledge, attitudes, and self-efficacy in intervention compared to the comparison group.

O'Brien (2001) suggests that prevention programs need to decrease male defensiveness by discussing how nonviolent men can play a role in finding solutions to the problem of violence. Sudermann, Jaffe, and Hastings (1995) report that their program includes content on how nonviolent men can help, and they believe this avoids "male bashing." The authors emphasize that most men do not batter their partners, focusing on responsibility instead of blame, and reminding adolescents that men will benefit from a less violent environment.

Some program staffers we interviewed talk about treating men as allies, which is related to the concept of bystander intervention. In addition to focusing on interventions to stop violence among friends and acquaintances, this theme suggests that men and women should be allies in the movement for the broader social change of stopping violence against women.

Content on bystander intervention can overlap with other subjects, such as how to help a friend and how to find resources that can help. Some interviewees pointed out that focusing on bystander intervention can decrease defensiveness. One person also spoke to the importance of empathizing with the bystander, who is often in a difficult position:

Because we take the bystander approach, it lessens defensiveness. Because you're not talking to men as perpetrators, and you're not talking to women as victims. You're saying, "When this happens to a woman that you care about, what are you going to do?" And one of the first things we do, like I mentioned, during an empathy exercise, we ask them to close their eyes and imagine the woman they care about most in the world being assaulted, and a bystander is watching and not doing anything. They choose to do nothing. They walk away or watch. And then we process that with them. Typically, it's a very emotional reaction and they're pissed and angry and mad and sad and all this, and they talk about how they think the bystander is just as bad as the perpetrator. Then you bring up the complication of if anybody empathized with the bystander. It's hard to be a bystander. It can be scary to be a bystander. And really bring up all these complicated emotions. Then you wrap up with, "Who in the room wanted the bystander to do something?" And everybody raises their hands. So, basically, that's one of the first things we do. And with that exercise, we're repositioning the statement, "It's none of my business."

Another interviewee stressed the importance of understanding the adolescent's social environment and the types of acceptable interventions within that environment:

> Most importantly, we discuss options with them. So we say, "Okay, what are you going to do? You're a bystander and see that somebody . . ." Encourage them to be really real. For example, a lot of times the kids will be like, "I'll beat him up. I'd get in his face. I'd yell at him. I'd get really mad." Then I say, "Okay, that's a good choice. Let's talk about what's going to happen if you do that." You explore the consequences with them and you get them to think, "Okay, you might get in trouble. You might get hurt. You might get [the victim] in more trouble." So we really explore the options for them. . . . I was in a session once where the kids were adamantly saying that calling the police would be the worst thing you could do. And I sort of had to recognize their reality and say, "Okay, why?" We had a conversation about it. I said, "Okay, what are other alternatives?" So really getting them to explore what the best option is for them and their realities. The only things we discourage are getting physically involved and doing nothing.

> We try and pump up the guys, you know, "most guys are good guys and speak up." And maybe they are at a party and they see another male kind of targeting someone, maybe they will speak up.

Statistics or Scope

About a quarter of those who participated in our study said they discuss national statistics, or the scope of dating violence and sexual assault in our society today. This is especially common when the presentation is on sexual assault. A few also mentioned that they discuss local statistics, because they believe that hearing about the prevalence of dating violence and sexual assault in their own community has a great deal of relevance for youth.

Most programs present statistics together with other topics, so researchers have rarely attempted to specifically measure the effectiveness of using statistics. Schewe's (2003b) literature review suggests that presentations of facts alone are not effective. Schewe and O'Donahue (1993) noted that presenting statistics to mixed audiences may have negative effects: "Men in the same audience may learn that rape is a common experience (i.e., 'normal'), that, if they do commit a rape, the chances of being caught are very slim, and that if they find and rape a woman in a risky situation, it is her own fault for being there" (679).

The interviewees emphasized that statistics can dramatically affect adolescents. Many people believe that adolescents view themselves as invulnerable, and some practitioners believe that statistics help teens realize that they are not invulnerable and neither are their friends and families. The message is that dating violence and sexual assault can happen to anyone. Presenters have developed creative ways to present statistics that allow the audience to actively participate:

> In the high schools, I use that one in four high school girls have been abused by a boyfriend. What I do is pass out Life Savers to 25% of the class, because I know ahead of time how many will be in the classroom and then the other 75% get the Jolly Ranchers. I have the Life Saver students stand up to physically show the rest of the class what 25% of the class is. Then I explain that they are the ones that were given the Life Saver because they represent the population, where at some point in their life, may need a life saver.

> There's the statistic that every nine seconds a teenager is abused in a dating relationship, and depending on the class I'll tell somebody at the very beginning, every nine seconds I want [him] to stand up throughout the whole class. And so then [he'll] do that. And the kids will do like, "Why is he standing up?" And then you get to that point, and you say, "every time he stands up somebody's been abused in a dating relationship."

Another presenter pointed out the interconnections between people, and tried to show that violence occurring in other parts of the community or even other parts of the country affects us all.

Empathy for Victims, and Who Can Be a Victim

Twelve percent of the participants suggested that programs should include a unit on empathy for victims, which is a corollary for both dating violence and sexual assault. One investigator notes that empirical research supports targeting empathy for victims in college prevention programs (Schewe 2002). This could be problematic, however, as some college programs experienced negative outcomes, such as men reporting decreased empathy after the intervention, as a result of trying to encourage men to empathize with female rape victims (Berg, Lonsway, and Fitzgerald 1999). Schewe (2002) reports that it is more effective to have males empathize with male rape victims and that programs with males in the audience should have at least one such vignette with a male perpetrator.

A few programs present material to indicate that anyone—males, females, rich, or poor—can be a victim of dating violence or sexual assault. Research suggests that it is important to select gender-neutral materials that do not consistently describe males as perpetrators and females as victims, as it is considered counterproductive to alienate male students (Avery-Leaf and Cascardi 2002). Some highly respected programs such as Safe Dates (Cascardi, O'Brien, and Avery-Leaf 1997; Foshee et al. 2000) are not based on the assumption that girls are victims and boys are perpetrators. Harned (2002) stresses that research on risk markers shows that those who perpetrate dating violence are more likely to be victimized. She believes, therefore, that prevention programs should emphasize the risk of bidirectional aggression.

One of the prevention educators in our study described an innovative demonstration showing that all types of people are victims. Recognizing this reality also assists in empathizing with victims:

From there, I move on to another activity where I pass around a bag. And just to show the lack of funding that I have for materials, I have a big bag of Mardi Gras beads. It's about all I could get. I really kind of don't like using them. But there's three different colors. I pass the bag around and the kids are automatically intrigued because they all like these beads. I tell them, "Just pick one. Pick whichever one you want and put it on." So, they all pick beads. They'll pick out which color they find most appealing. Then I show them a video clip of a physically abusive relationship that involves both a victim, an abuser, and bystanders. Before they watch the clip, I just ask them to observe what we're seeing in the video. "Make some mental notes about things you thought were wrong and things that you thought were right." Just their own observations. We discuss it after the clip. The clip is about five minutes. Then once it's over, I ask all of the students who are wearing a purple necklace to stand by their desks. I ask the other students to make observations about this group of people. This is the reason why I like to have a larger class, like 30 students. They are able to make observations like, "Oh, there's both boys and girls. There's different races, different sizes, different economic background, different styles of clothing." As they are making these observations, I facilitate them. . . . I ask them questions to lead them to the conclusion that these look like average, everyday students that we would see at the mall, at school, in our neighborhood. And I introduce this group as "these folks represent victims and survivors of abusive relationships. Because it could be anybody. You can't just tell by looking at them. It could be a boy or girl; it doesn't matter."

Whereas some programs emphasize that both males and females can be victims, others believe that it is important to primarily target violence against women:

> With dating issues, certainly sexual assault, we get into victims and offenders. We cover that boys as well as girls can be assaulted and can be offenders as well, you know, girl-on-girl sexual assaults can happen as well. So when we try to identify with the activity more than the offenders, so that they can recognize, whether it's a girl or a boy doing this to you, whether it's a stranger or a relative.

> When we talk about the issue, we talk about men's violence against women. And we name it that. And the reason being is that studies have shown that over 90% of all violence is committed by men. And we feel like if we didn't analyze it from the gender perspective, we'd be missing a piece of the puzzle. Needless to say, because we take that perspective, we are frequently accused of being heterosexist. And we acknowledge in all of our workshops that this is the approach we're choosing to take, this is the reason we're choosing to take it. We do acknowledge that it happens in other relationships. There are relationships where women are violent and we acknowledge that, but that we're going to choose to talk about it from this perspective. When we can, we use inclusive language. So, when we're doing an exercise about the types of abuse, we say "partner" instead of "boyfriend" or "girlfriend."

An interviewee reiterated a controversy in the literature about whether it is a good idea to describe both males and females as potential victims:

> The push is to [be] gender neutral. Our coalition says "violence against women." Our coalition also sponsors this whole training project and it is showing a great investment in how LGBT [lesbian, gay, bisexual, and transsexual] issues as they should, but there is a lot of push/pull in the whole state around these issues. I think the kids will hear—half of them will hear—"men can abuse men and women can abuse men." . . . they want to believe that women can abuse men at the same rate.

Some programs use survivor stories to help youths recognize that anyone can be victimized:

> We also recently have started having a teen volunteer come in, and she tells her story of her sexual assault and so that really makes the kids con-

nect and go "okay, this isn't just something that happens to random people. It could happen to my friend." Our volunteer is great at telling her story, and so I would say, the changing attitude is a big part.

Other Dating and Domestic Violence Content

More than 10 percent of our interviewees said that they present information on stalking. One program described it as follows:

> This year we concentrated on stalking, because those were the stories that we were hearing. So, our drama really had two stalking stories. One involved stalking in a dating violence relationship that had ended and the perpetrator wouldn't allow it to end. . . . The other one was a guy just inappropriately not knowing how to ask for a date and stalking with gifts and too many phone calls and that kind of stalking.

One or two of the interviewees said that their programs address types of adult domestic violence that adolescents might be exposed to at home. Some also discuss special issues relating to immigrants and domestic violence.

Other Sexual Assault Content

We learned that about 25% of programs present information about incest. For broader audiences, this content usually consists of definitions and information on where to get help. Some programs conduct groups for at-risk youth, where they are very likely to be working with incest survivors. In that case they concentrate on the effects of incest on survivors.

About 20% of programs mentioned including content on date rape drugs or drug- or alcohol-facilitated assaults. Research on middle school and high school prevention programs does not investigate the effectiveness of including this content, even though the shocking nature of drug- and-alcohol-facilitated sexual assaults makes this a logical subject to cover. This content can also be presented as part of a unit on warning signs and safety planning.

Another 20% of the interviewees pointed out that they include discussions on cyber safety, and a couple of program representatives mentioned content on pornography. No research supports the effectiveness of including these topics, but the popular media emphasize how common it is for sexual predators to find child and adolescent victims on the Internet (Mitchell, Finkelhor, and Wolak 2007). The practitioners address issues related to adults who prey on adolescents over the Internet, as well as how pornographic images on the Internet reinforce gender stereotypes. They also reported that teens are telling them about new, technological ways that some adolescents are using to harass and bully their peers:

> In one of the classes that we're doing now, we're doing four sessions and they want us to do a little more about the Internet. So, we'll talk a little more on that and the abuse that goes on over the Internet and how kids might be misusing IMs [Instant Messaging]. And there's a lot of bullying that's been going on.

> We get into the unsafe practices on the Internet, which almost all of them are doing . . . It has become the method of choice for any stranger to meet their victims. So, we talk about that.

Sexual Harassment

About two-thirds of the programs teach the definitions, types, and effects of sexual harassment. Some programs use this material for younger students and wait until high school to discuss dating violence and sexual assault. Some mentioned that parents or school administrators believe that middle school youth are too young to be discussing dating or sexual assault.

No literature was found on the effectiveness of including sexual harassment content. Casey and Nurius (2006a) report that almost no evaluated sexual harassment curricula for adolescents are available, but they believe that recommendations from college programs are applicable to programs for younger people.

Literature on adolescents does argue, however, for the inclusion of sexual harassment materials in dating violence and sexual assault prevention programs. Fineran and Bennett (1999) point out that sexual harassment rates in high schools reportedly are higher than they are among adults and that this type of harassment can be very damaging, especially for girls. Foulis and McCabe (1997) compared high school students, college students, and adult workers and found that high school students were more tolerant of sexual harassment than the other two groups. They also found that sexist attitudes can lead to the acceptance of harassment. Roden (1998) reports on a prevention program that presents, during its first session, "non-touching" forms of abuse, including sexual harassment. In her view, this content helps teens begin to identify feelings of shame and fear but is less threatening than discussions of incest, molestation, or rape.

Program Content

A common theme of sexual harassment presentations, mentioned by several interviewees, is that sexual harassment and flirting are different. This material includes definitions, clarifying that both males and females can be victimized by sexual harassment and that making fun of a person's sexual orientation is also sexual harassment:

> I start defining sexual harassment as behavior that is sexual and unwanted. Talking about identifying different types of sexual harassment. How boys can be harassed as well as girls. How sexual harassment and flirting are different and then we will use a little role-play to illustrate that. Then at that point I talk with them and tell them the Katie Lyle story and about how Katie Lyle was sexually harassed at her school in Minnesota and I walk them through the story. After the story, we talk about how Katie felt being harassed. We talk about some of the options that she pursued and how those didn't get her anywhere and we talk about some of the other specific ways, how it affected her life in addition to her emotions—so how it affected her social life, her academic life, those kinds of things . . . so that is kind of an empathy piece . . . Then we shift gears and go through about three or four role-plays that I call the red light, yellow light, green light role-plays. This is where we have two people—one person goes up to the other person and says they have a nice butt or something like that. Then the second person has, as part of their script I have given them, whether they are supposed to show if they like it or don't like it. Then after they run the role-play, the kids in the audience will talk about whether they are seeing red, yellow, or green as a reaction and what that means, and how specifically they know if it is red, yellow, or green. So, we break that down and talk about ambiguities. We talk about if you are seeing this color, what does it mean you should do?

> It happened because of what a kid shared with me. He kind of quietly on the side told me about a way that he had been harassed, and so I used that in the role-play that we were doing with the kids and, of course, they laughed at what I said. I talked to them about that and I said, "When you laugh about that, what do you think that does for me as the person doing the harassment?" And they said, "Well it makes you want to keep going" and I said, "Yeah." I asked, "Where do you think I came up with that line to harass the person in the role-play?" And they couldn't figure it out. I told them that, "I got it from somebody here in this room." And you could kind of feel at that point the whole feeling in the room changed, that one of their classmates had had that said to them, and it wasn't something that I just made up. It was real. I guess those are the

times that I feel that stuff comes together when kids share something from their own perspective, when they share how they are putting material together in their head, the connections that they are making; those are the moments that I feel "Wow."

It always gets brought up, however, when we are doing sexual harassment and we are talking about calling people "gay" or anything like that. We say, "Well what if they are or what if" . . . I say, "Can males sexually harass other males, and they say, yeah, when they are looking at me" . . . or, you know, that kind of thing. So, we definitely address the issue that way. Just say . . . it has nothing to do with someone's sexuality . . . talking about how that can really hurt someone and try to be as diplomatic as possible.

Other Topics

Many prevention educators we interviewed mentioned that they spoke to children in elementary schools about bullying, but only a few said that they present the subject of bullying to middle school or high school audiences. Two program representatives said that they discuss HIV, and one mentioned including substance abuse, independent of its role in dating violence and sexual assaults. Programs sometimes also include content on eating disorders and teen suicide as consequences of dating violence and sexual assault, but they rarely have other information on these problems. A few of our survey participants present information on current events or famous cases, such as those involving athletes or celebrities. Some said they would answer questions about these cases, or discuss them if someone in the audience brings them up.

Summary of Program Content

In summarizing trends in program content, we remind readers that we did not interview a random or representative sample of prevention educators. Our sample tended to combine dating violence and sexual assault, and to discuss definitions and types of dating violence and sexual assault. A common focus was awareness and myths, and strong attention was given to how to build healthy relationships based on respect. Discussion of gender roles and stereotypes, societal violence, and media and music were also common. Limitations of presentation time force many programs to focus narrowly and to eliminate topics that presenters would, in fact, prefer to include. A few programs addressed topics that were barely within their purview or training, because school or community members asked them to include coverage of these subjects.

It seems that most programs recognize that many adolescent participants have already been exposed to violence as victims or observers of dating violence, sexual assault, or neighborhood or family violence. Therefore, they were convinced that program content should be sensitive to the possible presence of victims.

A major controversy within these types of prevention programs is whether to focus on women as victims or to be gender-neutral. Some programs focus on males as victims to decrease male defensiveness, but others believe that females are the most common victims of serious, frightening dating violence and sexual assault, and that programs should be honest about the fact that most victims are females.

Throughout the prevention field and in the literature, a great deal of controversy surrounds the question of whether prevention programs should equip females with skills that might help them recognize assaults, respond assertively in relationships, or even fight back. Although interviewees clearly never want to imply that girls are responsible for their victimization, some do view it as a service to offer girls skills that might help them recognize or escape a dangerous situation. Some programs addressed this content to girls because their school districts wanted them to do so, and they were reluctant to jeopardize important school relationships by refusing.

Clearly programs did not always select content based on evidence that it was effective. As our literature review points out, relevant evidence is scarce. Chapter 13 discusses how program evaluation intersects with program content and structure. Additional details about how content is developed and presented are given in chapter 10, which discusses the use of manuals, and in chapter 14, which discusses the personal characteristics of prevention educators.

9

Diversity Issues in Prevention Programs

We asked the prevention educators how their programs responded to the diverse cultures and sexual orientations they encounter among the adolescents they serve. We also investigated the importance of matching the race/ethnicity of the presenters to that of the adolescent participants. (The diversity of prevention educators is discussed in chapter 14.) The interviewees' responses to diversity can be loosely grouped into four types of program content: approximately the same content for all adolescent groups, special content related to cultural diversity, some specific content for gay and lesbian youth, and other content particularly relevant to their diverse audiences.

Giving the Message That Violence Occurs in All Relationships

More than half the interviewees address diverse ethnicity and sexual orientation by pointing out that violence occurs in all types of relationships and among people of all racial, ethnic, and socioeconomic backgrounds. They want to convey that the dynamics of violence are approximately the same across all groups:

> I feel we teach the same content . . . We teach the students that domestic violence doesn't discriminate; it's not limited to any particular ethnic background or other type of background.

> When we asked educators if they included special content on gay and lesbian youths, our respondents were especially likely to mention that violence doesn't discriminate. They also usually use gender-neutral lan-

guage in the vignettes they present. Some also emphasize that everyone deserves respect:

So it comes up a lot and we have to say, "Listen, this is between two individuals who are . . . one person is abusive, the other person is getting abused. And that could be anybody [as a victim]: rich, poor, gay, straight, urban, rural, whatever . . . prostitutes."

Well, I use gender-neutral language for a couple of reasons, not just for gay and lesbian relationships, but also because . . . I will say "your partner" or "he or she." Because I am also learning more and more as I speak to students that there are a lot of females as well as males who are being abusive. And so I try to put it out there that any of us have the potential of being abusive if we choose to misuse our power and that it can take place in any kind of relationship, gay, straight, any type of friendships, it is not even in just romantic relationships that people can be abusive to one another.

Instead of saying "boyfriend" and "girlfriend," I actually use the word "partner." I explain that ahead of time to the students to mean that this is any relationship that I am discussing, no matter the sexual orientation, but I also use the term partner, because that's how any relationship should be, a partnership.

We don't specifically address that. What we try to do, however, is be cognizant of the possibility of someone maybe struggling with their sexuality or someone who is a gay or lesbian or bisexual. We try to keep our language as neutral as possible . . . like saying "a dating partner" or "boyfriend/girlfriend" or using examples with a boy and a girl. We try to be respectful of that.

Some of the educators stressed the need to communicate that dating violence and sexual assault can happen to anyone, while still focusing on violence against women. They want to make it clear to adolescents that women are the primary victims of these types of violence:

So, we really talk about same-sex assault, but it is always striking that balance between violence against women. When we talk about same-sex assault, we don't want to say it's the same thing . . . but you want to be able to give emphasis to both issues in a way that makes sense and doesn't say, "Okay, it's all just men against women, women against women, men against men," making all this kind of like it is all the same. Then the message comes across, "Well, see women are abusing men at the same rate." We want to be real careful about that. There are all kinds of articles that say that. And so we talk about same-sex assault, we talk about assault on males . . . it is not a gay thing.

One of our units is on homophobia. It doesn't necessarily deal with a gay or lesbian relationship, but it draws correlations between men's violence against women and homophobia. Something I should mention is that when we talk about the issue, we talk about men's violence against women.

Another way educators deal with diversity is to make a special effort to include media examples that show adolescents from various racial and ethnic backgrounds and to present vignettes using names portraying cultural diversity:

The only way that I think about it is we have a role-play and we ask people to give, like, would you name the mom and the dad in this domestic violence role-play. And kids yell out names, and, if it is a highly diverse class, I will purposely pick a Latino name as opposed to Mary or Judy or Carol or something like that.

Ethnic/Racial Makeup of Communities Prevents Culturally Specific Content

Forty percent of the interviewees reported that they presented their programs in racially or ethnically diverse communities. Larger regions often varied, so that, within a program's geographic area, some communities were completely diverse, whereas others had homogeneous or segregated areas. We learned from the responses that the question of whether programs tailored their content to particular cultural groups became irrelevant or impractical when audiences contained a mix of cultural groups. About 20% of the programs were presented in communities that lacked diversity, as described by the presenters we interviewed. Another one-fifth revealed that programs present the same content everywhere, regardless of the cultural makeup of the audience. Another common response was that content was essentially the same and tailored only somewhat for different cultural groups:

Each class is different; each school is different, and through all of those eight counties, we are hitting a lot of different cultural differences, economic differences, so we try to tailor . . . with getting the same core information out, but still tailoring it to our audience.

Just being open to each community, because it's true that some communities are—there are things that maybe they're not as comfortable talking about or ways that they're more comfortable speaking of things. And to be receptive to that. To be aware that you're gonna be getting signals and signs and adapt as you go. To make them comfortable or to kind of keep it going.

All Audiences Should Learn About Cultural Issues

One-fifth of participating prevention experts said that their programs present material on cultural sensitivity to all adolescents, even if the group is primarily or solely European American. They want all youth to be aware that cultural differences are important and that oppression of minorities exists:

> One of the things we talk about with all groups is sort of: what are the obstacles to getting help? Why would somebody who is in an abusive situation stay in an abusive situation? And there are different obstacles that are true for certain groups that we make a point of bringing up. For example, if you're speaking to a group of gay and lesbian youth, their fear of being outed might be an example of an obstacle to getting help. Now we mention this to every group, because, even if you're not speaking to a group where they have specifically identified themselves as gay and lesbian, there are always young people in that room or the potential of young people in that room who are gay and lesbian. And it's important to bring up those issues so that they feel they're getting the information they need. But we make special emphasis on it in certain settings. Another example is immigration issues. And if somebody is a non-documented immigrant, they might be more reluctant to reach out for help from authorities. And that is something again we always bring up. But we might put particular emphasis on it if we know we're with a group of young people who themselves are immigrants or their families are recent immigrants. There are a lot of examples like that we might emphasize more in terms of cultural influences on this issue, but we really make a point of trying to bring up all of these issues to all groups.

Obstacles to Presenting Certain Materials to Specific Groups

Some practitioners described the obstacles involved when presenting specially tailored materials to diverse groups, including financing, limited time, and the requirement that schools approve all the materials presented:

The content of the program doesn't really change according to what the audience, the racial background of the audience. I think that it would be nice to have the luxury to change some of the materials that we use. Some of them, whether it be the role-plays or the videos that we use, change those so that they match more closely with the audience, but that's something that is just financially . . . very difficult to do, to find the funding to be able to have three different videos, let alone three different videos that the school system would have to approve ahead of time for you to use.

Fifteen percent of the prevention educators we spoke with said that their schools or communities restricted them from presenting any content what-soever on issues of sexual minorities:

Not as far as in actually touching on gay and lesbian relationships. That is a very, very sensitive topic . . . I would say the three things that you try to avoid discussing are homosexuality, birth control or condoms, and abortion. Those are the topics that will, that strike fear in the eyes of the teachers in the room whenever students bring it up. Because [of] the parents, they are so afraid of the parents calling in to complain about an attitude or an opinion that was expressed that they disagree with. . . . So sometimes those topics of homosexuality do come up in kind of a peripheral way but not a direct conversation to sit down and say, "We are going to talk about gay and lesbian relationships and what violence occurs within those."

Special Content for Cultural Minorities

Although prevention literature often calls for cultural appropriateness (Eaton et al. 2007; Jaycox et al. 2006; Weissberg, Kumpfer, and Seligman 2003; Whitaker et al. 2006; Wolfe and Jaffe 2003), researchers have not evaluated whether culturally specific material is better than nonspecific material for dating violence and sexual assault prevention programming for adolescents. A few programs serving primarily minority adolescents have been evaluated, including Macgowan's (1997) and Weisz and Black's (2001) prevention programs for African American middle school students, but the culturally specific aspects of the programs were not evaluated separately. Jaycox et al. (2006) found that their program tailored to Latino youth was effective. Using a sample of college students, Heppner et al. (1999) showed that culturally relevant material did engage Black students more than material that was not culturally relevant.

Diversity Issues in Prevention Programs

Some research has suggested that differences exist in the dynamics of dating violence and sexual assault among the different cultural groups in the United States (Black and Weisz 2003, 2004; Levy 1998; MEE Productions 1996; Yoshihama, Parekh, and Boyington 1998). Therefore, programming might be more effective if it addresses these different dynamics, especially as victimization rates seem to vary within different cultural groups (Ackard and Neumark-Sztainer 2002; Halpern 2001: Howard and Wang 2003). Watson et al. (2001) found significant ethnic/racial differences in high school students' victimization rates, with African Americans reporting the highest rate of victimization (60%). European Americans and Hispanics had similar rates—47% and 41 %, respectively.

Adolescents' response to dating violence might differ culturally as well. In contrast to most research on European American youths seeking help (Ashley and Foshee 2005; Jackson 2002; Molidor and Tolman 1998), Black and Weisz (2003) found that middle school African American youths reported that they would go to their parents for help about dating violence. Most other research has found that adolescents are much more likely to talk to friends when dating violence occurs (Weisz et al. 2007).

Literature on the prevention of violence among youths in general also yields ideas that apply to dating violence and sexual assault prevention. Nation et al. (2003) maintain that prevention programs need to be culturally relevant in a deep, non-superficial way, so that the youth who are most at risk do not drop out. The inclusion of youth in program planning improves the likelihood of making content relevant. Yung and Hammond's (1998) work with general violence prevention directed toward African American youth concluded that it was important for videos to use role models that were relevant in terms of "language, dress, scenario content, mannerisms, and cultural 'feel'" (325). They assert that culturally relevant programs need to start with generally sound prevention principles, and then make those principles acceptable to youth by using culturally relevant content. For African American youth, it is especially important to address the issue of respect, because disrespect can frequently lead to violent confrontations. Yung and Hammond (1998) believe it is important for youth to feel that the program is applicable and feel comfortable in the program environment. Two approaches that might increase this comfort are the use of teenage slang, unless it is profane, and the use of scenarios based on the youths' own lives. It is important to display many positive slogans around the setting and to provide a number of positive African American role models:

> We recognize that shared ethnic background is not in itself a guarantee
> of cultural sensitivity but we believe that it promotes good rapport and

a positive modeling effect. For programs that are not able to provide an ethnically similar group facilitator, we recommend that they make use of African American parents or volunteers in some capacity. (Yung and Hammond 1998, 333)

Persuasion research suggests that curriculum and audio-visual materials should be sensitive to the primary culture of the program participants (Hovland, Janis, and Kelley 1953). Adolescents are more likely to pay attention to images and stories about other youth who seem similar to themselves (Stephan and Stephan 1990).

One-third of those we interviewed include specific content related to minority cultural groups. Programs might develop special materials after going to workshops, reading about cultural issues, or from their own knowledge of the community:

We have programs for high school students, specifically for African American students and for Latino students that absolutely do touch on that cultural piece—that talk about racism, that talk about machismo, that talk about the imbalance within culture and that also look at the unsaid issues of sexual violence within our community. So, we cover that information. I think for myself, I know within the African American community I see the issue around incest. Historically, it has been missed and I think that for us to be able to speak to our kids and to clarify some of those myths around that is very important. To create a path for them in regard to being in relationships with other people. And I know that we have a written curriculum for both African American students and for Latino students that touches specifically on that cultural piece of denial within the community, within our community of color. Males taking on roles . . . we do programs, specifically programs of males taking on their responsibility. To understand, being the culture, what they are responsible for, how they interact with the women within their own culture, within their own race. What does that look like?

I think you have to be able to adapt your material for the culture that you are dealing with. You don't have to change your curriculum, because those are the basics, but some of your illustrations or examples; there [are] different ways different cultures react in violent situations than others do. You have to be sensitive to that and recognize that. But I don't think you have to change the curriculum. I think you need to know ahead of time who your audience is going to be and give it some thought. If there is a list of materials that you need to gather or a different approach

that you need to take, then that is what you need to do. So, it is not good
to go blind into a classroom. You know, "30 kids, I don't know who they
are but to know that these are 30 twelve-year-olds and the class is pre-
dominately [a certain ethnic group], or half black and half Vietnamese."
So then, you have some way of kind of getting a head start in terms of
how to approach these kids and what some of their interests and needs
and thoughts and areas of discussion might be. It will vary from culture
to culture. It will even vary based on the age.

Some programs rely on their peer educators or youth advisory boards to
teach them about cultural issues in the youths' communities (see chapter
11). A few programs included content on how cultural background or immigration circumstances might create obstacles to obtaining help after one
has been victimized by sexual assault or dating violence:

We talk about power and control and also how sometimes a community
is closed or somebody feels ashamed. We try to deal with that perspective
because there might be people that think . . . if a community is closed
or people are ashamed then they are less likely to report, so that person
may make a good victim for an offender. Also, we come about it from
a perspective of saying . . . a lot of the kids we talk to are very positive
about who they are and they aren't having the same issues of being gay
or lesbian; so we might say . . ." sometimes it is hard to say that this is
going on, because you don't want the rest of the community to think that
something is wrong in this community." We also just talk about why it
might be harder for some individuals to seek help, maybe because of
immigration issues or maybe it's accepted in their culture, you know, to
behave certain ways or women may be viewed as property in different
cultures. And so we kind of address that and talk about why it's difficult
to leave abusive relationships.

Well, we do present the same content certainly, because a lot of it is they
need to know what's okay and what's not okay, what's appropriate and
what's not appropriate. But we do have to be very sensitive to culture issues, because some things might be totally different and we need to understand that. You might accept it in your culture, but here that might be
illegal. And so they need to know that. But again, be sensitive to . . . like
in the Asian community . . . we did a program on sexual assault and the
influence of the multi-cultural aspects. We had a few different speakers.
We had a panel after we presented the difficulties in servicing someone
that's been sexually assaulted, then to throw on that if this person is from

another culture. And we had someone speaking from the Asian community—Southeast Asian. Well, anyway, I remember the Asian woman spoke about how it's very difficult because she found that in her culture people won't come out of their culture to get some help. So those kinds of things, knowing that, just saying, "Well, here's a card. You can call these folks," might not work for them. So there are things, when we do present, that we have to be a little more sensitive to, and maybe even in the stories where who is getting help from whom and that kind of thing. But as far as the content and communication, those issues are presented in the same way.

Special Content About Gay and Lesbian Youth

Some literature suggests that material should address youth in sexual minorities, because dating violence is not limited to heterosexual couples (Levy and Lobel 1998). It should also address the vulnerabilities of youth with disabilities.

Thirty percent of our interviewees said that, in addition to using gender-neutral language, they also present information about special challenges for gay and lesbian youths coping with dating violence and sexual assault. Several other programs that currently did not include this content planned to develop it:

> We don't have any transgender persons, but we do have gay and lesbian people on staff, obviously. And we do, I mean that we make more of an effort, that we bring up—usually the facilitators bring up the same gender . . . We bring up things in our examples—to talk about and give people information about that. Our specialized outreach to gay and lesbian youth is because of recognition of a lack of services for them, not because of any particularly greater need within that community.

> Now we are developing specific programs on these three things just for the gay, well the GBLTQI [gay, bisexual, lesbian, transgender, queer, intersexed (and our friends and allies)] audience. They've added "questioning" and "intersex" and "transgender," so we're adding those. So, we're having all of those populations and are developing special programs for all those issues of sexual orientation. Basically, the three issues we're dealing with is the fact that if you are a victim of abuse, in same sex or transgender or whatever, you have that issue of "What is your stage of coming out?" So, [the issue is that] forced disclosure on a timeline that you're not comfortable with can be emotionally traumatic. The second

is the power tool element of your abuser knowing your orientation and nobody else knows it, and, therefore, they force you to comply or not to get help, because they're going to out you. Then the third is the whole internalized homophobia, that basically we do still live in a heterosexual society. So are you saying, "Yeah, but really is my lifestyle wrong?" So, that's our only consideration is those three things is that they feel more isolated and that we have to deal with that. That would be the only difference. Other than that, we would treat it all as the same.

We most definitely do address that. And we have people on staff, of course, who are gay and lesbian and we address that with them. If they want to talk more about it, fine. If they want to talk about it privately afterwards, sometimes, there again, that is another one of these—our society in America is backward. We are so ignorant about the idea that this could happen in same-sex relationships. We get all the nervous giggles. Of course, it is their age, too. We have to address it. We let them know, too, that there are people they can talk to. If this is an issue, something that is happening to you, and you are a female and a female is abusing you in a lesbian relationship or vice versa or a male relationship, that does happen.

Content on Sexual Harassment and Homophobia

Thirty percent of interviewees present specific content on homophobic harassment of gay and lesbian youth. They often talked about how they reminded adolescents that homophobia is implicit in "insulting" others by calling them "gay" and related disparaging terms:

With the guys-group curriculum, we do have specific scenarios around homophobia and addressing that issue in regard to harassment and bullying and also power and control and what does that look like? . . . I know we consider it very important, because the other thing is that it adds to objectification and that's part of what creates a sort of rape culture . . . the objectification of people, whether by age, whether by gender, whether by sexual orientation, whether by ethnicity, by status, whatever the situation is. Once you start objectifying somebody, it's a lot easier to assault them in some way or another. Whether it's with words, physically, sexually, or whatever.

One prevention educator noted that a school specifically requested material on gay and lesbian violence, "because there was an issue [in the school]," but this was an exception to the programs' typical experiences. Ten percent of the program administrators said that they would talk about dating violence and sexual assault in the gay and lesbian community if the adolescents raise the topic, but the presenters do not initiate the discussion:

> There are restrictions in the schools that don't necessarily allow us to bring it up, or give much information on it. So, if the students bring it up, we are allowed to address it, but other than that, we aren't allowed to. That can be difficult.

A small group of interviewees said that, although they were not forbidden to mention gay and lesbian youths, there was a great deal of discomfort in their communities around that subject:

> I don't necessarily see all of the teachers and schools that we are going to as being as open-minded about it. So I have treaded waters very lightly there . . . I also have to make sure that I stay within good standing in the schools.

> I know that in some of the private schools I have gone into, they have been a little uncomfortable about that, when I have said it. Nobody has not asked me back, but I notice some discomfort when I mention that.

Other Important Participant Differences

Lonsway (1996) encourages the assessment of the relevance of prevention programs for various ethnic, cultural, and socioeconomic groups, because socioeconomic status and cultural variables might affect rape vulnerability and the response to rape prevention programs (Barth, Derezotes, and Danforth 1991). Ackard, Neumark-Sztainer, and Hannan (2003) found that youth in lower socioeconomic groups were at greatest risk for any type of dating violence. Glass et al. (2003) note previous research suggesting that living in a rural community was a risk factor for dating violence, so there may be a need for culturally distinctive programming in rural areas.

A few interviewees cited significant cultural and experiential differences between urban and rural adolescents in their communities or indicated that their communities were exclusively rural and presented special challenges in addressing and preventing dating violence and sexual assault. Certain communities also have unusual environmental or economic circumstances affecting their culture:

One of the towns that I work in, . . . the majority of the parents work in a paper mill that is in the town, so I think in that town there is some different cultural things . . . just sort of expectations and there are definitely some differences in what I would do there. There is a large issue of alcoholism and that is actually the town that I had to write to the parents and say, "This is what is happening." Lots of domestic violence. So probably, the way I would address something in that community would be different than in a community that didn't have those [situations].

If I'm talking to a private Christian school, I'm not going to approach the topics the same way I would if I was talking to more of an urban, low-income school.

That's why I really ask them a lot of questions, particularly in the beginning, or before I make a point, I ask them a question. Like particularly about the images. I will ask each group, "Okay, who is popular now?" I can't say "Britney Spears" to everybody because not everybody in that class likes Britney Spears. You know, that's not the kind of music they listen to. They might listen to Fifty Cent or, you know, Eminem or someone. So, I ask them, and I get a real good feeling about where they are and who they're listening to and who they're looking at and what TV shows they're watching.

As mentioned earlier, age also influences the choice of content. Because adolescents' cognitive abilities vary, content sometimes must also vary, even within the same ethnic group and the same age level. One program's staff described how they make adjustments for some groups in which students require assistance in reviewing handouts, whereas students in other groups can review the handouts independently:

The special-needs program that we work with, high school students that are developmentally delayed or physically challenged, so that we create role-plays and scenarios for them that are specific to their needs . . . a lot of issues in regards to inappropriate touching and boundary issues on the bus. They all ride the bus together and then this whole issue in regards to their developmental issues. And the fact that they are physically teenagers and it becomes a very difficult, kind of a paradox for them.

Finally, one prevention educator thought that group dynamics in a classroom may play a more powerful influence than race on how she adjusts her presentation:

If my default was ever to go into schools and adjust based on racial de-
mographics, I learned not to do that real fast . . . It's every class, it's their
ability level: do they raise their hands or do they just scream out, or do
they like to sing, or do they like to sit and write? And it's different for
every single class. And it's almost as if race is not an issue compared to
all the other [aspects].

Summary of Diversity Issues in Prevention Programs

Discussions with these practitioners revealed that cultural appropriateness
is not always easy to implement. Although cultural sensitivity is important
to all the programs, many reasons were given as to why program content
cannot be tailored to specific cultural groups. One factor is that groups of
adolescent participants are rarely homogeneous; another factor is financial limitations. On the other hand, many prevention experts resist too
much tailoring, because they want their presentations to make the point
that dating violence and sexual assault can happen to people of all cultural
backgrounds and sexual orientations. Some interviewees noted that racial/
ethnic differences were not always the most significant variables among
the adolescents. They suggested that presenters might want to adjust program material to address differences in cognitive capacity or other varia-
tions such as rural versus urban audiences. Many program administrators
are conscious of including youths of all sexual and gender orientations, but
others found that their communities and schools were reluctant to openly
address gay and lesbian dating violence and sexual assault. This chapter,
therefore, reinforces an important theme found in other chapters: context
often limits a program's ability to live up to ideal approaches such as tailoring material to specific cultural groups. Many experienced educators recognize other important differences between youths that programs should address, and many believe that adolescent culture supersedes ethnic culture
as an important factor for prevention programs to consider.

10

Curricula Development

All the interviewees said that they develop their own curricula but also often borrow parts of curricula from other programs. One practitioner reported that sometimes she used another program's curriculum and sometimes her own. Half the interviewees noted that they like to expand and improvise rather than adhering strictly to a manual.

Researchers often endorse the idea of using standardized curricula, because they believe that, without standardization, evaluators cannot compare programs nor can others replicate a program (Corcoran and Vandiver 2004). Experts who talk about the importance of monitoring fidelity to the program design (Mihalic et al. 2004; Weissberg, Kumpfer, and Seligman 2003) usually imply the use of a standardized program or manual. At the same time, however, experts assert that programs must continually update themselves to remain effective (Schewe 2002). Johnson, Farquhar, and Sussman (1996) also note a dilemma in trying to apply empirically validated programs in new settings; they raise the question of "how to promote constructive reinvention, given that modification seems to be an important ingredient to maintenance" (941).

Writing about empirically supported dating violence prevention programs, O'Brien (2001) emphasizes the need for standardization and guidelines for delivering model programs so that others can replicate and evaluate them. Replicating standardized state-of-the-art programs across the U.S. will help assure that programs are relevant in a variety of locations, beyond the geographic area where they were developed.

Galinsky, Terzian, and Fraser (2006) observe that many people support the use of manuals for group work, as long as they integrate current evidence that leads to more effective practice in several different settings. Standardized curricula can provide guidance for practitioners and therefore increase the number of practitioners who are able to meet the needs of different populations. On the other hand, Galinsky, Terzian, and Fraser (2006) point up the criticism that the use of manuals can lead to mechanistic and unresponsive practice, a "cookie-cutter" approach that ignores differences between participants in various settings; they encourage a balanced approach and also the need to collect empirical evidence on the use of manuals, but they also emphasize the importance of allowing practitioners to incorporate their knowledge and experience when working with particular groups.

A national survey of domestic violence prevention programs, with as many as 526 respondents, found that few teen dating-violence programs use complete curricula developed by other programs (National Violence Against Women Prevention Research Center 2003). Meyer and Stein (2004) reported that the majority of programs they studied use books or manuals from other programs. However, 93% indicated that they were concerned that some curricula are outdated (12.9%) or not age-appropriate (11.9%), and they noted certain topics were missing from curricula they used: AIDS, male victims of sexual assault, and fighting among girls. A few pointed out that the materials are too expensive and that the videos quickly become dated. Some believed that the curricula do not have enough interactive components to encourage participation and discussion. The respondents mentioned a need for materials that have more diverse content about race, sexual orientation, and physical challenges, and they thought that programs should develop materials to reduce male defensiveness. Meyer and Stein (2004), in questioning whether the same presentation was given to all audiences, found that 4.3% gave the same presentation; 61.8% varied their presentation by age; 53.3 % varied their program content by subject matter; and others varied the presentation by the topic requested, taking into account gender and the nature of the students.

While some researchers call for stable curricula so that programs are sufficiently consistent to be evaluated, Schewe (2002) sees the value of frequently modifying a curriculum to maintain effectiveness:

Prevention educators should be constantly trying to improve their curricula. Even if a program demonstrates initial positive effects, it is likely that these effects will begin to fade after a few weeks or months. By always working to increase the quality of the curricula and by increasing the number of sessions, educators will greatly increase the likelihood that a program will have lasting effects. (123)

How Interviewees Developed Their Curricula

All the interviewees said that they developed their own curricula, and they strongly believe that the material should be adapted to the local audience and to their own presentation styles. Often, however, they did borrow or adapt program material from others:

> I have taken a lot of different information from different places, and I have kind of compiled that into a curriculum that we use. So, every single thing in that [our curriculum] did not come from just me. There are resources that I have used just by working with them [teens] for many years or different prevention programs that I see, and, obviously, those programs are receiving credit in the curriculum.

> We started with a curriculum and then the group workers have just put their own spin on it and get their own material . . . I've hired the second male worker now. . . . And he put together his own agenda for the men's program, just based on a lot of sources. So, it's kind of a hodge-podge. Well, I borrowed the Rutgers program, the theater work. The other, I started based on a curriculum in 1998 and from then I have just taken it from all different sources of what I want these kids to know. So, I don't have one set curriculum that I use, but I use something from a lot of different places.

Program staff expressed confidence in the quality of their materials and in their ability to design appropriate activities for their goals and their audiences:

> It's still evolving to be honest. When I started I drew heavily—I created my own thing, but I adapted pieces of other curricula that I had worked with and other tools that I found or somebody had shared. And I put it all together in a kind of a menu of tools and topics and I would—depending upon the particular group and the requests and the time allotted—would mix and match, according to that group and what that group needed and how much time I had. And there wasn't that much that was written down, except guidelines for exercises. That works really well if it is just me and I know how to do these things backwards and forwards, eyes blindfolded with my hands behind my back. But for the purposes of having other staff begin to do some of this, or, perhaps, in some point in the future, use volunteers or parents to do some of it, we needed to formalize the curriculum a

little bit. Now I still use some of those same pieces, but it is all put down on paper with facilitator instructions, and not only discussion questions, but the points that the facilitator should elicit or offer if the audience doesn't come up with it on their own. So, we have created it and are still creating it, but [I have] definitely swiped pieces from other things that I had seen or ideas that I got from other . . . you can take an icebreaker that you learn in college and turn it into a great learning tool with a little bit of creativity.

I love my education background and this job because I can make it creative and informative and fun. And [my supervisor] totally supports it. She totally supports everything I do. I'm creative and get ideas. I see something and I think, "Wow, that would be great." She'll tell you. I'm constantly at her door saying, "Can I bounce this idea off of you? I want to do this." And she'll drag me around and make me show the other people at work and I get embarrassed.

Some states require that programs include certain topics in order to receive state money, so that is another influence on curricular development. Sometimes state coalitions offer ways to learn from colleagues:

A lot of what I have learned and what I use is through other children's advocates within the state. The coalition for domestic violence sets up meetings with children's advocates regionally and often . . . the topic is school presentations or dating violence or sexual violence, so I have gotten a lot of things from them. I don't really have a curriculum that I get things from. Sometimes I will go online and do research and find things that I would like to use in the presentations, but it kind of becomes a hodge-podge of things. Especially after I have been doing this for a couple years now, I tend to use what students have given me [for inspiration].

Each of our ten rape crisis centers [in the state] has an education department, so we have meetings and we share [curricula] that we've used or share presentations that we've used . . . That is really helpful. People have tested them out before you do, so they know what works and doesn't work and they can share that with you.

The Importance of a Manual

Participants in our study are aware of how important it is to preserve their programming ideas for colleagues and future prevention educators within their organization:

I did almost all of it totally on my own. Hopefully, when somebody re-places me, they won't have to do that, because we now have file drawers full of information on all of these types of things [program ideas].

We have a manual that some of the past presenters have put together where they put their outlines in and all of the handouts and the activities that we use: warm up and follow up activities that the schools can use, if they want to help us out with that. We will send them warm-up and fol-low-up activities to kind of get the kids primed and to finish off the topic. We do have a manual, and that is, when a new person comes in . . . It has tips on how to prepare, frequently asked questions, and appropriate re-sponses—classroom management stuff. Yes, some of the handouts and stuff that we have or activities might have come from other books, but as far as the flow and content, it is stuff that our group has put together.

Modifying Curricula

The next chapter, on peer education, discusses programs that use youth ad-visory boards to formally and actively guide curriculum development and modification. In this chapter, however, we relate how some of the educa-tors we surveyed benefit from informal feedback from past or prospective audiences, including students, teachers, and school administrators, as they modify curricular content:

We developed the curriculum ourselves with, early on, the input from teachers that met with us. It has continually been adjusted as we get feedback. I think this is one of the critical things if you are going to be in schools. You can't just go in and say, "This is my curriculum, take it or leave it." You need to work with the teachers and the administrators. They wanted it [to be] more interactive. There were some things early on in the middle school that they did not want. . . . We are just responsive to the input, without compromising our values. There are a lot of ways to get messages across, and so I think the curriculum has constantly evolved to respond to input from different schools.

I think we've kind of gotten to the point now where we do have like a "101"-type presentation that we can draw from; we have outlines; we've gotten a little bit beyond that now. But, yeah, when people do ask—like we'll have a teacher say, "Can you put it in the context of healthy relation-ships?" or like "kind of put a little different spin on it," then we would.

We've stolen pieces of things over the years from other people's [curricula], and then we've developed our own units. . . . We continue to, like on a yearly basis we review and continue to modify and . . . I'll give you an example for instance, with our sexual assault units that, it's sort of like the concept is spread out over these, say three or four units. We realized that we weren't focusing enough on the significance of oral sex, that we were just sort of glazing over it. . . . But the various cues that we've gotten from the kids and things we've learned from them—we've modified our program. . . . We tend to change things, like our Internet safety unit that we do, stuff that we ask the kids what they're doing and . . . how do they interact with the Internet and what is it that they, what are they looking for? And then we change that to fit into make it contemporary and real for them.

Interviewees sought guidance from youth and teachers with suggestions on improving their curricula and tailoring them to their own community context:

At one point, while we were reworking the curriculum, we went into some classrooms with our curriculum at the time, did it with them and then talked to them, invited them to give us some feedback like, "What's missing from this?" Like, "Do you get it? What should we also be saying? Are there parts that are really conspicuously left out?" We wanted to know from the boys, you know, "Give us some feedback." And from the girls as well. Yeah, I mean we've had to, because I think there are things . . . there are different cultural things that don't take here.

The initial curriculum was . . . 32 different activities and we, every year we go through and we decide what we are going to revise or change and what we are going to use or not use. And then the facilitators, the educators, pick the five or seven sessions they want to use and they've pretty much stuck to the same ones over the last couple of years. They just revise those every year. If they need to add something, then they do . . . During the summer time, that's pretty much what we do. When we are not in the classrooms as much, [we are] going over our curriculum, and we are updating it. We bring kids in that have worked with us throughout the school year and say, "Okay, what could we change, what should we change?" And they correct our terminology.

One very experienced prevention educator pointed out how updating curricula can help maintain interest for long-time staff members.

Improvising

Although at least half the interviewees sometimes improvise rather than precisely following a manual, there appears to be a continuum of improvisation. It is sometimes difficult to know where programs are situated along that continuum. Sometimes improvising can be done within the curriculum, and at other times it is done by disregarding the manual and paying attention to the interests of the audience. A common approach is to have certain basic points that educators must present and then to allow modifications, as long as they cover those basic points. Educators described how presenters could improvise by drawing from different parts of the curriculum:

What they [presentations] are based on is an assortment of materials, handouts, and videos that we put together into scripts that we've written. The scripts are really ones that we've written and put together. What we've done, is we've drawn from a wide variety of sources. But we don't do any one canned curriculum. We have scripts that we've developed that we utilize with the critical points for all of our different topics on them and then we tailor whatever else we're doing to our audience.

I think that's one thing that's so great about the curriculum is that there is . . . so much information that you can vary it, based on the group. It's not that there's only enough for you to do to take up 90 minutes, and then you have to say everything you know. I mean there's a lot of variety, and so I think you can definitely tailor it. We would tailor it, as well, based on age. I mean we wouldn't get into some of the things with the 6th grader that we would with the 12th grader, necessarily. So that's definitely a challenge for [us], too, is to kind of read the crowd as we go and adjust things as we need to, because we're not doing any good if we're not being relevant to the kids.

Others we spoke with emphasized the importance of informality and the willingness to set aside the curriculum and follow the interests of the adolescent participants:

I think [the educators] better improvise. I think that they need to absolutely be the facilitator and all. They need to create an environment of learning and, you know, but I think to be rigid with kids could be detrimental, because I think the kids can bring forward some information that they need to have and to try and stick to the script or an outline and bypass that [giving information] I think is disrespectful and discounting to them. And I do not, as a supervisor, encourage that. Where kids bring forward something, chat about it. Incorporate it in a way within the material that, you know, you are giving them the information you were going to give them anyway.

If someone does a new activity, we tell each other. So, "This is what I do." Like I have one I'm doing tonight, which is not in the curriculum, that I started doing. So then when we have, we have program meetings twice a month or we will also do that kind of thing like, if we have to get our story straight on something like how are we going to answer questions about Kobe Bryant. Whatever our curriculum is, because our curriculum is facilitated discussion, it really is decided by the group, so [we discuss] whatever they get stuck on. Different things with different groups. It really has changed. But whatever they get stuck on or whatever they have a lot to talk about is going to be how it goes.

Any time I go to a group I don't know what I'm going to end up doing. I'm being honest. That's why I said, what we've got etched in stone is [minimal]. Each group is different. You may have a group that is really talkative, and you may need to kind of cool them down and I'll do more talking. Or we have a group that doesn't talk too much and I'll say "you, you and you, come here" [and do a role-play], and I'll do something like that or I'll pull people. I've even gone as far as, when there is little dialogue and they are a really quiet group, I'll pass out pieces of paper and say, "Okay, write down some questions you have and I'll answer the questions that you are proposing."

Programs with less restrictive timeframes are more likely to include content that coincides with the youths' interests, because the presenters do not have to use all the allotted time in order to make sure they can include some essential concepts. Conversely, with a one-time, short presentation, it is often important to adhere, as much as possible, to the planned content:

You ask how much they adhere to the script per se. It's pretty close, because we only have the 50 minutes . . . But there is room for people to use their own style. There is room, if somebody mentions, like let's say a student speaks out and says, "Well, I think all faggots ought to be shot or something." And there have been a few times when there have been dramatic things like that. You don't let that go and just say, "Well, we're not on that right now" . . . The whole curriculum might change for that day to deal with what has just been said in the classroom. Pretty much, we pretty much stick to the script with not exact wording but with the contents of the day.

The educators spoke about the advantages and disadvantages of allowing improvisation. One advantage in improvising is that the presentation can be more compelling by following the interests of the adolescents and not repeating information they already know:

Sometimes I will go into the classroom with the intention of doing, talking about one specific thing, and when the students don't want to go—you know, their questions are on the other end of the spectrum. You have to go to where they are . . . Well, 'cause that's what they need to know about. And I incorporate what I intended to talk about even if it does not go the way I planned for it to. I try hard to meet the young people where they are. If they don't need to know the information that I thought they needed to know, they need to know something else . . . it is constant improvising from wherever they are, whatever they need to know.

Experienced educators know that there is a balance between following adolescents' interests and allowing the discussion to become tangential:

I'll have the outline. But if the students want to start talking about something else—like oftentimes . . . some of the conversation will get going that we don't get [to] 'til the next part [in the outline]. Because the students are just so interested in hearing what each other is saying. And you know, "What can we do? As students, how can we change this? We know it's not right that this is going on, but how can we change it?" So, if that's where the conversation has gone, that's where I'll let it go.

A disadvantage of improvisation is that the presentation of different material to subgroups can make it more difficult to have a dialogue afterward, when the group is reunited:

We stick with the curriculum fairly closely. There's room for discussion and so if we're talking about, you know, sexual harassment and it goes off on a related direction, we'll talk about it. But we always stay under the umbrella of sexual harassment. So, we have pretty strict agendas and formats that we go by. Like timeframes that we spend on each thing. I think that's especially important when you co-facilitate because you need to know where you're going. You need to know your beginning, middle, and end points. So you know, if I'm in a room and the boys are across the hall and they totally go off the topic and they talk about something different, then we come back, that conversation's not going to work together.

Several educators from one agency, when interviewed together, noted that the requirement to adhere strictly to a curriculum would make them feel like actors, not educators:

There's a movement in the state to start to do that [have a standard curriculum] . . . Now, I don't know what that means—whether it will mean guidelines, which I would prefer, or whether it means, word for word. [Interviewer: So you'd like to have the ability to kind of be creative?] For our sake, as well as the students', yes. If we had to go in and follow the script and say what we needed to say, then we are actors, we're not educators. And it's reciting; yeah, we're not there to recite someone else's words, and we have stories and we have experiences . . . it's about connection, how you connect with a group of people. If you just have to say, "Okay . . . point one, everyone listen." You know and you can't expect them to put themselves out there if they don't see you putting yourself out there and they . . . Again, if I really feel like every single classroom almost every week is a different situation. And when they respond to you—I often have five different ways of asking the same question or five different ways of teaching the same material, and if one doesn't seem to resonate, I'll move on to the next and feel out what they understand, how they understand things, what gets them going. And I think if we didn't do that, we would just not have any kind of success at all. That's a big thing actually because we always, we spent a lot of our time as educators not only in the classroom but always trying to come up with new activities and trying to go over our lesson plan with each specific upcoming class in mind.

If a program is using a pre- and post-test, educators may need to adhere to the curriculum to make sure they cover the concepts included in the evaluation instrument. Otherwise, the program may test as ineffective. In addition, presenters' accumulated experience contributes greatly to their effectiveness in improvising. If presenters are new staff members or volunteers, there are advantages to having them adhere strictly to the curriculum:

Certainly, for a presenter that's relatively new, I have them stick to the program because of the pre- and post-questionnaire. So, if we're going to do that, we're going to cover the concepts that we're supposed to. But should a child or a student start talking about something—where something becomes important, I really make it known that you don't have to worry about moving onto the next activity. If this is making more sense, which is part of a discussion, don't feel like, "Okay, we need to stop now . . ."

We go through trainings with people, I want them to follow that curriculum, know that curriculum really well. Not word for word. And then they can use their own style to deliver it. It has to be the basic same message and that we are all consistent. Everybody has their own style . . . It still works as long as it is all the same message . . . And we had somebody in our program a while back that was saying, starting out with statistics that really weren't true . . . She was saying one thing, and the rest of the staff was saying something else, and the agency philosophy wasn't being followed.

Summary of Curricula Development

The predominant trend in our sample is that program presenters develop their own curricula, but often it is based on borrowing parts of other programs' curricula. Many believe strongly in the importance of expanding on a topic and improvising rather than strictly adhering to a manual. Our participants feel confident that improvising curricula is most effective in working with various populations of youth. Strict adherence to a manual or outline is advantageous, however, for new prevention educators, volunteers, or when the presentation time is short.

The educators we interviewed, perhaps because most know they are involved in respected programs, were confident of the quality of their materials and in their own ability to design or adapt activities that work well within their own communities. They seem to have a great deal of respect for their own practice wisdom and believe that their knowledge of the youths in their own communities makes them best qualified to design programs for those communities. Researchers may question some of that self-confidence, but we did not observe or evaluate interviewees' programs; we simply convey their views.

11

Peer Leadership Programs

Peer education is the most common type of youth leadership program mentioned by just over one-third of those we interviewed. In a quarter of these programs, adolescents conduct community education projects, and 10 percent have teen advisory boards. However, 20 percent of the programs represented in our survey have neither peer education nor teen advisory boards. One or two programs have adults mentoring at-risk teens, but discussed in this chapter are only programs in which teens act as mentors within the context of peer education.

Most of the literature that treats youth-leadership and peer-education programs favorably is based on theory and opinions rather than empirical evaluation. Shiner (1999), writing about English drug prevention programs, notes that peer-education programs have not been sufficiently evaluated. When evaluations find that dating violence and sexual assault peer education programs are effective, it is difficult to separate the effectiveness of the delivery method from the content (Lonsway 1996; Smith and Welchans 2000; Ward 2001). Much of the literature on peer education focuses on college students but probably could apply to programs that work with pre-college adolescents (Heppner et al. 1995b).

A major reason why several authors favor peer education is that adolescents communicate better with one another than adults communicate with youths. Edelstein and Gonyer (1993) emphasize that peer educators might increase the potential for change, "because they effectively convey information and communicate with their peers in ways that professional staff cannot. They can influence peers' behaviors, be a role model and disseminate information using the language of peers . . . in a nonthreatening manner" (256). Simon (1993) asserts that peer educators capture attention and put students at ease to discuss difficult subjects. Sloane and Zimmer (1993) describe peer education as an excellent health education and motivational model, designed to empower students to help one another promote positive health beliefs and behaviors:

> Peer education continues to be an effective means of delivering messages to any target population . . . People are more likely to hear and personalize a message that may result in changing their attitudes and behaviors if they believe the messenger is similar to them. This is particularly true for youth, who are often at a stage in their lives when they are unable to trust, communicate with, or identify with adults. (242)

Adolescents may view themselves as invulnerable, believe that risks do not apply to them, and resist material presented by adults (Pohl 1990), but peer educators may provide credible role models for them (Sloane and Zimmer 1993). Durlak (1997) writes that programs benefit from using "credible, high-status peers" as peer educators (190). Peer-education programs with multiple peer educators can potentially meet Silverman's (2003) requirements for behavioral change by offering teens "access to models of behavior change and [the option] to select from among the models that best fit their view of themselves and the contingencies that must occur" (36).

Researchers point out that youth turn to peers for advice and support when experiencing dating violence (Ocampo, Shelley, and Jaycox 2007; Sudermann, Jaffe, and Hastings 1995), but adolescents may not know how to give support that truly helps a victim (Weisz and Black 2008). Empowering peer leaders helps them to become informed and increases their ability to help. Avery-Leaf and Cascardi (2002) recommend including a peer-counseling component in dating violence prevention programs, because research shows that youth are more likely to seek help from friends than from adults.

Economic arguments also favor peer education. Fennell (1993) points out that peer educators in college settings increase the number of students that can be reached and cost less than professional presenters. Peer leadership also benefits the leaders themselves (Durlak 1997), as it leads to "improved communication skills and personal relationships" (Paciorek, Hokoda, and Herbst 2003, 11).

Although there is much support for peer education in the literature, some authors question its actual value. Tolan (2000) asserts that no research exists that strongly supports targeting peer groups or implementing mentoring programs in general youth violence prevention. Paciorek, Hokoda, and Herbst (2003) point out that most of the peer-education programs that have been evaluated have been college programs, and that support for these programs is not unanimous. Gould and Lomax (1993) note that peer education "is not a panacea" and should be used as "one component of an educational whole rather than as a universal remedy" (235). They suggest that, if peer educators are, in fact, different from the audience, it is not really peer education: "peer educators' viewing themselves as equals of program participants is of little value if the participants themselves do not share that view" (236). In one of the few studies examining the effectiveness of peer education versus professional presenters, Anderson and Whiston's (2005) meta-analysis of college-level sexual assault prevention programs found that professional presenters are more effective than peer educators.

Peer Education Programs: Descriptions and Advantages

In the remainder of this chapter we discuss, and transmit the reasons for, peer education programs that our survey participants gave us and continue with information on how those programs are implemented, including the training of youth leaders. We conclude by discussing other types of youth leadership programs, as well as potential problems with and advantages and disadvantages of peer education.

Although more than one-third of the interviewees include peer education components in their programs, these components vary from a few peer educators doing a few presentations a year to programs with high numbers of peer educators presenting in multiple settings. Some work with, or help train, peer educators who address various topics, not just sexual assault and dating violence, but our focus is not on general peer education programs. A few interviewees no longer had active peer education programs but were able to share what they learned before that component lost funding or was otherwise discontinued.

Reasons for Peer Education

One program added peer education after internal research showed that peers had the greatest credibility with adolescents. Interviewees echoed the literature in discussing the advantages of peer education, such as increased credibility and access to role models:

> We have a peer leadership program where we work with three different audiences of young people. High school students, college students and

also our . . . clients from our legal services program, and help grow them into the next generation of leaders in this movement. . . . Of course, their voices to educate their peers are incredibly powerful. A high-school-student peer-educator has a very different but a very powerful voice, [compared to] an attorney coming into the classroom . . . Partly, related to our clients, is also about just helping empower them to recognize the ability that they have to make a difference in their community. So it's everything from getting, in exchange for their services, getting our clients to volunteer for our organization, speak out in the community, do outreach, various things . . . write a story about their experiences, you know, whatever fits with their comfort and skills to help them recognize that they have value to offer, that they can be a powerful voice to help others. We find that to be a very empowering experience for our clients who have had their self-esteem really worn down.

[Our program did research that asked youth,] "Who is a credible presenter to use?" and that sort of thing . . . Some of the results, I know, were [that the] the advocates and adult teachers, other adults and celebrities were not credible. It was primarily either peers, their mothers, or adult survivors of sexual abuse would have credibility, in that order. And so that's what the youth were saying.

They [presentations] are usually done by a group of peer educators at a time, sort of as a panel presentation. We also believe that for the audience to really hear the messages from the peer educators, that they need to in some way feel like this is an issue that could touch them. So, they have to feel some vulnerability to it. So we also try to, when possible, send peer educators who the audience can identify with . . . as somebody who is up there that "looks like me, or in an organization like I'm in, and they are talking about these things and know or have had personal experiences on some occasions with these things, like this could happen to me." When you bring in kids, they are more prone to listen to kids than even myself. . . . When I started here even though I was 24 or 25 years old, so maybe I am not that much older than them, but they still think that. If the kids are saying, "We have researched this and looked at this as an issue" . . . it gives them somebody within the school to talk to. Sometimes after a classroom [presentation], they may not approach me, but they may approach the peers or they may talk to them later about certain things. Even some of the teachers in their classrooms will turn to them [peer educators] if they are talking about a particular subject to get more information. I always think that anytime you can use students to teach other students . . . of course the biggest component is that . . . part of their mission statement is they are positive, nonviolent role models. If I had a kid who just got in trouble for beating up another kid the day before, then that has no merit . . . Sometimes I will think that eighth graders will react to this certain presentation and they [peer educators] will say, "No, this is what you need to do to get them to interact." That's great because they were there and they know. They know how to motivate a classroom and get them talking about certain things or what kind of activities are going to work. . . . They [peer educators] aren't mandated reporters like I am, so they can talk to them and get more information.

How the Programs Conduct Peer Education

Program administrators varied in how strictly they planned presentations and controlled the content presented by peer educators. Some used scripts or manuals and others allowed adolescents and their adult sponsors to tailor the content to their local audience. They varied in the level of adult involvement in developing the content and monitoring the presentations:

> We are really leaving a lot of the details and a lot of the flexibility up to the local youth and their sponsors. So, it's primarily a prevention program for sexual assault and presenting programs, initially in the schools, but as the teens get more experience we are hoping they will present to other community-based youth groups or in other sites . . . And they are primarily presenting sexual harassment, dating violence . . . date [rape] and club-type drugs and how they are used and that sort of thing . . . Some teens are experienced enough and feel confident enough to present all four topics. Some teens only focus on one or two maybe throughout the whole year. . . . It is heavy on information and, of course, they are coached, and the sponsors are trying to encourage them to come up with creative ideas to make it interactive and use whatever their talents are, if it is in art or music or whatever.

> And at that point, they prepare to do presentations to their younger peers, which is where we evolved into the middle school. So, through that they can choose the medium they want. They can do a skit. They can do a formal presentation. They can do art, creative writing . . . We design the format for them. So, we sort of give them all the paperwork and let them put it in their own words . . . But then I would say about 50% of them want to do skits and create their own skits. And we teach them, "These are the topics that you can cover, topics we covered in [our program]."

[We] teach them how to introduce it, how to introduce themselves, do the skit and then create an educational unit after. So, they are coming up with questions to ask after. And facilitating a discussion with their peers. We ask that they go a minimum of twice [to present to other adolescents]. The first time, we go out and we observe. Then after that, it's sort of the teacher or our contact at the school . . . The hope is that they go many times so they begin to get really comfortable with it and get really good at their presentations.

We usually have 3–4 [presenters] so that they kind of divvy up parts and do it as a group. . . . I think we have done that because it is a lot of information for one person to take responsibility for learning . . . So, I think it has taken some of the heat off the person to be one person in front of the group, talking about such emotionally charged issues . . . I think in some ways it has been more interesting for the audience because with more than one person presenting, they do some role-plays and kind of some interactive things during the presentation, which, always, the audience comments [that] they love that part. . . . When they do present, however, we do always try to send a professional staff member with them.

In some programs, peer education is only one aspect of multilevel interventions:

We also try to then support our peer education program with a variety of other types of work that we think is related to prevention, such as awareness events and bringing in more well-known national speakers. Then we also use sexual norms marketing as a tool to kind of bring all of that together.

Most of these programs face many logistical challenges, and various ways are found for organizing the presentations:

We hire teen educators and we train them for about two months in the fall. It's a community-based program and they go out to different middle schools, high schools, after-school programs, and they teach. They do workshops on dating violence and healthy relationships. They do about two to three a week . . . Right now we have four educators . . . This fall we're hoping to hire six and it's actually a paid position for them. They get $8.50 an hour and it's typically about five hours a week that they'll commit to. Two hours of that is a meeting with me and program development and then the other—the workshops are about an hour and a half long.

Yeah, they get out of school . . . at least once a week. . . . We have two teams of nine. So, we take one team at a time. That makes it possible to do more and not get them out of school quite so much. But we probably do 35 programs during the school year. They give us one night a week . . . [they go to] churches, youth groups. We are doing quite a bit of parent education now, so they will come and give some communication skills for parents . . . We always go with them but they introduce themselves . . . Usually the format is some kind of attention-getting kind of a beginning . . . They define the problem or the issue you are talking about and they usually demonstrate the issue by doing a bunch of skits and then we break the group up into small groups and they work. Near the end of the year they can handle groups by themselves, but in the beginning they have a co-leader and they have a bunch of interactive activities they do with the small group to give the kids a chance to talk about the subject more and relate more and then come back to the large group usually for some kind of skill building . . . and then closure. It is about 90 minutes. . . . Oh, and we have these youth self-defense instructors . . . usually we co-lead, like an adult and a youth instructor will teach.

We try and do it on a rotating schedule . . . So, they're rotating through and not missing the same class. I think that's one thing, in the long run, that would really work is if schools got the group and did it as a leadership class, so students would not necessarily [be] missing class to be there. It would be like an elective. But we haven't progressed that far yet. . . . But basically, a lot of that ownership falls on the school. If you're the contact and we come in and do a training, then it's sort of on you to find places for them to do their presentations.

Theatrical Approaches

Most of the peer education programs involve theater or skits. After the skits, the peer educators usually lead discussions or answer questions from the audience:

We have gone to some places with some "thug" kids who you think, "they are never going to watch our little play and don't want to pay any mind to it," but the plays that we have used or the different types of theater experiences, if it is authentic, if you are using work that kids have really had an input into; it is really hard to find a play that an adult has written that is going to be completely what you need. Most of the plays that we have used have been done where an adult was guiding it and the kids had a lot of input into how the play was written, where they could use their lingo and they have to really be able to tell you, "That word is stupid. We would never use that word." . . . But I have seen it be completely trans-formative, where audiences are watching. Now I think it is important to do the talk back . . . that is some skill how to facilitate the talk back, but I wouldn't want to do it where you just perform and leave because the learning part . . . the most important part is in the talk back.

They went to a special camp . . . they learned how to do improv scenes. So those are scenes that they have a starting line and an ending line and it stays the same and in the middle, they kind of stick to what they origi-nally came up with, but if different people are doing it, it might change a little bit. . . . In some classrooms, it works really great, and in some, it doesn't . . . The majority of our skits are set up to end at a climactic point where you are not sure what the character is going to do next, so that you can start a discussion about it and then they can ask the character as well. Once it ends, they stay in their characters, and I ask the class, as the facili-tator, I will ask them what they saw, what went on in this scene, to make sure that they understood everything that went on. Then I will ask them how they felt about it, if this is something that they think happens . . . de-pending on the type of scene, "Is it something that you see in your school?" Then I may ask them how they think the characters felt. Then after that, I give them a chance and say, "Help us make more sense of this, why they did certain things or what they are planning to do about it?" We'll talk to the characters. Then I let them ask questions of the characters. Then the peers will answer as their character would answer. Then once we are done with that session, I take them out of their character so they can help with the class and we talk about solutions. "What should somebody in this situ-ation do? Or what if you had witnessed this situation? What could you do or if this was your friend, how could you help them?"

Some of the prevention educators also mentioned the benefits for peer educators as well as the audience:

Well, in the current drama that we have for this year, there are six [peer educators]. But it changes every year, depending on the stories that they do. . . . The process is we just write them on the board. We just start with all kinds of aspects of dating violence. Then the kids get to choose. You know, "What themes are you getting from this?" It's all about empower-ment. One of the greatest joys of this is to know that these kids are doing this work. And the work doesn't end with the presentation that we make.

You know, the kids take this out into their lives. See, I think this is where the change is really happening.

Programs sometimes blend mentoring and theatrical peer education, and two actually organized competitions for theatrical productions:

We do have an auxiliary organization . . . and it is an organization that is men in the community who want to make a difference being either mentors or public speaking and education-based to reach a lot of different groups of people. Also, I'm involved with that organization right now. We're working on a theater competition for high school, middle school, and college students that is allowing these students to produce and direct and act in various types of theater work that portrays the reality of domestic violence and ending violence against women.

It was really important that we made sure that the participants who were submitting any of their theatrical work that they were creating their works based on factual information and researched information. We certainly didn't want someone to invest all of their artistic time creating a play that was very victimizing. And so the training . . . was a required training that anyone who was entering any kind of work into this theater competition had to go through this training. . . . There are going to be two judges for each area of the competition . . . one being someone from the theater community and one person being from the Violence Against Women community.

One program includes a theatrical presentation with trained actors. Because the actors are young, this program might be considered peer education, and it is expanding to recruit youth in schools to develop presentations. It seems likely that the theatrical start-off contributed to the high level of interest in an after-school club:

That [theatrical presentation] allowed us to expand something that we began a few years ago . . . which is an interactive theater performance about a high school couple and several of their friends and the audience members watch as this relationship unfolds between the couple and it seems very normal and healthy in the beginning, but by the end, it is very obviously abusive, and, in between each scene, the audience can interact with the characters. They can challenge them; they can question them. . . . But this prevention money from CDC has allowed us to expand that, so that we have one partner school for a 3- to 4-year period. We work with one school in the state where we are targeting the ninth grade population in that school. Every ninth grader sees this performance at the beginning of their health class rotation and then weekly throughout their half-year health class, I go in and do workshops on dating violence prevention. It will end up being about 15 sessions on a weekly basis, in addition to the play that they see, and then we have also formed an extracurricular club at the school where students take their time and are learning even more about relationships. It is a co-ed club so that we have a lot of dialogue and discussion about different aspects of a relationship: what's healthy and what's not. It is good for the boys and girls to hear each other's perspectives and right now we have contracted with a local theater company to come in and work with the club members and they are developing their own production for the end of the year. . . . In recent meetings, they have told us they know what abuse is. They would know an abusive relationship if they saw it, but they are not sure if their peers would know a healthy relationship if they saw one. They really wanted to show some healthy relationships. . . . Then the other part of this prevention program is doing teacher in-service training . . . The play . . . actually, they are trained actors. They are very young, some of them are just out of high school, some are college students, a couple of them are out of college.

Sometimes, the programs collaborate with classes or other community agencies, such as this program that presents a peer theatrical one-time event:

Something unique that we have done now, for the second year, is that one of our local high school drama clubs, they do a community service project with it and they do a mock trial each year in the community. It's really a great program. . . . Last year, the case was an acquaintance date rape. It was where a woman met a man at a bar and then he put a date-rape drug in her drink. This year, the case is a little bit different, where it's a boyfriend and a girlfriend who had broken up, had had sex in their first relationship and then a year later they got back together. And he forced her to engage in sex. So, the whole premise is, "If you have sex with someone before, do you have the right to still say "no?" And the students are actually writing the script this year.

Whether an adult always accompanied the peer educators to their presentations varied among programs, and where adults did accompany the youths, their roles varied:

But at [one high school] we thought it was necessary because they were younger kids—and they needed the support. But at [another high school] I would go sometimes. They were like, "Oh no, she's grading us." I would sit back and never hold a pen or anything. I would try not to say anything, but then they go, "Oh do you know the answer to this?"

[Interviewer: Now if you're there and the peer educators get stuck in some way, do you jump in?] Yes, I do. And they ask me to or look for me to. And I would actually schedule the workshops. November and December I would go with them to kind of facilitate, make sure everything is going okay and then the rest of year, January through May, they pretty much go on their own. . . . They're just able to talk in the language they're used to talking in, using slang or if they're comfortable using curse words they tend to—because that's just how they normally would talk among their peers. But when adults are present, I guess they probably don't express certain things as often.

Other Types of Youth Leadership Programs

Some of the educators we spoke with mentioned other types of youth leadership programs. The most common alternatives were youth advisory boards, youth outreach or youth action programs, such as those that assist adolescents in doing outreach or designing a social action campaign, and peer-counseling programs.

Youth Advisory Boards

As our participants described them, youth advisory boards usually enabled adolescents to play important roles in directing the development of an agency's prevention program. This approach is consistent with national calls for opportunities to "promote youth as constructive civic activists and community leaders" (Irby et al. 2001, 1). Irby et al. report that "a growing body of research indicates that young people are more likely to avoid problem behaviors, make healthy choices, learn effectively and become lifelong engaged citizens if they have opportunities to contribute and make a difference" (9).

Bloom and Gullotta (2003) suggest that, when participants are involved in designing prevention activities, the process builds on their strengths and promotes wellness. Promoting psychosocial wellness "assumes that an important part of primary prevention involves enhancing wellness in order that people may attain some desired state of well-being. Promotion is a positive activity in its own right and is not simply a reduction of risk for illness" (13). Zeldin (2004) supports programs where youth participate in advisory boards or do outreach or media campaigns, because, he argues, involving youth in community decision making about youth violence helps youth "acquire the competence, confidence, and sense of belonging necessary for a successful transition to young adulthood" (624). Zeldin believes that adults tend to think of teens as wild, rude, lacking in positive values, and unwilling to give to their communities, but research suggests that most youths do want to contribute. The positive youth development movement asserts that society must provide daily opportunities for youth "for self-directed and challenging learning, participation in the adult world, feelings of group membership, and emotional and strategic support from non-familial community adults" (627). Involvement in community decision making is key in this, and research supports positive outcomes for youth when this happens.

Our interviews indicate that youth advisory boards are growing as a facet of dating violence and sexual assault prevention work. Several programs already have these advisory boards, and others want to start them. One program had both teen clubs that do outreach and a youth advisory board, and another program has a youth advisory board with members who sometimes serve as peer educators:

Obviously, if you want to find out how to reach youth, the best people to ask are youth. So, we proposed and put together a youth advisory coalition which is a youth group, for kids 13 to 21, but we've never gotten anyone above 17 or 18 to come. And that being a way that we can do some education, and they've done some peer presentations for some different groups . . . and just various other outreach kinds of projects. . . . We've had probably 20 or 30 kids come to meetings at some point in its about-a-year's existence. Never have we had all those people at one meeting, and attendance has been a struggle—trying to motivate youth to come to the meetings and working around scheduling, and I think that we've tended to get a group of youth who are active in a lot of other activities, so they've got a lot going on . . . Lately it's been more like four or five. . . . They made up a Jeopardy game, sort of, an idea, with different questions and point values and so they spent a lot of time working on that and it seemed to work out as a tool for presentations for getting some involvement of people in the classroom . . . They're also working right now on putting together a presentation that's a little more about, sort of gender, the media and how the stereotypes interact with the issue of violence against women for another student youth group that works on discrimination . . . issues. So, that's going to be a slightly different, more focused presentation that they're excited about.

We have a youth advisory board that meets usually monthly . . . They direct the program and they look over any materials we might print, handouts that we do. . . . The STOP [youth clubs in high schools doing prevention activities] clubs meet once a week during lunch—usually at the school. We have youth, like youth coordinators [college-age] . . . a lot of them went to the high school that they were the president or whatever . . . and then they have these meetings once a week and they plan their activities. And part of that is, the coordinator identifies or asks people, "Would you be interested in being in this?" . . . And then people who are interested come to the meetings. . . . Some kids have cars. We do have these two vans. We are having our annual meeting this Saturday and they are coming to the annual meeting. . . . And usually we go into a health class . . . or Life Skills Class. . . . That is how we recruit kids for the club. And then the kids in the club, they usually, they do awareness raising events on their campus like in April they will hand out lollipops with sexual assault facts on them.

I do think the lesson that if you get [give] youth the opportunity to voice their concerns and their thoughts about something, they really will do that in an appropriate way. Sometimes I see a lot of reluctance to getting youth involved in things that are considered more like management or planning or leadership, but really I have found when people really let go of some of the control and kind of realize that: let them make some of the decisions, that they really [are] doing things that are even better than what we probably would have thought of.

Youth Outreach or Social Action

The inclusion of a social action component in prevention programs may help adolescents retain information (Begun 2003; Irby et al. 2001). Grasley, Wolfe, and Wekerle (1999) reported on a prevention program for adolescents that finished with an action-based segment. They assigned tasks to pairs of youth, such as interviewing staff at an agency that helps domestic violence victims and then sharing their findings with the group. The adolescent group also plans a social action event in their community, which gives them a feeling of empowerment and that they are contributing to the community. The youth-action components of the program were not evaluated separately from other components, and the authors note that youth-action activities require intensive efforts by adults. They reported that they sometimes needed "graduates" of their program to encourage current participants to complete the projects.

Some school- or agency-based peer leadership programs do community outreach, such as poster campaigns or similar projects:

Last year we worked with a group of students in an art class and we did a banner on dating violence and sexual assault. Then this year we began . . . an opportunity for teens to volunteer on their campus to change the climate at their school. So, they receive six hours of training; they have an adult sponsor on their campus and then they are the outspoken leaders on their campus for reducing and preventing bullying, sexual harassment, and dating violence . . . It's kids with, maybe not academically strong, but strong in other ways. . . . Those are kids that are in there because they want to make a difference on campus. They go through the six-hour training and then they brainstorm a project for their campus . . . So one school, the group that broke into smaller groups and created . . . skits which they then videoed and I want to use it to train other younger kids. Another school decided they wanted to do a presentation to administrators on these issues. Another school wanted to have a drop-in, peer-counseling center.

These kids are from a variety of backgrounds, but they're tops in their class. These kids are among the top grade getters, and they are kids that are very ambitious. And what they wanted to do, they proposed to start a group that goes around and maybe attends agency fairs with us promoting nonviolence in the school. They put up posters, hand out things like that. Distribute literature around the school. Talk to kids about dating violence: [help them determine] if they are in a violent relationship. And some of them have set up like peer mentoring, peer counseling in their schools. We are not necessarily part of that per se; that depends on the school . . . different projects, projects that promote the anti-violence message in middle and high schools. . . . Right now it is about 10 [teens involved]. A small group but from the different high schools throughout the county, along with private schools. . . . I think some of them may consider that it looks good on the resume, "I was part of this group," which is fine. Some of them see the issue and realize how important it is. Others are about, "I've got to do something, I am more privileged, in my Maslow's hierarchy of needs. I've got my food, I've got my shelter, I've got all these things and I want to start understanding how I can help my fellow man." . . . [We provide] literature, information, resources. And they want to get the word out about anti-violence. What we don't want them doing right now is going out and substituting what we are doing, delivering the message. Because we have a specific way of doing that and we don't take volunteers.

Mostly they help us with promoting the organizations and activities. We do drafts over the summer, literally go door-to-door and put a flyer in a door, or we teach them to talk with people, almost like a campaign. . . . That [number of participants] varies, that really varies, I would say, I think at our largest we had forty. . . . I wish we could [pay them] . . . some of them like to come in for two hours, some of them like to come in for five, others will stay a whole day. So, but what we do is offer the internship as a two-hour project.

Media Outreach

Some programs involve teens in media campaigns, including activities such as designing posters and business cards, and participating in cable TV shows:

The part of the program that is the youth-mobilization piece where we are working with teens to develop—they've done some plays, they've done public service announcements, they've written poetry—that part of the piece where we are capturing the youth voice and hearing from them in terms of media messages. . . . The students have created their own public service announcements. Those get put on our cable stations. The plays we talked about, those have been on the cable-TV network. . . . We had a lot of students creating media messages, creating posters, T-shirts. Creating different kinds of things that we put in the community, that are up in the schools. We had a student not long ago: "Oh my gosh, I can't believe that poster is up there. I saw my friend's work." . . . Our business card for teens used to be very formal. Then teens actually created a card with a heart on it that says, "Love Shouldn't Hurt. Do you know violence isn't just physical?" With our emergency number on the back. And then most recently, out of one of the posters, we created bookmarks that is their design with two arms being, one arm grabbing another one. You don't see any faces and it says, "You are not property."

Peer Counseling

A few interviewees described programs that included a peer-counseling component:

We also have done some training in peer counseling . . . If a student has a problem with a partner, that they can go to the teen health clinic on campus . . . and tell the coordinator that they would like to speak to one of our peer counselors and then arrangements are made for the two to meet with a facilitator and they can talk about what they need to talk about.

Recruitment of Peer Leaders

Shiner's (1999) research on English drug-prevention peer-education programs found that a peer is usually defined simply by age, but some programs find tensions between peer educators and their audiences because of gender, social class, or ethnicity. A potential advantage of having a diverse group of peer educators is that the programs may become more accessible for different adolescent groups (Gould and Lomax 1993). Youth can more easily identify with peers recruited from the youths' school or club, who might be from a similar ethnic background or social class. Simon (1993) believes it is important to have both males and females as peer educators.

The interviewees often spoke of the importance of recruiting a diverse group of adolescents in terms of gender, socioeconomic status, ethnicity, sexual orientation, or type of peer friendship group (clique). Several programs recruit peer educators by issuing an announcement about the peer-education program when adult educators are presenting programs to classes. Few programs offer academic credit or pay for participating:

> We send flyers out to different community organizations like health centers and community centers where a lot of teens may go to, [and to] schools, we post flyers up and we just say, you know, "Do you like public speaking? Do you want to be involved in spreading the word about dating violence?" And then so we get different applications and then we do interviews and then we hire in September [for paid positions].

> We define "student leaders" really broadly. So, we encourage schools to get us a cross-section of students from each of the subcultures in the school. So we're saying, "Don't just get us the traditional leaders. Get us leaders from all the different groups." . . . There's the athletes, the student government, the peer leaders, the newspaper, drama, skater kids, alternative kids and even encouraging teachers that leaders aren't necessarily always the best students. They may be the kid in the back of the classroom that gets everybody riled up and laughing, but they're the one that has the attention and the power over their peers. . . . What we don't

do is we don't go in and work with an already pre-formed classroom. . . . We typically don't do that because they already have a dynamic amongst themselves formed. And what we really want to do is come in and get a brand-new cross-section of kids and create our own dynamic. And the power of that is that you also get the kids that, because we have such a cross-section, they wouldn't normally be talking to each other. Once I watched a presentation with the captain of the cheerleading team, who was co-facilitating with the kid who had tattoos and piercings and purple hair. That, in and of itself, sent a message to the students that were receiving it . . . tenth and eleventh graders is who we work with. . . . We explain to [teachers] that it's not a good idea to put in a couple . . . You know, where there's a potential perpetrator and victim in the room. We find out if there are any special needs that we need to know about. So, we don't screen the students, but that's sort of on the school to screen them and get students in however they want. . . . One thing we like to do is go in and do a faculty presentation. We sort of give the spiel on the program and say, "This is who we're looking for." And then have them write names down. That's how we get kids nominated. And you tell kids that they were nominated as a leader and that gets them in the door. And once we get them in the door, we can typically keep them. You're probably aware, if you tell a kid, "Oh, you're going to come and talk about violence against women," . . . especially the young men aren't going to come. But, "You've been nominated to be a part of this great program," and they come. Our catch really is that we're very interactive and we listen to them and we have real conversations with them. So, that keeps them in the room. . . . And you know, we ask for 30 students because you need that many to have a good conversation going . . . Yes, trying to get teachers to match the cultural diversity of the school. There are some schools that we go to that are primarily all white. So, I say, "Okay, try and get some diversity in there that you can." But obviously, that matches the school. Whereas, we have schools on the flip side that are all students of color. So, you have students representing all racial and ethnic groups in the school. . . . To be honest with you, there have been gay and lesbian youth in our groups that have loved it. And there have been gay and lesbian youth in our groups that have left.

We have equal numbers of girls and boys. You can't teach violence prevention without boys. We select 18 seniors from area high schools. We do our recruitment; we put out applications every year. We go around the schools and talk about the program, so we recruit in the spring of the junior year. So, we have about 60 kids who apply and we take 18. . . . We do certainly have more white students that are interested but we have, out of the, how many do we have, maybe 10 from [one high school] this year, we have three African Americans and one Asian. Sometimes we will have a Hispanic kid. It's not a lot but we do have some diversity. . . . Their parents have to sign off on it. They pay $500. Obviously we give scholarships, but we are a very poor nonprofit and as you know, it is harder and harder to stay alive as a nonprofit.

It is a very progressive suburban school . . . The high school is progressively open and it is 95% white. The people who make the difference are the administration and then their student activities coordinator and they are heavily, heavily invested in sexual assault and dating violence issues. . . . The hand-selected kids were already highly involved in the school as peer conflict mediators, what they call PCM—it's an interview. There are maybe 80 applicants and they take 12–14 kids a year. That have this first hour and their whole mission is to solve conflicts through mediation and serve as role models and are very much visible in school. So, most of those kids became involved and we did open it up to other kids too. . . . Sixteen was too much. We always had an even number of boys if not more boys. I don't know how we pulled it off, but we did. They were heavily invested in having males represented. . . . We recruited through the student council if there wasn't enough of the PCM kids. . . . We recruited out of those groups and then did the interviewing. I don't believe there were any kids that were denied. . . . And again, I think the boys are really impressive. Not that they deserve more credit than the girls. I'm really careful about that. Thank the boy for being here, but thank the girls too. Because I think that as a movement, we just bow at the knees of any man who is involved. . . . I think it creates an uncomfortable situation for those men . . . idolizing . . . I think you have to be careful about that, but I think just seeing, like when we were doing the training and we were watching one of the videos, and, of course, there's all these survivor stories and this sweet teenage boy, he says "I think that is the saddest thing I've ever heard." You just see this sensitive side of boys. It is so nice. Then they get back in the hallway and they are punching each other and all that.

In discussing recruiting, one person we spoke with pointed out the strengths and potential problems that teen leaders might bring with them:

Members of that program have been victimized, are referrals, because they've been victimized by domestic violence, sexual assault, sometimes sexual harassment and stalking crimes and it's, they've been participating in a support group or now have interest in using their voice to end the cycles of violence against women. . . . But the Young Men's Leadership Program is somewhat similar to what we do with our women's projects, but we're trying to teach young men, again, how to relearn behaviors, healthy behaviors, learn to be leaders, that domestic violence and these other kinds, are not just the women's problem. They are men's problem too, and that's, that's kind of the philosophy behind the design of that program. And for all eleventh-grade students we offer a summer internship program . . . That is not just offered, in other words, to people who have been, who have survived these types of crimes, but it's offered—open to the general public, and we try to advertise with the schools and foster partnership with not just the public schools but the local private schools as well and other youth programs.

Although what we do have sometimes, is people who want to be peer educators who we just choose not to take, because we feel like they want to do it for the wrong reasons or we feel like they may be over committed to other activities and not have the time. We do tell them that if they commit to do this and we accept them, that it will take on the average of two hours per week of their time and that we would like them to make at least a one-year commitment to it, because of all of the training we have put in for them. Also because they do present as a group, they have to spend a little bit of time just working with their other group members just getting their presentation ready . . . They need to be able to work together like a team.

Having current peer educators nominate younger teens as potential colleagues or successors seems to work well in some settings:

I just started asking kids, "Who would be good doing this work?" Why I didn't do that in the beginning? I don't know. Because the kids know, and so really now we just had a meeting on Sunday and they came up with almost 30 names of kids that they want to nominate to be part of this. And so they came up with those names. The other way that we get names is that when we go out and do presentations, if there are people who come up to us after and say, "Oh my gosh! I'm a survivor," or, "I want to do this work," or, "What you do is so interesting. How do I get involved?" I take their name and number and that's another way that they can get involved.

Some programs required parental permission for participation. One interviewee mentioned that they needed teens to have permission partly because the material in the training was very "adult." (See chapter 5 for more information on issues of parental consent.)

Training Peer Leaders

Literature on training peer educators is scarce. Simon (1993) maintains that peer educators require a lot of opportunity for dialogue at the beginning of the training, because they may hold "a variety of views and opinions on sexual assault" (290). Adults involved in the program might assume that only those who are "quite evolved in their thinking" (290) have volunteered, but this may not be the case. The views of peer educators who are less "evolved" may be the same as those of future presentation audience members, so early discussions in peer education training are doubly important. Edelstein and Gonyer (1993) recommend rigorous training of peer educators at the college level, while maintaining opportunities for some creativity and individuality. Gould and Lomax (1993) note, "Critics of peer education have questioned the volume or quality of training that peer educators receive in preparation for entering the field" (236). The length of training should relate to the complexity of the skills that peer educators are supposed to teach.

Some of the nine students Paciorek, Hokoda, and Herbst (2003) interviewed were unhappy with their peer leadership training, believing it was not thorough enough. At times, the program had experienced peer educators train new ones, which was not always adequate. Paciorek and colleagues report that most of the peer educators they studied had personal experience with violence and that this "points to the importance of close monitoring and supervision" (17) if students are acting out violent scenes that could trigger an adverse reaction or "interfere with their effectiveness" (17).

Our interviewees offered useful details about how they trained peer educators:

> And then September and October we do training and get them ready for the workshops. We train on public speaking, domestic violence 101, teen dating violence, the cycle of abuse, different forms of abuse and then we practice the curriculum, do a lot of practice . . . Well, when they go through their training we have a curriculum and one of our main things is to really stick to the curriculum and what is said in the curriculum and not to say things, you know, like your opinion, because that could kind

of put us into trouble. . . . We give out cards at every workshop; if there's a question they're unsure of, they kind of encourage the person to call [the hotline] or they say, you know, "Come talk to me afterwards," and, you know, if an adult's there, they can talk also. But, yeah, we try to stick extremely close to the curriculum. And I don't think we've ever had any problems really. None of the educators have ever told me that someone asked a question and they were unsure what to do.

We work with those students for a total of 22 hours. The first part is 15 to 16 hours and it's what we call "basic awareness-raising training" and it's basically where we go through the fundamentals of preventing men's violence against women. And we go through sort of our curriculum, which progresses with some like introductory stuff about our approach. And then we go into some empathy-building exercises. And then we cover battery, gender roles, sexual harassment, rape involving alcohol, homophobia and then some wrap-up exercises. And that's our entire awareness-raising curriculum. The primary focus is the bystander approach to prevention. So, because we have student leaders in the room, we're encouraging them to make a proactive stance against acts of violence in their community. . . . They have an option of moving on to what we call "Train the Trainers" which is an additional 5 to 6 hours . . . And we offer to continue to do "Train the Trainers" with, quote/unquote, old kids. So, for example, in the fall we may go in and do a kick-off with the old troop and get them settled for presentations, and start a new group. . . . A big piece of where we're coming from is that if students challenge each other in their thoughts, as opposed to us, that's much more effective learning. You know, if their friend is like, "Wait, that's totally not cool what you just said," as opposed to me saying, "Wait, why do you think that way?" They're going to hear that message.

I do an initial four-hour training and that's where the new ones [peer leaders] will come and meet with me. I have a manual that we go through that goes over all of the topics that we cover. Usually I am giving more information to them than what I expect them to give to a classroom. They are also a pillar in their school that kids might come talk to them and ask them questions about stuff. . . . Then each summer all of the kids get to have the option of what we call a retreat. . . . We focus on team building and bonding with the team. . . . That's where they develop their presentations and come up with things; they evaluate what we did in the last school year and if things need to be changed or worked on. Then we talk about any new things that they want to do, and that is usually two and a half days.

One program trains both adult educators and peer educators, often mixing adults and adolescents in the same training groups:

> I would rather mix them in because I think that it gives a couple of things. I think it gives those adults the opportunity to really hear youth say, "You know this would work, or this wouldn't work." Or "you know, if you're going to talk about it that way, you're probably going to lose a lot of people's attention." And plus I think it also gives that youth, those youth who say "I want to be a peer educator" or whatever the situation is, I guess that place that honors that work that you're doing above and beyond. And that has maturity to it, and so, to me, it seems like a respectful place to say, "We are all working on this issue and I'm not dividing it out by age." Now sometimes youth will say, "I'd feel more comfortable with just people my own age."

Challenges in Peer Leadership

Walker and Avis (1999) published an excellent summary of difficulties with peer education based on their practice experience in England. Peer education programs, they write, often underestimate the complexities of the task. The programs, they note, must be designed to fit the context, have highly skilled leadership to perform the many complicated tasks, and provide thorough training and support for peer educators. Program staff also needs to continuously monitor boundary issues between adult leaders and peer educators, and between the educators and their audience.

Several participants in our survey cautioned about the important challenges and difficulties involved in running youth-participation programs. One challenge is recruiting a diverse group of adolescents:

> I think that's a fault of our youth advisory coalition, that it doesn't reflect the geographic or cultural whole of the county. It's pretty much white kids from [an elite college town]. And so we—it's something we've been talking about, how to change that and, you know, about the sense of privilege that that enables kids from [elite college town] to do after school activities versus the type of outreach we need to do.

Scheduling meetings, training, and multiple presentations was also a challenge, having to work around peer educators' school schedules and busy after-school calendars. Several programs were forced to discontinue their peer education programs, as they were unable to overcome difficulties in getting the teens together for meetings and presentations:

We've been talking about that. It feels like, oftentimes, it's not a priority in their schedule. Like for whatever reason, that—and part of it is that we don't really make anything mandatory. Like part of that, it's almost like the flip side of trying to have an empowerment-focused teen advisory board, it's that we're not holding anything over their heads, so then four people come to a meeting when we know it would be so much better if there were ten or fifteen people. And that's been a struggle for us for sure. . . . And I guess I'd like to see a group where you can get at least a little more consistent attendance. It wouldn't bother me so much if it were four or five people if it were the same four or five each time. So what happens is it's four people one time, the next time it's totally different people and only one person is the same and it's hard to have any consistency to get anything done or to plan.

We tried, probably four years ago now, to implement high school peer ed, and it was a disaster. What we found was that we do not have enough staff to coordinate an intensive peer-ed program. To do peer ed successfully, in my opinion, you would need it to be your full-time job. It was a logistical planning nightmare. And for the three of us working part-time on this project, and also having other jobs, we just did not have the staff resources to be arranging bus tokens and cab vouchers and calling parents and, oh my goodness. It was the worst experience I've had in this respect. I would say it's the year we tried to do peer ed. And it wasn't that the kids were bad. It was just that it took way too much. We were really stretched to the limit. Also, the kids we work with, you know, they don't have a lot of home support in some cases. So, it was just too difficult.

Walker and Avis (1999) observe that "many young people who volunteer for peer-led projects do so because they are working through personal difficulties" (575). Peer leaders might bring their own troubling personal issues that require a great deal of help from adult prevention-program leaders:

It really does take up a lot of time, coordinating the teens and a lot of the teens, they have problems also, you know, just other teen problems. And so it's kind of hard to balance some of the issues that they may be going through and then also the job itself. And so I think that's a big challenge and so I think it would be helpful to have maybe two coordinators. And it would be great if we could have a male and female coordinator.

Another potential challenge is that survivors of abuse or assault might volunteer to be peer educators. Program administrators vary in their views on how to handle this:

A lot of [the peer educators] were survivors . . . An 11th-grade student and her cousin, they were both victimized and they were part of the group, so it was really challenging to work some of that out. Although, because there is lots of support at schools, the health centers and all that, there was enough support to keep them going and constantly assess if they wanted to stay involved, and they ended up kind of very appropriately telling their story to some of the students; and it ended up kind of working out, so the kids felt very supported and were getting their needs met, as far as issues that were triggered in other ways besides our program.

We don't want them to answer questions personally. . . . If they want to share something about a relationship to the group, that's up to them but it's not something that we really encourage, their personal sexual behavior. Other than, we expect them to be responsible and discrete and. . . . So when a question comes up in a program . . . we kind of teach them to field it like, "Well actually at [our program] we recommend that da, da, da." Or "most teenagers, in my opinion, it seems that most teenagers in my school do such and such" rather than answering how they do it.

What I've told my speakers is that if they choose to share their story, here are the pros, here are the cons. That's just based on my experience. . . . And it's their decision if they choose to share that. I have one student who is a speaker who currently is in a stalking situation, so her story lends all kinds of credibility to the theater work that we're doing. So there has been a time when I've asked her if she's comfortable sharing that story with the audience. But that is her choice and her decision. On one occasion, I have asked the audience to be careful with the information that they're hearing and the reasons for that.

A common reason for discontinuing peer education programs was lack of funding. Cuts in the budgets of agencies where those we interviewed were employed or school funding cuts ended some peer education programs. One resource that requires staff time and money is training for the adolescent leaders. Experience with the lack of training led one interviewee to question the value of peer education:

In the past, when we've done work with peer-ed classes and the students have developed their own skits . . . so all the judgments, all the misinformation comes out, and then we can process it. But what the peer-ed teachers have tried to do is have those students go out and replicate it [the process of bringing up and clarifying misconceptions]. And the students aren't able to prepare to really address some of the misinformation . . . We still do it. It's just . . . I'm not enamored with it. I don't think it's the best way to develop leadership on this issue, student leadership.

There are situations where teens have stopped presenting after a presentation goes badly and generally that comes from questions from the audience. [Questions that are] kind of challenging, or the guys in the room kind of gather in and reject the whole thing. And I know sponsors [staff from the local rape crisis center and from the school] have stopped. They may have a whole schedule of presentations arranged and after the first one or two, something like that happens and the sponsors will pull them from the schedule and stop them from sharing. Go back into training and coaching. . . . Other times where the sponsors are watching the presentations and notice there are some problems with the presenters. Either, for example, one sponsor called and just talked about, "We are pulling off of our presentation schedule because a couple of our presenters just have this wrong concept" in the sponsor's mind, "about girl power and that it is sensual and sexual and all this sort of thing and the way they are dressing and talking and giving presentations" in the sponsor's mind, is not real . . . So, she stopped that . . . and is working with them now. That sort of thing. And really, I mean, from our role in kind of facilitating this, we don't know what all is happening. We just don't know. And we can try and just survey randomly to find out what are some of the experiences happening on a team, but my experience with this program so far is that we don't get information back. We get very little information back from the sponsors or the teams.

Regarding training issues, one very experienced person we interviewed described how a member of her staff attended an anti-bullying, peer-education program that invited youth to come forward and discuss upsetting experiences. This story reinforced her fear that peer educators might not be able to appropriately handle the concerns of those who have survived dating violence or sexual assault:

Our issues are so life-threatening and so traumatic. . . . And I totally disapprove of that kind of evangelical type of stirring people up. So, my educators said, "Well, they had therapists ready in the wings for anybody who wanted counseling." And I said, "If you're going to stir people up so much that they're going to need a therapist, that is totally inappropriate in a school setting. And as a parent, I would be really, really upset that you did that." So that's why we've been staying away from peer education, because it is so easy in the way that you say something or are doing in education if you don't pick up the facial expression, body language or something like that, that somebody is being impacted by what you're saying. You could actually put someone into a crisis and not be able to handle it. That's why we've always shied away from it. Plus, there's the whole thing about confidentiality.

Summary of Peer Leadership Programs

Many of the program staff we interviewed are very aware of the importance of empowering youth. They also see the active involvement of adolescents in their prevention programming as a way to keep their programs fresh and relevant to youth culture and to diverse adolescents in their communities. The interviewees' comments often were consistent with the literature in suggesting that peer leadership engages attention and offers role models for youth. They also pointed out that participation in peer education or peer leadership can be rewarding and educational for the peer leaders.

The interviewees also suggest, however, that those who provide peer leadership programs are constantly challenged both to empower youth and at the same time to protect the peer educators and the adolescent audience. If programs do not provide sufficient training and support for peer leaders, the peer educators may feel incompetent and their peers in the audience may receive inadequate knowledge or help. Programs that allow peer educators to give presentations without adult supervision may be considered unethical by some, because they may not offer adequate protection to survivors in the audience or they may not be able to challenge myths that support violent behavior. Similarly, allowing peer educators to relate their own traumatic histories publicly can increase survivors' vulnerability in ways that program staff may not have anticipated. In addition, coordinating and facilitating peer-leadership programs can be complex and challenging, suggesting that peer leadership offers exciting possibilities but must be developed and implemented cautiously.

12

Parental, School Staff, and Community Involvement

The literature and experienced practitioners agree that parental, school, and community participation are strongly needed in prevention programs targeting youth. For example, Repucci, Woolard, and Fried (1999) argue that violence-prevention programs need to address multiple domains with a coordinated strategy. In focusing on parental, school, and community participation in prevention programming, this chapter explores how programs cited in the literature have brought these individuals and groups together in their prevention programs. This is followed by examples of the various ways in which prevention educators have effectively involved parents, schools, and communities in their work.

Parental Involvement

Parents are vital to any work with youth, and an increasing number of prevention programs recognize the need for parental involvement (Fredland et al. 2005; Nadel et al. 1996; Weist and Cooley-Quille 2001). Experience with substance abuse prevention programs for youths has made us aware that excluding parents from other prevention work directed toward young people is unrealistic (Jansen, Glynn, and Howard 1996). Parental involvement is important, because parents need to know what their children are learning so they can be in a stronger position to reinforce the program's messages at home. Both the literature and interviews with prevention educators yield ideas for involving parents, including the use of orientation sessions, presentations, written information, newsletters, and group sessions. Suggestions in the domestic-violence and sexual-assault fields often center on increasing parents' knowledge about these issues, as well as improving parents' ability to educate and work with their children on the topics (Sanders 2003). The literature also notes the challenges associated with involving parents (Salazar et al. 2004).

All the educators we interviewed felt strongly about the importance of involving parents, and only 18% acknowledged that they had been unable to involve parents in some way:

> We need to do a better job, would like to do a better job of talking to the parents of teens . . . you can't just work with the youth, as you know. I know, it is working with who surrounds the youth . . . We provide, in the brochure, we just basically provide like a resource to a helpline for parents. But we don't do specific work with parents.

> We know that kids are going home and talking to their parents about it . . . But we don't have any real parental contact. It is an area we'd like to grow into at some point.

Even prevention educators who have been unable to involve parents in some way agree that parental involvement is important:

> Parents really need to be onboard with this. In order for this to make any sense, you really have to be in all settings giving the same message and stuff. And that parents and caregivers are the prime protectors.

> I think involving adults is really positive. And I think that sometimes just because somebody's an adult and a parent doesn't necessarily mean they have to be in the same group with their child. So I think that there's a lot to offer in that. I think it is very difficult to talk about what is really going on in my life with my parent there. I think I would have a problem even at 47. I completely understand that, although I do think there's a lot of parents who can be very helpful for youth saying, you know, "As a mother, that would really scare me to hear you say something like that."

Prevention educators described how they were able to involve parents through school and church activities:

> To have parents and their kids come in to the schools for an evening and talk about it, so that is one way to get more parental involvement.

Sometimes . . . we do go to the after-school programs as well; sometimes parents are there. Sometimes parents are the volunteers at the after-school program.

In fact, the Department of Health grant that gave us the funding for the three-day pilot wanted desperately for us to include some kind of parent component after the students completed the three-day pilot.

One of the targets is teachers and parents. So we have specific targets to try to reach out to those people. We . . . in our literature . . . say that we are doing this, because if we just educate the kids, then they are least able to use anything that we are talking about. So it needs to be a community effort. So again, some of them take us up on it and some of them don't. A lot of the schools we go to in general have pretty small PTO [Parent Teacher Organization] attendance. So the only programs that I have ever been to, where I have shown up and there have been attendees, have been PTO meetings.

Orientation Sessions

Many prevention programs offer some form of orientation session for parents whose children will be participating in programs. The sessions typically are one-time events where parents can learn about the program and its content. It is an ideal forum for parents to learn about the program and to ask questions. A secondary benefit is that, besides informing parents about what their child is learning, educators can influence parents' attitudes and increase their knowledge. Skuja and Halford (2004) suggest that information learned at orientation sessions may educate and assist parents who may have been involved in domestic violence, thus possibly reducing youths' exposure to violence in the home. Twenty percent of the programs whose staff members we interviewed conduct orientation sessions for parents. Many of them use the orientation session to answer questions and address concerns:

We did orientations for the parents and teachers before we ever got to the kids. We would send out a sheet saying, "This is a new program. These are the things we're going to talk about. Parents, teachers come in, listen to us tell what your students are going to be learning about." To kind of put parents at ease.

I went out there and did parent information meetings and talked about statistics and talked about the programming and then the parents had to sign permission forms for their kids. I think it started out more their parents telling them they had to go, but it was a pretty positive response by the end. But interesting enough, when we only offer parent information nights, we don't have a lot of parents show up.

We always offer to our schools to do parent in-services . . . I'm going to . . . go over our curriculum and let them [review it], calm any fears that they might have of our program.

Information Letters and Newsletters

Because high attendance at meetings is difficult to attain, some prevention programs have alternative ways to reach parents. Some use letters to inform parents of meetings, and others use the same letter to secure parental consent. The use of letters is common in studies cited in the literature (Serge and Webb 2005; Weisz and Black 2001; Wolfe et al. 2001). Parental consent was discussed in chapter 5, but here is what one prevention educator said about the use of letters to inform parents:

In our one-page-flyer description of what the program is, it says it [the program] is going to look at media and criminal sexual conduct law and dating and healthy/unhealthy relationships and alcohol and sexual violence. We list more the topics of the sessions, not the theories.

Some prevention programs use newsletters as a primary vehicle for keeping parents involved in what their child is learning. If programs are more than one or two sessions, it is helpful to send home a newsletter periodically to inform parents about what is going on in the program (Black and Weisz 2006; Sudermann , Jaffe, and Hastings 1995). One of the prevention educators we spoke with talked about the use of newsletters:

I am creating some parent newsletters based on the different topics. So we send out one newsletter per topic to the parents. The way I am sending them out actually, I pass them out to the students and then they are writing their address on it, I put a stamp on it and put it in the mail . . . there is an area where they could ask their student to kind of discuss the issues with them. So this is kind of a way for them to engage with their children about the topics and it kind of brings a reason to come together, because they got this thing in the mail and what this is all about and stuff.

Parents on Program Boards

Discussions in the literature point out the importance of involving parents in program administration or program policy and on planning boards (Sudermann, Jaffe, and Hastings. 1995). This is how a few of the interviewees involved parents in their programs:

> Parents sit on each campus as a leadership team that's made of administrators, teachers, and parents. In addition, there are parent seminars offered at the school each semester.

Parent Presentations

Offering specific parent training or directing entire presentations toward parents can be helpful both to parents and youths (Binder and McNiel 1987; Sudermann, Jaffe, and Hastings 1995). Parent presentations typically include content about dating violence and sexual assault in society and often focus on warning signs for parents and how parents can help youthful victims or perpetrators. Almost half the educators we spoke with confirmed that they offer parent presentations:

> We have it set up where we can do a parent workshop . . . It's just a lesson plan for the parents. It talks mostly about what dating violence is and how to recognize it if their child is in that type of relationship and also how to help them.

> Parents, I usually stress upon them the effort that we are making in educating their kids and that, you know, we need their help to express what their role is, and that it does exist. If my group of parents are all of high school kids, I'm going to be like, "Okay, when they go to school [laughs] you know, when they go off out of your house to college or whatever they do and they're on their own" . . . things like that. And I really, in addition to just the basics, like the basic I do with any of my groups, sexual assault 101, so to speak. So in addition to that, I will do more from the parent approach of things to look out for and how to react if your child tells you that something has happened to them, or they make some kind of disclosure to you. You know, how do you react? And [we discuss] healthy reactions versus non-healthy reactions and the repercussions from non-healthy reactions. And we go over the reporting process. I usually get into the laws a little bit more in detail.

Invite Parents to Sit In

Prevention educators also mentioned other ways they involve parents besides specific parent presentations. Some invite parents to sit in on the programs they present to youth:

> I found when we go into a church or something like that, and occasionally we have a parent who would like to sit in, which is fine, of course, and so once they hear the statistics and kind of find out, then they really get interested and then they want to know more, because they're realizing how much this is going on that they were not aware of.

> I've had parents come to observe and then they're all over me, "this is wonderful, this is wonderful."

> For the media program, we're hoping that the last night, when they present their findings of the TV Detectives, that's going to be open for parents. We really want parents to come to that. So I'm hoping that the kids can share the information with their parents. They might be more receptive to it than if I'm up there saying, "You need to watch what your kids are watching on TV."

A few program representatives we spoke with cautioned against having parents sit in on the presentation or program, as parental presence might inhibit young people from speaking freely:

> Normally I don't like to have the parents there, because I find a lot of time the children won't share their experiences or give me feedback with their parents there. That may not be for all, but it is for some of them, I find. They are a little shy.

Parent Groups

Ten interviewees said that their programs actually conducted ongoing or multi-session groups for parents. Some were specifically for parents, and some were for parents together with their adolescents. One Latino agency has a program for mothers and daughters geared toward helping them work through cultural gaps that often occur because the mothers are more culturally rooted in Mexico or Puerto Rico compared to the daughters, who are surrounded by the American culture:

We did it at night in the home economics room, because they had a meal with every group and that was a 6-week program, where every week they would come in. The whole purpose of that program was to get them at the sixth- or seventh-grade level, when they are still okay about talking with their parents, to help build a stronger network and communication with their mothers, so that when they get older and are into more serious situations, they feel like they can still talk to their mom about it. I had four parents and three students. The school wants to try it again this coming school year, and they are hoping they can recruit some more.

Challenges of Involving Parents

According to participants in our survey and as indicated in the literature, getting parents involved in programs can be extremely challenging. Parents often fail to attend orientation sessions and parent presentations. McKay and Bannon's (2004) work on engagement offers several suggestions that might be useful for increasing parental involvement, including making the need for their attendance apparent to them and reminding them of meeting times. Despite their efforts, prevention educators had much difficulty involving parents:

> It is like, [the parents feel like] "we don't need one more thing to organize or attend or whatever."

> Many times, to be perfectly honest, with middle and high school kids, I'm lucky if a handful of parents come in. It's not unusual to have a no-show. So it's discouraging. But I still think it's important to at least let the parents know that we're at least having that outreach, so if they do have any questions, and we do feel that their input and their, um, their consent is important to us.

The few parents who object to their children participating in a dating-violence or sexual- assault prevention program can be particularly challenging:

> We've had times when a parent, one particular parent, just is almost a thorn in your side. Didn't like the program, wanted it out of the school and just kept hounding the administration and kept taking our time and I would say, [what helps is] just continually keeping the communication open with the administrators.

What we did is we gave the parents the curriculum in advance to look over . . . and, oddly, the part that she objected to wasn't the part about rape and sexual assault. It was the section that we spend on healthy and unhealthy relationships.

School Staff Involvement

The participation of schools in prevention programming for youth is critical (Nadel et al. 1996). Coben et al. (1994) recommend that schools make violence prevention a long-term priority, incorporate it into the schools' health services, and appoint a full-time violence prevention coordinator for each school district. The prevention programs that are located in schools today most often target students, but the literature often cites the importance of involving the entire school community, including teachers, staff, and principals (Coben et al. 1994; Nadel et al. 1996; Rones and Hoagwood 2000; Wekerle and Wolf 1999). Many researchers advocate that schools educate their teachers to integrate violence-free principles and materials directly into their curricula (Jaffe et al. 1992; Jones 1998; Levy 1998). Teachers need to model healthy relationship behaviors for students. Some prevention programs are now beginning to target teachers, staff, and administration officials (de Anda 1999; Foshee et al. 2001).

The practitioners we interviewed discussed their efforts to involve the school in their prevention efforts. Eleven stated that they specifically conducted training and workshops for teachers, staff, and school officials in the schools:

We'll come in and do an in-service for all the teachers on sexual harassment. What is the school policy? How do you handle this? What is mandated reporting?

We do it [provide information] for the teachers a lot, actually, at our implementation sites. We'll do like a staff in-service of an hour or two hours, depending on how much time they want us to do. And we'll just talk about what we're going to be talking about. A lot of times, well most of the time, we'll put in there about mandated reporting and child protection laws. It's amazing to me how many teachers do not know about that. And so we cover what the curriculum covers. Then they're also comfortable with what we're talking about . . . so they can provide support to the students when we're not there. Usually it would be like on teacher day when the kids aren't there. We've done those pretty regularly. Then the other thing we do is come and train the trainers. We do that probably two or three times a year. It's a two-day, full-day training, 16 hours. And we just send out a mass mailing and we always have anywhere from 6 to 12 teachers, school counselors sign up. And they come to the two-day training. It's free. We give them all the curriculum materials. They get practice implementing and teaching the curriculum back to us, and we provide a critical review of what they did. So we do that quite a bit as a way to get new schools interested in our program.

I do trainings usually every fall, I've been doing this for years, and it is a big chunk of teachers that attend these . . . they'd be from different schools . . . It sort of gives a lot of exposure and then it, and it also creates a format with where you can promote the programs. And then what we do, every August . . . we sent out reminder letters to all the guidance counselors and to the various teachers that we have connections with, and we tell 'em what's the update, like if we've changed units.

The compliance officer, one of her jobs is to make sure that the district is meeting the requirement as to the education code. And the education code calls for students to have violence prevention information during the course of the school day in some form or another. So with that in mind and with her cooperation and support of our program she has organized a couple of huge meetings where we've had sign-ups. She's had all the principals, all the vice principals, all the counselors and all the teachers of middle schools and all the teachers of high schools come together and sign up for training for us with domestic and dating violence. So that has been really good. That has taken us a long time. It has taken us awhile to get to that point. But the last few years for us has been very, very productive.

Community Involvement

School-based prevention programs show promise but need to be part of broader community efforts to be effective (Close 2005; Fay and Medley 2006; Foshee et al. 1998; Knox, Lomonaco, and Elster 2005). Working with community partners in the initial stages of program development is essential to creating a successful linkage with community agencies (Hammond and Yung 1991; Wolfe et al. 1996). Although little empirical knowledge exists about the kind of community involvement that is most effective, the literature is consistent in stressing the importance of involving the community.

Prevention programs can actively involve the community in many ways, and the interviewees discussed some of the methods they use to promote community participation.

Community Agencies

Community agencies must be seen as key participants who are actively involved throughout the whole prevention process (Coben et al. 1994; Dryfoos 1990). Prevention programs involve community agencies in various ways, but particularly important is to involve the community in the start-up phase of programs in order to build community recognition and support. A few of the prevention educators we interviewed discussed the ways in which they seek input from the community as they develop their programs:

> It's a three-year grant and the first year of the grant is doing . . . a community assessment and focus groups with the students and things like that, so we have set up an advisory committee for that program, that piece of our programming, and that advisory committee is comprised of people from the community.

> So we actually did focus groups . . . with the African-American community, the Hispanic community and the Native-American community here in [our city]. And we also did . . . interviews with people that we identified [who] know a lot about working with our population. So we interviewed teachers, youth counselors, people that worked with juvenile sex offenders, people that worked with victims of sexual assault.

Over 55% of the prevention educators had some involvement or worked with other community agencies in some way. Some of the educators' involvement was informal and short-term, whereas others were involved formally and on a long-term or ongoing basis.

COLLABORATION

The literature consistently stresses the need for prevention programs to collaborate with appropriate agencies to most effectively reach youth (Foshee et al. 1996; Molidor and Tolman 1998; Wolfe et al. 1996). The importance of collaboration comes through strongly in one prevention educator's comment:

I'm really big about collaborations, because I think that nine times out of ten, it is all the same people doing the work anyway, so we might as well be working together. We all end up at the same meetings. It is almost always the same people, so we want to collaborate and use our money effectively.

Many of the prevention educators we interviewed described how they worked in concert with other agencies in planning or presenting their prevention programming. Seven programs collaborated for specific and special events; eight cooperated in presenting programs to audiences. Community collaborations for specific events took on various forms:

We also partnered with the [local] Theater for Youth last year in supporting and engaging in a performance named "War." I don't know if you're familiar with it, but it's a piece about, again, conditioning and socialization of boys in the culture which engenders violence. And they went out into the schools statewide. And then we had a community performance of "War" and the publicity and visibility around that. We tried to infiltrate, again, the community's consciousness about dating abuse.

We've got two major things that go on in [our city]; one is October Domestic Violence Month, and we have what's called, "The Week Without Violence," that about 40 agencies come together for, and we have all kinds of stuff going on all over the city, for kids, for adults, for schools, churches . . . that's why we need 40 different agencies to help us do this. We have a planning committee that I've been on for seven years . . . and it's all over the media; it's—we're everywhere.

What I think has also been important to the program is that there have been two groups of people who have helped lead this effort. I guess you would say and one we would call is the "Design Team" and they are all the collaborators that work on the expressive arts, the evaluator, the Center for Human Development with the parenting project. Probably about 12 people who have sat over the years and met once a month to actually work out details of the project, of our whole prevention project. Another group we have is . . . a broader group of the community that met to do broad, long-range planning for our prevention effort.

Some programs specifically collaborate with other community agencies in their program presentations:

We are working with the [local] Rape Crisis Center and together we are providing . . . we do those three workshops: dating violence, healthy relationships and the action project, and they do sexual assault, child sexual abuse and sexual harassment, so when we get a group of teens, we cover all the whole range of physical, emotional, and sexual violence and finish up with a positive action project. That way we combine our expertise to address all of these issues. We find that many of our clients have experienced multiple forms of violence and personal violence and dating violence.

Partners in the violence prevention field that go in with us, like we don't do the expressive arts piece. That is a partner that comes in and works with us to do that. The parenting piece was co-taught by Center for Human Development, one of our partners. We used to have several medical agencies that worked [with] us, helped to develop materials and partner with us in our educational effort. We still have partners. The school district, the PTA, the expressive arts component, the Center for Human Development, the [local] Police Athletic Association, that is one of our collaborators.

TEAMS/NETWORKS

In addition to collaborating, some of the interviewees discussed their involvement with various teams or networks that often met regularly. Some discussed how they participated in their communities' coordinated response teams:

Any other agencies providing services in these schools would probably be working with that person to coordinate services [and] may have collaboration meetings on a monthly basis with all organizations that provide services in the schools and with a county-wide, school-based, mental-health advisory group where we work with [other] agencies and schools.

Because we are so small, we have that opportunity to work with all the different agencies. And we do monthly meetings where we all come to the table and talk about how we can improve not just individual agencies, but the whole system in our community.

We have actually started meeting with them and other people who are doing this sort of programming in the area to develop a network specifically for prevention educators. So that has been really great.

We definitely do a lot of collaboration with other organizations. Either through specific collaborations on different projects that were funded to work in collaboration, or, if it is a community group, that meets monthly to talk about common issues or work on projects together.

Representatives of four programs also stated that they often attend community fairs to increase awareness of their program in the community and a few of those surveyed pointed out that contacts with other agencies were a result of referring youths to these agencies. Representatives of two programs mentioned how they included businesses in the community to enhance their programming efforts:

Our agency sends out a quarterly newsletter to about 700 individual business[es] and agencies in our area, and sometimes we do some articles in there.

For the sexual assault programs, April is "Sexual Assault Awareness Month" so we're doing a lot. Next week, we'll be doing a "Jeans for Justice Campaign" where employees pay a dollar to wear jeans to work that day. So different businesses and community agencies are getting involved with that.

EDUCATIONAL PROGRAMS

Community involvement for many prevention programs entails educating the community in as many forums as possible. The general public is often uninformed about the myths surrounding rape and dating violence and thus often cannot see the need for prevention programs. Five of the prevention educators we interviewed described their efforts to provide education and training for various community groups:

This is going to be our fourth year, that we have a seminar in the summer . . . Each year we filled up; we do it here on-site. It's a two-day seminar and we recruit nationally, school district people and agency people. And the whole two-day seminar is on how to work together; how to start doing these things; and we give them our materials and it's very experiential and we have wonderful trainers that we bring in to chair.

CHALLENGES

Community collaboration is not always easy to accomplish. Several prevention educators discussed the challenges they face in working and collaborating with other community agencies:

> I think also different agencies have different perspectives. My perspective is different than an agency that I might collaborate with and we might be able to provide the same information from different perspectives. You know, might have a different impact on one of the people that we are talking to. So I think there is a huge amount of advantages to cooperating with outside agencies.

> Sometimes territorial issues come into play. For example, we have a youth-service bureau that's like about two blocks away. And we've had that conversation several times. You know, "We're so close, why don't we do more things together?" And one of the things that we realized was the barriers for us was that they get a certain amount of client dollars for client hours. All of our services are for free. And so what we've been able to say to them is, "Listen, even though we might come at it from a clinician standpoint, for example, there might be a therapist that comes there and co-facilitates this conversation with you or helps you with this group, we won't be taking away from your getting access to that client's money or insurance or whatever for those hours." So we've had sort of those frank kinds of conversations.

However, despite the challenges, prevention educators saw great value in working with many others to address the issues:

> I really believe strongly in working with community in individual communities, so that we don't have everybody come right here to the center or only go to one place, but to work within communities and with leaders in their own communities to develop these types of things, and the library has been a great resource for that. So that [is] right in someone's neighborhood, if you will. They can just trot down the street and hear about these types of things, and then we are keeping all of our information out there.

> Well, I think that due to funding and that we can't work in a vacuum, it is absolutely imperative that we do collaborative work . . . It is important

for us to do that work, not to work in a vacuum. Not to assume that we know all, be all, do all. It has been very effective.

Wherever there is a possibility of collaboration, then that's where we are, because it is not a work that can be done by one group. It is too big a problem. And different organizations have different specialties that they bring to the table, and so each person can bring their piece.

Media

More than half the interviewees confirmed that they involved the media in their programs in some way, an involvement that can take many forms.

PRESS PELEASES

Some programs tried to gain exposure for their program and wrote press releases for the programs' activities and special events:

We're very lucky to have a PR firm working with us as their pro-bono client and they do a lot of media; have been on TV, like Oprah, do lots of radio talk shows; send out notices of events.

I set a goal for myself last year to get on TV, on radio, or in the news-paper at least once a month. That was just for myself and I was suc-cessful in doing that, so . . . I have been interviewed on local radio sta-tions a number of times on different stations. In October of last year, I was interviewed about teen dating violence on the, on Z104, which is our radio station that their demographic tends to be ages like 13 to 16.

The [local media] are really good about taking the materials we provide them and putting it on. Also, the media has been involved, particularly early on when we were doing some larger events, to get them to ad-vertise for us and get out there with supporting, mentioning what is going on.

ADVERTISING CAMPAIGNS

Representatives from seven programs discussed advertising campaigns that they had successfully launched. The advertising media included bill-boards, newspapers, radio, and television:

We have several billboards around town promoting healthy relationships as well as commercials that aired on the news channels that we use.

We had undertaken a pretty colorful public-awareness campaign. We produced some television commercials and some large, powerful posters and some bus posters. . . . We did radio commercials. This is also laying the foundation for this development of the program in the agency. So we were able to raise quite a bit of money for the public-awareness campaign. It really caught on. The media was very interested in it and did a lot of stories and whatnot. It was, for us, really, the beginning of letting the community understand that we cared about this and we knew something about it, and we wanted them to know more about it.

PUBLIC SERVICE ANNOUNCEMENTS

Other programs took advantage of public service announcements and sometimes included materials produced by teens:

We did one project with a group of students where they recorded a public service announcement, and the kids created the announcement and then they read them and they were aired on local stations.

STORIES ABOUT THEIR PROGRAMS

Nine interviewees discussed their success in having stories about their agency and programs published in newspapers or featured on radio or television:

In April we have an article series that we do educating on different topics. This year we had one on . . . from a victim's standpoint, the aftermath of a sexual assault. We did one on male sexual assault. We did one on educating about what is going on in our community, what are we seeing in our community as far as what is happening, the kind of services that are offered to victims.

Our coordinated community response team and the [peer educator] team, they put on a mock trial for the community on date rape and that was just on Tuesday. So that got taped on the cable channel.

Because we're such a small community, it's real easy to, you know, have something printed in the paper, so they print our things all the time and it's great. With the mock trial coming up, that's a big thing that the media does. Last year, we got front page in the one newspaper.

There's a local cable show that we're on every week as a center . . . And we've done several appearances on that show on the topic of violence against women.

MEDIA PROJECT

Two prevention educators described their effective incorporation of a media project into their prevention program:

We have a community media center which is Public Access TV. We had them come in and train the kids there to use video cameras and to use the software programs, you know, the video making software equipment. And the kids made their own public-service announcements [containing] information about sexual violence.

DOCUMENTARY

One program coordinator described how they had worked with the media to create a documentary:

We did that public-awareness campaign and then produced a documentary video featuring the lives of four people: two young women who were survivors of dating abuse and two men, one a young man who had been convicted of a felony, a dating-abuse crime. He had pushed his girlfriend and broke her collarbone. The other is the brother of a young woman who was killed by her boyfriend. The video is called "Four Stories" and we began showing it everywhere and including it in the development of a curriculum that we were going to use.

OUTREACH BY MEDIA

Representatives of programs often were contacted by media outlets, primarily to ask for a reaction and comment on a new domestic violence case or statistic reported in the media. Five of the prevention educators noted that they are often called upon to respond to such events:

ABC News Magazine [had a show] a long time ago on dating violence and featured the kids in our programs in their group. So we got a lot of mileage from that for training. Every time there's an incident in school or even a rape or a domestic violence, homicide, the media [contacts us].

Very often we are asked to speak to media, print media, the news people or whatever. If it is a particular program, for example, April is sexual-assault [month]. October is domestic-violence [month].

INCREASING MEDIA USE

A few of our interviewees noted that they really had little contact with the media, and a few outlined their plans to increase media exposure and involvement:

Because the public perception is going to be, "Well I guess they got a problem with it." And so instead of saying, "Hey, here's a school that's proactively trying to work on this because they're saying 'gee, we really think this is really an issue' and this is a group of people that are really putting their efforts behind their words," that is not the first impression that people have. So they and school districts and school boards are real reluctant to, they just don't want any media contact at all. So it's been kind of an interesting dilemma for us.

We're going to be pursuing the idea. You know, when you go to the movies, before the movie . . . there's like PSAs [public service announcements] before the movie starts, not movie previews, but PSAs. We're going to try and produce some of those with some private money.

Summary of Parental, School Staff, and Community Involvement

Practitioners described various ways that they work with parents, school personnel, other community agencies, and the media to prevent violence. They all stressed the need for parental involvement and recognized that it was important for parents to model positive interpersonal relationships in the home. Several educators also noted how difficult it is to involve busy parents, and they discussed some methods for overcoming the obstacles, including orientation sessions, information letters, newsletters, encouraging parents to sit on policy boards, and special programming. Many programs offer training sessions for school personnel.

More than half the programs whose representatives we interviewed collaborate with other community agencies to sponsor fairs, conduct programs, and serve in networks. They advise that, despite the challenge of dealing with agencies' different perspectives and territorial issues, working together is essential for success.

The majority of programs also worked with the media in their communities, and others were attempting to increase their exposure in the media. They solicited news stories for events and programs, wrote press releases, and conducted advertising campaigns. In sum, the participants in our study were keenly aware that prevention messages are far more effective when reinforced by the family, the school system, and the community.

13

Evaluation of Prevention Programs

Few of the numerous prevention programs for adolescents across the country have been empirically evaluated, and many of those evaluations have significant limitations. This chapter shares prevention educators' thoughts and experiences that may help others meet the challenge of evaluating a program. The first step is to examine the various sources from which prevention programs receive funds and the evaluations that the sources require. This is followed by discussions of the content of program evaluations; the kinds of evaluation mechanisms that interviewees are using; evaluation results; and, finally, the problems posed by conducting evaluations of youth dating violence and sexual assault prevention programs.

Rigorous and comprehensive evaluations of dating violence and sexual assault prevention programs can contribute a great deal to the development of the prevention field. . However, relatively few prevention programs have been evaluated beyond their immediate effects on attitudes and knowledge and few evaluations have examined actual behavior (Foshee et al. 1998, 2000 2004; Gidycz et al. 2006; Wolfe et al. 2003). Even fewer evaluations have used samples of minority youth in the inner city (Salazar and Cook 2006; Weisz and Black 2001). Those of us in the field know little, therefore, about the program characteristics, components, and content associated with program effectiveness.

Researchers are calling for more rigorous evaluations including, minimally, the use of behavioral measures, random assignment to control and treatment groups, larger samples with higher retention rates, and follow-up measures over an extended period (Pittman, Wolfe, and Wekerle 2000;

O'Leary, Woodin, and Fritz 2006; Whitaker et al. 2006). In addition to the problem with random assignment, the logistics of randomly assigning youth or even entire schools to control and treatment groups often can present formidable obstacles to program evaluators. However, the use of alternative methodologies, including wait-list controls and quasi-experimental group designs, can improve program evaluation.

To advance research on dating violence and sexual assault prevention, future studies must address four critical issues: behavioral outcomes, control groups, follow-up, and sample size and retention rates.

Few studies evaluate whether attitudinal changes translate into behavioral changes. Even fewer reports include reduction of dating violence and sexual assault as outcome variables (Sochting, Fairborther, and Koch 2004). It remains unclear, therefore, whether changes in knowledge and attitudes translate into relevant behavioral changes (O'Leary, Woodin, and Fritz 2006).

The inclusion of control groups is critically needed in evaluation studies (O'Leary, Woodin, and Fritz 2006) to further our understanding of factors that moderate the effectiveness of dating violence and sexual assault prevention programs. We need to understand, for example, how the participants' gender and age influence program outcomes, as well as such factors as prior victimization. We also need to know how the number of program sessions and the program content relate to effectiveness. The use of control groups is especially complicated, as it is unclear in many school settings how to rationalize the idea of some students receiving ten sessions, others receiving only four, and still others receiving no program at all. Not providing some students with crucial information that programs could give them raises ethical issues for many staff members who might want to conduct evaluations.

Follow-up data is a third area in need of evaluation. Sochting, Fairbrother, and Koch (2004) note that successful sexual assault prevention programs have been unable to demonstrate whether their successful outcomes are maintained over the long term. The results of multi-year follow-up surveys by Foshee et al. (2004) and Wolfe et al. (2003) suggest that some initial behavioral changes are maintained over time and others may not be sustained. (The specific behavioral changes are provided later in the follow-up section of the chapter.) Longitudinal studies can also help us better understand which "youth escalate from mild to moderate partner aggression and from moderate to severe aggression" (O'Leary, Woodin, and Fritz 2006, 155).

Evaluations of prevention programs also need larger samples and better retention rates. Attrition is often an obstacle for longitudinal studies, but without high retention rates, studies will be unable to answer with confidence many of the important questions about program effectiveness. If retention is low, for example, studies may not be able to determine whether the students who responded to follow-up surveys were more interested in the topic and therefore probably more likely to report changes in their attitudes, knowledge, and behavior compared to students who were not included in a follow-up survey.

Meyer and Stein (2004) offered additional recommendations for program evaluations:

(1) design clear, measurable program objectives; (2) ask school staff who help implement the program about which aspects of the program seemed to be the most effective; (3) include qualitative analysis to lend meaning to survey based evaluations and understanding as to why some students change in undesired direction; (4) review of curricula to see why some programs are more successful than others and also comparison with other prevention curricula such as smoking cessation; and (5) clarify what are significant changes and what changes imply program success/effectiveness. (203)

Much information exists on how to evaluate a program including how to create measurable objectives, analyze qualitative data, and identify significant and meaningful change. Two books that may be especially helpful in learning how to evaluate programs are *Practical Program Evaluation: Assessing and Improving, Planning Implementation and Effectiveness* (Chen 2004) and *The Handbook of Social Work Research Methods* (Thyer 2001). The Center for Disease Control (CDC) also has useful information on its Web site on both quantitative and qualitative program evaluation. The *School-based Violence Prevention Programs: A Resources Manual* (Tutty 2002) has a chapter titled "Evaluating School-based Prevention Program: The Basics," which describes the steps in conducting an evaluation. It is available at http://www.ucalgary.ca/resolve/violenceprevention/English/evaluate.htm.

Eighty-five percent of the program representatives we interviewed reported that they perform some kind of evaluation. Some of those representatives whose programs are not being evaluated recognize that this creates problems. As one interviewee stated:

We are not even collecting data to look at to see if it is effective. So we don't have any idea. And that's, of course, the problem.

Funding Sources and Evaluation

The literature rarely mentions the relationship between program evaluation and funding sources in general or the specific issue of how funding sources participate in program evaluation. In talking with prevention educators, however, we found that funding sources often require some form of program evaluation, and some provide financial support for programs to analyze evaluation data. Twenty-five percent of interviewees said that their funding sources require some form of program evaluation:

> We are doing pretty extensive evaluation for the Teen PEP program, because the state [requires it], in order to justify the funding . . . So it is built into the Teen PEP program and the state pays.

> When we write grants, one of the things that funders really want to know is, "How are we going to know that the program you are doing is making any difference at all?"

> The state coalition, because they're the ones that are accountable to the CDC, are forcing us to use these pre- and post- things on any audience that we meet with [where the program is] more than two hours long.

Two programs evaluate and engage in extensive data analysis:

> We have a wonderful data management department here . . . Each program has its own evaluation tools, and some of our funders fund multiple programs, so it's up to our data department to really enter and report all of this wonderful data to all of the funders . . . A few years go we actually created our own system for this purpose with a software development company, so we have our own tracking system. It has, I think, been key to us growing the agency.

> We've finished the data collection and now we're in a data-analysis stage. It has been a multi-year project. The project we worked on with them was specifically to assess how effective our program is within the Latino community, with Latino youth. And so we had specific schools that we targeted as part of that evaluation. It was a very in-depth evaluation.

Evaluation Mechanisms

The literature discusses various mechanisms for evaluating prevention programs, including pre- and post-tests, follow-up surveys, and qualitative methods. The prevention educators we interviewed discussed their use of these and other evaluation methods.

Pre- and Post-Tests

Pre- and post-tests are the most common means of evaluation cited in the prevention literature, even though youth may be more prone to tell evaluators what they think is socially desirable on these tests (Bachar and Koss 2001). Although most post-tests are given immediately following the program (Hilton et al. 1998; Pacifici, Stoolmiller, and Nelson 2001), a few programs report that they delay administering the post-test for a couple of days or several weeks (Avery-Leaf et al. 1997; Jaffe et al. 1992; Krajewski et al. 1996; Proto-Campise et al. 1998). Some of the stronger research studies using pre- and post-tests also used a comparison group (Foshee et al. 1998, 2000; Pacifici et al. 2001; Wolfe et al. 2003).

Of the programs we surveyed, 65% used pre- and post-tests to evaluate the effectiveness of the program. About 75% of programs that conduct evaluations used pre- and post-test designs, and almost all of the programs administered the post-test at the conclusion of the program. Only four interviewees stated that they waited to administer the post-test. No one mentioned using a control group in the evaluation. Programs that presented multiple sessions were more likely than shorter programs to conduct pre- and post-tests. A few interviewees noted the challenges of doing a pre- and post-test of a one-time presentation:

> We don't do pre and post testing because, first of all, it's only a 45-minute session and you're not going to make any big changes.

Follow-up

Researchers agree that it is unclear how prevention programs influence youths' knowledge, attitudes, and behavior over time, and many are calling for follow-up studies over long periods (Gidycz et al. 2006; O'Leary et al. 2006; Whitaker et al. 2006). As noted early in this chapter, some programs are beginning to use follow-up evaluations and several of these are discussed in the literature. Results are mixed. One program, *Ending Violence: A Curriculum for Educating Teens on Domestic Violence and the Law*, which targets Latino youths in Los Angeles, found that, six months after the program, youths only maintained added knowledge and the perception that an attorney might be of help (Jaycox et al. 2006). Other changes in their knowledge, attitudes, and perceptions of helpfulness and the likelihood of seeking assistance from various sources were not maintained. Wolfe et al. (2003) found that, over a period of two years, adolescents that participated in the Youth Relationship Project were less physically abusive toward dating partners and reported that they were less often the victims of physical and emotional abuse. No influence, however, was detected on healthy relationship skills. Foshee et al.'s (2005) evaluation of the Safe Dates program three years after its conclusion found that significant effects of the program were maintained regarding the perpetration of psychological abuse, moderately severe physical victimization, and sexual dating violence. Changes affecting psychological victimization and severe physical victimization were not maintained at any of the program's four follow-up periods. Salazar and Cook's (2006) evaluation of their intimate-partner violence-prevention program for adjudicated African American adolescent males found that increased knowledge and changes in attitude were sustained three months after intervention.

Some research shows the importance of follow-up evaluation of programs for college students. Breitenbecher (2000) reports that seven out of sixteen studies using the Rape Myth Acceptance Scale (Burt 1980) had long-term follow-up and that four of the seven evaluations showed rebound effects (positive changes found at post-test were not maintained). Other studies evaluating the effectiveness of showing a movie on "campus rape" found that it was successful in changing attitudes about rape myths initially, but the changes were not sustained several weeks after the presentation (Johansson-Love and Geer 2003; Heppner et al. 1995b).

Only one of the practitioners we interviewed stated that her evaluation, which was a study for a student's dissertation, used a follow-up instrument. Other interviewees, however, acknowledged the importance of including follow-up in the evaluation of a program:

> We had one dissertation done on our men's program, where they used it and looked at . . . they did kind of a control group for people who didn't get any information on our program and then they looked at the group of men who did. Then they also did some follow-ups . . . evaluations of those men like three months after the program, looking at how much

information they had retained and if they still kind of were at the same level they were immediately after it and they did find that it was effective in terms of that.

I would say I feel really positive about the results we get. Some things . . . limitations that I see in it is that it's a pre/post test. I would like to do six months, or even later; go back and do a follow-up survey and see if the kids are retaining the information.

Qualitative Methods

Few studies discuss program evaluation in terms of qualitative measures, but several authors advocate for qualitative and other types of program evaluation methods (Grasley et al. 1999). Weisz et al. (2001) found that qualitative analysis provided useful information about the ways in which audio-visual displays, emotionally intense vignettes, statistics, and peer educators contributed to their program's effectiveness in dispelling myths about sexual assault.

In contrast to the scarce literature endorsing qualitative program evaluation, almost 50% of the educators we interviewed use some form of qualitative data collection to evaluate their programs. Many of these evaluations focus on what the students learned from the program:

We also do more of a qualitative feedback form. This is what we [use to] get a lot of good information; they write their answer to some [open-ended] questions; they also do some check boxes about what they got out of the group.

There's a qualitative piece to that and a quantitative piece, in terms of talking about the overall importance of the group and "What the most important things were that you learned about the group? What changed about your beliefs about dating violence?" and on that we didn't find any students [who] basically didn't think that it changed.

One interviewee described the varying reactions one can obtain from qualitative data:

You read one evaluation that says, "This was boring, I knew all of this information." And then the next one you read says, "This was great. I wish we could have met longer; this really helped me to know how to help my friend." So you get such a wide range of reaction to these things.

One program asked its participants to write an essay about the program's impact on them:

> They actually have to submit [an] essay to us, it's a one page essay that we require and they, almost like a survey, as to "Was there a benefit to the program? What did they learn from the program?" that sort of thing. That way we can measure out our teaching mechanisms.

Four of the prevention educators mentioned they had conducted focus groups as part of the program evaluation:

> We're only going to be able to do one focus group per school, per gender. It will be an evaluation strategy and also to look at what we need to do to improve and what additional things would students like to see.

> We did a focus group in the beginning of the . . . program and at the end of that 9-, 10-week program to ask, to find out what students got out of it. What they liked and what they didn't like. How their attitudes had shifted.

One program asked students to keep a journal as a way to evaluate the program. Four other programs asked students to develop a safety plan as part of their program evaluation:

> For the sexual harassment presentation, our outcome is that the kids will sign a pledge . . . they will pick three of those behaviors that they think they can complete in the three months. They will sign a pledge stating that they are going to do that. Then I follow up with them three months later to see what they have done.

> I have a little safety plan and an evaluation in their little packet. So what I will do, once everything is done, I will ask them to sit down and I will have them do the safety plan and ask them to complete the evaluation.

One-third of all programs evaluated the adolescents' level of satisfaction with the program. Evaluation forms were collected for both multi-session programs and one-time presentations:

> On the back of the post-test we have an evaluation form for the students to comment on how effective they thought the program was, what their

favorite part was, what did they like, what did they think could be improved upon.

Anecdotal Evidence

The literature rarely addresses the use of anecdotal evidence to support the effectiveness of prevention programs. Coben et al. (1994) suggested that anecdotal evidence can support the implementation of various forms of prevention programs, such as peer mediation, relevant curricula, and the teaching of conflict management skills, areas where there is scarce empirical support. About one-third of the prevention educators in our survey mentioned anecdotal evidence when asked how they knew whether their programs were effective. Many were convinced that their programs were effective, even without quantitative or qualitative evidence. For them, "evidence" was manifest simply in adolescents displaying more amenable body language during a presentation, remembering the presenters long after the program ended, and asking questions after the presentation or confiding their own experiences with abuse:

> I find it effective because students come up to me afterwards and confide in me. I also find it effective because when I come back into the schools, they approach. Even if not on the topic, they say hello to me, which tells me that I am a reachable adult to them.

> I'm talking at a church at Christmas time, one Sunday morning, and there was a young man there speaking from a cancer society and this young man was a junior in high school and we were both speaking briefly with three other agencies and afterwards he came up and talked to me and he said, "Do you go to classes and talk?" And he said, "I knew it was you." I said, "Did I speak to your class?" And he said, "Yeah, last year." And this was, I felt, especially rewarding to have a young man [remember] and I said, "Well, hopefully, you remember some of the things that we talked about." And he said, "Oh, I do. I've shared it with lots of people. I have every piece of information you gave me." He said, "I will keep that always."

> The fact that these kids choose to come, something must be working if they choose to come and are engaged while they're there and they beg for more. That's for me is evaluation enough.

> I think when we take those small gifts of being able to tell that our programs are effective, versus being able to say we have the data to back that

up, it is more the anecdotal kind of thing, that when you leave a classroom and a student comes up to you afterwards and they tell you that a situation like that happened to them or a friend and you realize that the information that you gave them had an immediate impact and that they might be able to share that with somebody else. Like I said, you look out and see those expressions on the kids, that "aha" moment, "I got it," that is one way that we keep going.

I would say based on the calls that we get from kids after we go. The letters we get from kids. All the different stuff that we see from kids. It's amazing because sometimes I feel like "Gosh, are we really doing our job?" . . . and the next day I will get a call from a kid saying, "Thank you for coming. Can you please help me?" So that's how I know that we are effective because, you know, these calls that come in.

Involving Others in the Evaluation

Most programs are evaluated without the involvement of teachers, other school personnel, or outside evaluators, although a few programs do use these extra resources. Twenty-five percent of those we interviewed said that they involve teachers and other school personnel when evaluating their programs. (The general involvement of teachers and other school personnel in prevention programs, outside of evaluations, was discussed in chapter 12, "Parental, School Staff, and Community Involvement.") They may ask teachers and school staff to distribute evaluation surveys before and after the program to avoid taking time from the actual program presentation. One interviewee noted, however, that involving teachers may create a lack of confidentiality among students. Twelve of the programs stated that they asked teachers and school personnel to evaluate the program itself:

The teacher in the classroom usually does an evaluation of the presenter and has a specific form that they use.

We do end-of-the-year evaluations with students and teachers and faculty to see if they have noticed any systemic change, school-wide change.

After I speak at a school, I send them a letter thanking them, with an evaluation form, asking them to return it to me, and in the evaluation form it asks if they know of anyone who might be interested in a presentation.

Outside evaluators can improve the quality of program evaluations because of their technological capability to conduct objective and scientific evaluations. They also can assist practitioners in developing their research questions and survey instruments, and in analyzing the data. Funding sources may view evaluation results with more confidence when outside evaluators collect and analyze data rather than the same people whose jobs and well-being depend on particular outcomes of the evaluation (Myers-Walls 2000). Five prevention educators reported that they had used someone outside their program to conduct the evaluation:

We, since the beginning of the grant, have had it analyzed by [a local university]. So it's an independent evaluation . . . This will be our first year where we are going to do an in-house evaluation. And we are going to use our planners . . . We have a planning department here . . . to do it. So, it's not like I will be evaluating my own program. It's going to be another staff person, which I haven't even met yet, who is actually going to be doing the evaluation.

We have been evaluated and underwent a three-year, mixed-method evaluation by an independent contractor, and we're proven to be effective at changing attitudes and behaviors.

Although outside evaluators can be helpful to programs, the literature suggests that program staff sometimes finds it difficult and frustrating to work with them. Some practitioners feel that researchers are unaware of the severe time constraints most practitioners experience or that researchers or outside evaluators do not understand the "real world of clients and providers." One interviewee discussed problems associated with using outside evaluators:

The reports that came out were not user-friendly. I'm not a dummy about statistics. I understand the concepts. I've taken several courses and they were very hard to understand. None of our staff could understand them. I could barely understand. I didn't understand exactly what they were saying. There were a lot of really complex terms that come in SPSS [a statistical data analysis program]. . . . We've asked them for some kind of summary that would be user-friendly for the teachers and students and parents, but never got it. We were real disappointed with that, but the one thing that came out of that relationship was that they had made that recommendation [to look into same-sex groups].

Evaluation Content and Results

The many program evaluations cited in the literature report, as stated previously, mixed results (Coben et al. 1994; Sudermann et al. 1995). The majority of published program evaluations focus on measuring knowledge and attitudes, and some programs measure behaviors or behavioral intentions. Studies measuring knowledge and attitudes, and reporting evaluations immediately after the prevention program, yield positive results (Cascardi et al. 1999; Feltey et al. 1991; Krajewski et al. 1996; Macgowan 1997). But evaluation data from some of the current dating violence prevention programs that use follow-up data and include behavioral changes also look promising. Some initial changes in behavior, knowledge, and attitude were maintained over time at the conclusions of the Safe Dates program (Foshee et al 1998 2005), the Fourth R Program (Wolfe et al. 2006), and Ending Violence: A Curriculum for Educating Teens on Domestic Violence and the Law (Jaycox et al. 2006). Anderson and Whiston's (2005) review of sexual assault programs for college students found that the programs had the most influence on participants' knowledge and attitudes about rape, but the influence decreased over time.

Like the studies reported in the literature, our interviewees' programs rarely included measurements of youths' behaviors. Forty percent of our interviewees reported that their programs used evaluation instruments that focused only on measuring youths' knowledge and attitudes:

> Our evaluations test knowledge gained, as well as changes in attitude, as well as their attitudes related to how important this issue is, how prevalent this issue is in their lives and whether they have seen situations of abuse among their peers.

> We measure, basically, attitude, because we ask questions like, for sexual harassment, we ask things like, "Pinching, touching, grabbing or making sexual comments. These are all forms of sexual harassment. Yes or No or Not Sure."

> We're just measuring, "Do you know more about sexual assault? Do you know more about how to help a friend? Do you know more about where to go to get help?" And that's really all we can do.

In addition to measuring knowledge and attitudes, most of the programs' instruments contained a limited number of questions. The representatives of many programs noted that their instruments were limited to only five or six questions because of time constraints. A rare exception was a program that used a survey with nineteen informational questions and five demographic ones.

About one-third of the program representatives we talked with have results from the evaluations of their programs. The kinds of results they had varied, but many had analyzed their data:

> They have found significant changes in the attitudes and behavior of . . . peer educators and in the classes that they teach. So that is very exciting.

> They did show significant differences and then what they found with the other project, the other schools, was that although we were doing three presentations, really presentation one was the most effective and presentations two and three were kind of just there. They are reinforcing information but it wasn't making any statistically significant difference.

In response to the question of what they do with the evaluation results, several interviewees acknowledged that their programs do little with the data they collect, others use it to complete reports for their funding sources, and some programs use it to modify their programs. A typical response was the following:

> We're trying to improve on our evaluation process. We've just obtained a small grant, an evaluator for very small money. So our evaluation isn't as . . . the truth of what's ended up happening until recently is that we've collected these evaluations and it's been very difficult to have time to do the full running of the data to find out what happens. I mean, we kind of look over it. We garner the information from what we see, but we haven't translated it to any kind of official data, per se.

Several interviewees talked about how they use evaluation results to assist in completing reports for funders:

> We collect all the data and we organize it and input the data into an Excel spreadsheet. I went through all of the training for building them and worked through MPHI to create the pre and the post and the final surveys. So we input all the data, I analyze the data and give a report at the end of the year.

Other interviewees talked about sharing the evaluation results with the schools or others who might be interested:

I give a copy to the school. And when I initially started doing the evaluation, it was more to prove to the school how important this was, and now
that the schools see how important it is, they are all onboard with it, now
I'm just kind of collecting the data so that if we ever have a funding opportunity that comes up for this program, then I'll be able to show that
we have made some differences.

Some prevention educators described how their results lead to changes
in the coming year's program:

When we have the post-test, we will do the same thing and then compare
the different percentages and if anything is changed. I use it . . . it is part
of my grant requirement, so then I send them into my grant and then
the kids and I look at them in the summer and see if there is anything we
need to be changing. To look at the questions and see if this is something
we are not talking about in class.

Challenges of Evaluation

Any attempt to evaluate the effects of multiple interventions on the long-
term goal of reducing violence is a daunting task. The challenges most often identified in the literature include (1) definitions of dating and violence;
(2) participant recruitment and follow-up; (3) instrumentation; (4) design
issues; (5) the value of evaluation; and (6) lack of evaluation skills (Lewis
and Fremouw 2001; Pittman et al. 2000; Wandersman and Florin 2003).
The practitioners we interviewed echoed some of the same challenges
presented in the literature but they also mentioned additional difficulties
they encountered.

Definitions of Dating Violence

Researchers often find it difficult to establish operational definitions of variables in teen dating relationships in a manner that captures their variation
in form and meaning. For example, the definition of "a dating partner" is
difficult to capture with adolescents, and equally difficult is the definition of
"dating." Adolescent dating relationships are often brief, so youth often differ in their conceptions of dating. Teens also use different words for dating
relationships, and the words describing dating partners change frequently
and vary in different parts of the country (Pittman et al. 2000). Definitions
of violence are also difficult to capture. Adolescents may form different
opinions and judgments about violent incidents based on the context of the

situation, as well as the identity of the perpetrators and victims (Pitner et al. 2003). Culture also plays a vital role in adolescents' perceptions of violent incidents (Lee Takaku, Ottati, and Yan 2004). For example, White (1997) found that African American adolescent girls defined physical assault, but not sexual assault, as violent.

Recruiting Participants

Researchers recommend multiple sources of information, including parents, friends, and dating partners in evaluation studies (Pittman et al. 2000). Recruiting participants presents difficulties, including the protection of human subjects and obstacles that may be raised by laws governing confidentiality, which differ between states (Hickman, Jaycox, and Aronoff 2004). Recruiting a random sample is particularly difficult for community programs, because it is difficult to maintain contact with youth for follow-up data collection to determine the success of abuse prevention efforts. Helpful strategies may include the use of flexible meeting times, and the selection of locations that are most convenient for participants (Gregory, Lohr, and Gilchrist 1992; Pittman et al. 2000).

Instruments

One of the best resources for instruments that measure attitudes and behaviors is *Measuring Violence-Related Attitudes, Behaviors, and Influences among Youths: A Compendium of Assessment Tools*, which is available, free-of-charge from the Centers for Disease Control (CDC 2005). Most standardized instruments measure attitudes and knowledge about relationship violence and rape myths. Instruments measuring actual behaviors are most often self-reports. Researchers are often cautious about self-report responses because participants may give socially desirable responses (Lewis and Fremouw 2001). This is especially true following participants' completion of a prevention program. Although "acts scales" can provide some important information about actual behavior, they have shortcomings. Foshee et al. (2007) state that "acts do not capture the ontological status of violence, including the context in which it is developed, interpretations of the contexts, their consequences, and the meanings attached to them. Acts scales typically treat very different violent acts as equivalent" (499).

Few instruments also ask respondents to report on their intentions related to dating violence. Sheehan et al. (1996), in discussing Ajzen and Madden's (1986) theory of planned behavior, suggest that "intention to perform or not perform an act is the strongest predictor of future action" (299). However, few programs inquire about intended behaviors in their evaluations, perhaps, at least partially, because few adolescents will report their intentions to be aggressive. Most adolescents, in fact, report that they know the use of violence in relationships is wrong (Black and Weisz 2004).

Design and Measurement Issues

Design challenges complicate many evaluation studies. This is especially true when evaluating community prevention programs. Wandersman and Florin (2003) discuss program practitioners' difficulties in obtaining the results of community-level interventions, because practitioners are given minimal training on assessment and evaluation. Holder et al. (1997) discuss the difficulty of finding comparable communities when evaluating programs. A comparison community may have its own prevention efforts or differing community characteristics. Often community programs have multiple components, and it is difficult to determine which components are effective. Orlando et al. (2006) suggest that one of the most important constraints on measurement is that many of the behaviors that programs attempt to prevent occur infrequently and are socially undesirable, resulting in highly skewed responses. The questionable validity of survey responses blunts the drive to conduct evaluations.

The Value of Evaluations

Many schools and programs recognize a need for program evaluation but operate on very limited budgets. Many are forced to choose between putting resources into a program or evaluating it, and some prefer devoting scarce resources to instruction, not evaluation. Many program presenters, moreover, are not trained to conduct evaluations. However, once program administrators understand the importance of evaluations and realize that they can use the results to continually improve their programs, their initial resistance because of time constrains and limited resources may decrease (Farrell et al. 1996; Mouradian et al. 2001). In conducting school projects on intimate-partner violence, Jaycox et al. (2006) note that each research team has to find a way to help schools see the value in the proposed prevention program and its evaluation.

Nearly 20% of the practitioners we interviewed struggled with evaluating their programs and identified various challenges in conducting program evaluations. They appeared to recognize the large time commitment that proper evaluation requires, as over 20% of the interviewees pointed to their lack of time as a deterrent to conducting effective evaluations, especially the difficulty of using program time to collect data:

> In order to do a really truly effective evaluation with the students . . . pre- and post-test, it is impossible to do that in an hour setting because that is going to knock out at least 10 if not 15 minutes of my program. So I think that if we were able to have an optimum situation, we would be in there for more than one session, multiple days, and we would have these mechanisms in place to have a really, really truly effective pre- and post test, and we would be sending that pre-test out days before we come, and the post-test would be days or even weeks after we've gone.

> For the three- and four-day programs, the kids get the pre- and post- and that is a big consideration, because sometimes, depending on the reading level, and depending on the grade level, the questionnaire can . . . be taking out 15 minutes of our time, which is a really difficult amount of time to give up.

Some program presenters mentioned that, in addition to not having enough time to do program evaluations, they lacked funding and expertise:

> We've always found it to be a very difficult thing to do because, for a lot of years we would have kids fill out evaluations at the end of the program. But then what do you do with them? If you don't have the time, money, and expertise to evaluate the evaluation, it is really not worth anything. So we really, I think that is something that we have not done a good job in evaluating what impact we have.

> At some point, I would love to have a mechanism where we could have some sort of formal evaluation of our programs, but we don't have the money or the time to be doing that.

Finally, a few interviewees clearly recognized the general difficulty in measuring program effectiveness:

> I don't think it is like a program where you teach kids to brush their teeth, and then you know if they brush their teeth every day that you've been effective. So I think it is a longer-term evaluation process. So I think it is hard sometimes to measure that.

At one time, we were trying to not only measure pre- and post- but even see where one student went from pre- and post- and then we got so piled up.

Summary of Evaluation of Prevention Programs

Evaluation is a critical tool for the presenters of violence prevention programming. Although evaluation poses many challenges for programs, the large majority of practitioners we interviewed recognizes its importance and conducts some form of evaluation. The requirements of funding sources create a great impetus for conducting evaluations. Most of the programs evaluate participants' attitudes and knowledge, and few evaluate behavioral changes. Programs use various forms of evaluation design with pre- and post-tests as the most common instrument, and many also gather qualitative data.

Program results look promising to interviewees, but few programs use evaluation techniques that can match the ideals summarized in the literature review for this chapter. Some programs receive assistance from school personnel to gather data or they employ outside evaluators to analyze the data, but most programs find it difficult to gather and evaluate their own data. As the literature suggests, interviewees faced many struggles in conducting evaluations of dating violence and sexual assault prevention programs. Practitioners' limited time, money, and expertise make it especially difficult for them to engage in the ideal, rigorous evaluation that would include behavioral measures, control groups, follow-up studies, and larger samples. It is difficult, therefore, for most practitioners to live up to or advance the "state of the art" in program evaluation. We call upon funding sources to provide more monies and resources to prevention programs to assist with program evaluation.

14

Qualities of Ideal Prevention Educators

This chapter summarizes the thoughts of those we interviewed about the qualities that an ideal prevention educator requires. But apart from their views, the literature scarcely covers the topic and is usually limited to describing the roles prevention educators play and the professional types who are drawn to this work, without evaluating their effectiveness. A recent review of prevention programs summarizes eleven published empirical evaluations of dating violence prevention programs and notes that teachers (n = 6) or community-based professionals (e.g., social workers, advocates, police officers, and abuse survivors) or both delivered the programs (Whitaker et al. 2006). The evaluations offer few details about the training that was provided to prevention educators, and in some cases failed to mention whether they received any training at all.

Several articles address the need for extensive training for prevention educators. Nation et al. (2003) published a review of research suggesting that teachers working as pregnancy prevention presenters need almost a full day to three days of training. They note that presenters need to "buy in" to the program, and that low morale or high turnover can be a problem. Avery-Leaf and Cascardi (2002) used classroom teachers to present their dating violence prevention program, and they suggest that a manual is insufficient for teachers, as teachers also need training. They note: "Perhaps the most important key to successful programs is the competence of the facilitator or implementer" (98).

Who Should Be a Prevention Educator?

A number of those we interviewed were the sole prevention educators in their agencies, so they could tell us only what in their own style or persona they thought worked well. Conversely, several were also responsible for hiring and supervising other prevention educators, and they described the qualities they seek in an educator. A number of programs focused primarily on peer education, which perhaps lessened the importance of the adult educators' characteristics in those particular programs. However, many interviewees contributed useful thoughts about the requirements of an excellent prevention educator. One described the importance of selection and training:

> One of the things about doing prevention education is that you become aware very early that one unprofessional or inappropriate comment can kill your program in a school. And they won't ever have you back. And so we're very particular about who goes in and what they say and how they say it.

Cultural Diversity in Prevention Educators

We asked the educators whether they believe it is important to have a cultural match between prevention educators and adolescent participants. Some programs never attempt a match for practical reasons: the prevention program may be small, with only one or two educators, or the program may have several ethnicities within one audience. Thirty percent of those we spoke with, however, said that they do not believe an ethnic match is necessary, as similar backgrounds or ethnicities does not guarantee similar understanding:

> I think . . . well, I'm Philippino and so I never go into a classroom that is all Philippino. It just doesn't happen in [my city], so I never am ethnically matched, but I think all of the kids relate to me. I think what is more important than a racial match is just the presenter being willing and able to translate the information they have in their head to what kids will understand and relate to. So, I think it has more to do with the presenter's ability to be sensitive and aware of developmental issues and certain issues in the community . . . I don't think that it is necessary to have a barrier between races.

> I think we were mostly looking for the people who knew their stuff and worked with the kids, and if their race matches the race of the kids, then great; that's a bonus, but it is not always how it works out.

I have had no problem speaking with the opposite gender students, students of different racial backgrounds. . . . I have had no trouble. I often will try and tune into things that are real for the group that I'm dealing with. And by no means do I sit there and try and pretend, "Yeah, I'm African American, too. I'm down with you guys."

I find that's only important if there's a language barrier. . . . It's your knowledge and your sensitivity that we push rather than the fact that, "I look just like you."

You know when I first started doing this work; I thought that was going to be so important. I thought for instance, it was going to be so important to have a guy on staff so he could really relate to the guys. And then we get through this whole study. . . . And so I probably started out thinking that I needed diversity in order to really impact minorities with these issues but then I went into an alternative school myself, with kids that had all been expelled for different kinds of behaviors, as a middle-aged Caucasian woman, and I had no problem whatsoever relating to them or having them relate to me. And so I feel like, now, that is really less important than people want to make it be. That what is really important to kids is your honesty; and your directness; telling it really like it is; not using coercion, yourself, in trying to get them to believe something—that you're really laying it out straight and being there to listen.

One African American woman we interviewed described her program's experiences with diverse prevention educators:

Our Caucasian female gets rave reviews. Just like our black educators do. So, she is just good. She relates well, she is enthusiastic, energetic. She knows their language; she knows how to relate to them. She is nonjudgmental. She allows them to express their feelings. She gives them the respect. So, she doesn't have to be black to do that. She can be whatever. Cause that is fundamentally what is important. I think it is helpful to have facilitators that look like the kids. I do. I think it adds to their comfort level. Okay? And in some degree it validates the fact that "this person understands what I'm going through." But I don't think it is an absolute necessity. I know it is not, because I know from experience.

Qualities of Ideal Prevention Educators

Some interviewees said that they trained all staff members in cultural sensitivity and the relevance of cultural differences. Others discussed the importance of cultural awareness including awareness of urban and rural differences:

> I think that [an ethnic match] can be helpful, although I think that you can overcome those differences through, just, the educator themselves having a good understanding of different cultures so that they can be aware of some of those differences and speak to those [differences] if it is appropriate.

> A person doesn't necessarily have to be ethnically the same but has to really be aware of the cultural values of a particular community . . . like there's real distinctions here between rural and town.

An expert whose program involves ongoing discussions with small groups of youths pointed out that it can actually be advantageous when there are differences between adult leaders and the adolescents:

> I know of one group in particular—all the girls are African American and the leader was Hispanic and they have fun with talking about . . . [differences]. So we tried to get that out on the table the first few lessons in the curriculum.

An important point is that because shorter programs allow fewer opportunities to discuss these differences, some interviewees believe that ethnic similarities increase rapport when the program is brief:

> And that's another drawback that we have, because we don't have a whole lot of staff. . . . [W]e have some advocates that work with us. On occasion, we'll try to get someone in, particularly if it's a bilingual class too. I mean, it's important. And if we can't, then we try to get someone else from the school.

> [One] high school . . . really wanted us to get . . . they were hoping we could get an African American male. "Someone who looks like Denzel Washington," is what we were asked. And we joked about it, but yeah, it would absolutely be ideal. Because particularly when I talk to males, they are looking at me like, "First of all, you're a lady. You don't have a clue." And then, if it's a different culture, certainly you have that. I do feel as though we get good rapport with the kids, and after a while they certainly

would respond. But if we don't have a long time, it [ethnic match] really is more helpful. And I think the kids open up a little more if they really feel like they have a connection with you.

Sixteen percent of those we surveyed described their program staff as diverse, so sometimes there was a "match" between the educator and most of the adolescents in a particular setting:

Our agency has a very diverse staff anyway. That's a commitment we have, which is . . . those of us who are serving have to, you know, match the people we're serving.

On the other hand, several of the respondents noted that they would not restrict a white educator to working only with white adolescents. One or two respondents mentioned that schools or other venues sometimes request presenters of certain cultural backgrounds:

So we do try to [have an ethnic match] . . . because research . . . and just what schools and people have told us, the message does get across better or smoother. But again, if a person is not available on a certain date that would be of a similar ethnic background . . . unless the school requests a certain ethnic background, we will send a person that is available. For the most part one of our African American presenters, she focuses mostly on the urban core, but she also has a lot of context [knowledge about the community].

Twenty percent of our participants believe that visible ethnic similarities between prevention educators and the adolescents in the audience increases the adolescents' receptivity to and comfort with the presenters:

I'll tell you honestly, I think, too, in some instances they are going to listen a little better. I think they feel, even though I don't believe that is necessarily true, I think in some instances they feel that if you are African American and they are, you understand their struggles a little better.

I think [ethnic match is] important. It does make a difference with some of the teens when they see me present; that they see someone who has an experience like theirs. I do openly share that I come from an immigrant background, that this issue we're talking about is not something I don't know from . . . I do this work because of personal experience. I do feel like it affects the level of disclosure.

I think . . . it sends a correct message in terms of having the mixed-race teams; that this is an issue that is pervasive across all races and ethnicities. But additionally, it's a relational thing. I will fully admit that, as a white woman, it takes a while for the students of color to warm up to me. I'm a firm believer in the fact that if you show kids that you care about them and you respect them, they'll respect you back. But when a woman of color goes in, it's more automatic. There's not the history of oppression there. It's not the history of difference there.

Other interviewees, especially organizers of peer education programs, stressed that prevention educators should ensure that their programs reflect the community (see chapter 11). A few noted that prevention educators of color can be important role models for adolescents:

And not [as if] I go in as a white female, 40 years old, and talk to a predominantly African American group that I think they don't hear a thing I say, but I do think it increases their comfort level and their desire to share their opinions. And I think it's good for them to have a role model from their own community that has gone through similar experiences that they are experiencing to come and say, "This is what I've learned," and that type of stuff. I think that our trainers . . . our more diverse trainers . . . add their own life experiences to the program, and I think that helps.

So, they were able to see a Latina who went through the same school that they are at and was able to go to college and get a degree and then who works to teach others.

The presenter can also be a helpful role model for adolescents of different cultural backgrounds, as this African American interviewee pointed out:

The other issue is that sometimes I think it is good for the kids to see me in an area where they wouldn't normally see an African American, a woman in the professional world. So, there are some schools that we go into where there is not a person of color in the school. So, I think it is pretty enlightening and a wonderful experience for the kids to have that.

In a similar vein, 20% of the interviewees mentioned language issues, especially the need for Spanish-speaking prevention educators:

When we had five staff members to go out into the schools . . . When we did our hiring, we actually were conscious of trying to provide the gamut of male facilitators, female facilitators, Latino, African/American, sexual orientation differences. We just tuned in to that, so that the staff reflected the district. Obviously, you can't do that when you have one facilitator.

Fluency in Youth Culture

Many prevention educators who participated in our study urge their colleagues to understand youth culture, and they frequently spoke of the need for educators to like and respect adolescents and to skillfully build rapport with them:

> I think the cultural match that is more important is that they can connect with the young people, that it's less about ethnicity. . . . I think it is important for our organization to be reflective of the community we serve. But really, more than anything, what we have found in working with young people is that the culture that you need to be competent or fluent in is youth culture more than it is any particular race or ethnicity and that it is critically important for us to have presenters who teens are not alienated by, who they can connect to . . . understanding teens, and being someone that teens can relate to. That doesn't necessarily mean being young. It does mean having a level of youthful spirit and energy and being an engaging person. And also being respectful of teens and honestly liking teens.

> So, it's more personality traits than information . . . you know, how to lead a conversation and when each question comes up, knowing what to say and not to be just value-based and to really come from an empowerment philosophy. It's helping the kids make their own choices.

Importance of Being Trustworthy

Several prevention educators we interviewed stressed the importance of being honest, trustworthy, and empathetic, as well as highly motivated:

> Well, I'm looking for someone that really is motivated in the field, that really wants to do it. I also like to have somebody that has some experience, somebody that has some public-speaking experience.

> A couple of years ago, I would have said, it's not about the presenter, it's about the program. And I have made a real switch on that. I don't believe that anymore. I think it's about the presenter. I think doing prevention

work means that you have got the very finest professional people that you can have, who [also] have a heart. And being professional means you have a heart with kids. They've got to be really grounded in the issues. And very well trained. So I'm kind of reiterating that again, I realize, but those have been critical things. And I think to really be involved with the children that you're working with in an open, honest, nonjudgmental way. So that they feel that they can really trust you and that's much more about your character and integrity than it is anything else.

Our interviewees cautioned that adolescents are good at identifying insincerity. Because many programs measure their success by how many survivors approach them for help (see chapter 15), educators must be able to convey trustworthiness to survivors who may not have told anyone else about their history or experiences of victimization:

And as they go along in training, are they really listening to the kids? Are they so busy talking, getting through the material, that they're not paying attention? And how are they responding to questions at question time? So, a lot of this is done in the interview and just to see what they would do in a "what-if [situation]," but also how they think they might respond in a crisis situation or listening to this all the time. Have they thought about: "This is what might happen: you might have to call Child Services" . . . But certainly their personality and if they are enthusiastic about what they do. We want to see that the kids are going to be able to reach out to them. . . . Sometimes it's just the personality. You know, a person may do a workshop or come with us and see how they work with kids or interact . . . So, that's a big part of it, their personality and a little bit of passion . . . you know just that they can really project that they're really interested in the kids as well as the topic, and that they're someone the kids can trust and be able to talk to. . . . But if they've never worked with kids before I don't think I would hire them.

One interviewee underscored the importance of educators having positive attitudes toward parents as well as youth:

There seems to be some kind of a false assumption that anybody can do prevention. The truth of the matter is that it is a very specialized field. When I hire somebody, I have some very stringent interview questions [for] them. It centers around their attitude toward youth, toward parents. I want to know what they believe is the biggest challenge facing families, what they believe is the biggest challenge facing kids, why do kids act aggressively, what would you do to remedy this? I really want somebody that's going to be coming in with a positive attitude toward the kids and their parents and their families. . . . I also want someone who's had a lot of experience working with youth. I would not consider hiring someone who hasn't. Someone who's comfortable being up in front of groups. I don't care necessarily that they have a college degree, though the people that I've hired over the last couple of years have all had college degrees, but they must have had a lot of experience working with youth.

Ideal Age for Educators

A few of our participants thought that younger educators are better able to maintain rapport with middle and high school audiences, and some middle-aged interviewees believed that adolescents are more responsive to younger prevention educators than to older ones:

I myself have done high school presentations and I think they listen to college students more than they would me. I think they look up to them and really see them at this whole different level of where they want to be. I think they get their attention much better than I ever would.

I also have a male staff person and he facilitates the guys' group that we're doing at a middle school, and the truth is that he gets much more out of them than I ever did. Many of the kids said, "You look too much like my mother," and I can understand that too. So even before I had a male facilitator, I had a younger female who facilitated the group, because there were several young men who said, "You know, it just feels kind of weird to me." . . . which is great information because it just gives us the opportunity to say, "We want that information to be out there. We want you to have an opportunity to dialogue and if there's a way that we can find somebody else to facilitate that, that makes it more comfortable, we'll get that."

Some responders mentioned that being older can be helpful or at least not an obstacle. Older educators vary about the value of becoming familiar with and using the language of adolescents:

Even just talking to high school kids, my presentation style is pretty informal, no matter who I'm talking to. With the kids, I've made a point of learning some of the new words that I don't know, because I'm too old. And they think it's hysterical when they hear me say those things. They don't expect me to be saying them.

I have talked about this issue with other presenters, younger and older than I am, and they all discount it, and maybe it's because of how I present. 'Cause I'm energetic and I'm—I don't try to use their speech. I mean that's ridiculous—a middle age person trying to speak like a teenager. That would really be dumb, but I'm real straight; I'm not mincing any words.

A few interviewees emphasized that it is essential to maintain boundaries between educators and youths, and that maturity might make this type of boundary easier to maintain:

I think there are some people, programs . . . who go too far in that direction [connecting with adolescents], where they are just trying to be one of the kids. And that, we're not aiming for. And I think that teens are very, very astute at seeing through that. And I think that if you're trying too hard to be one of them, they dismiss you as a joke.

It is really important in youth programs, especially because we work so closely with our youth, to maintain a boundary at some level or else it is just a nightmare for everyone. My experience is that the youth try to push the boundaries a lot. When we have young people on staff, they will flirt with them, they will call them at the office, that kind of thing. So, we have to be very strict about it.

One interviewee, who was in her sixties, said she could "get away with saying a lot of things that the twenty-two- or twenty-three-year-old educator could not get away with saying in high school." She went on to point out that adolescents had told her that they thought a young prevention educator was "flirting" with them when she discussed sexual harassment. The older interviewee knew, in fact, that the young educator was just trying to be friendly and outgoing.

Use of Volunteers or Interns

A quarter of those we interviewed use volunteers or interns, such as undergraduate or graduate students, who receive course credit for their field experiences in the prevention programs. One interviewee described the use of volunteers as similar to establishing a speaker's bureau. Such unpaid help can be essential, especially when funding is scarce and the demand for prevention programming is high:

Just being able to, realistically, being able to pull in more trained volunteers, because that is really what we rely on a great deal—trained volunteers to come help us out in the schools and with our programs.

Some programs will not work with undergraduate interns, because they seem too young or only minimally trained. The agencies often know their volunteers well, or they may subject them to criminal background checks. They usually supervise volunteers carefully or instruct them to adhere closely to a program manual:

We trusted her to come in and present to students, because she has been here for so long. I've got three volunteers who do presentations, the classroom presentations, and all three of them have worked on our Crisis Line. They have that background . . . I think all three of them are survivors, too. So then they've been working with our program for a while. I don't typically take volunteers directly from training into my program; usually they come from other programs within the agency.

There are also disadvantages to using volunteers, unless they receive extensive training:

It really takes a broad knowledge of a lot of different issues to be able to think quickly on your feet and say to them, "I understand where you are coming from, but have you thought about it in this perspective?" That's something that is hard, I think, to train a volunteer to be able to do. An intern is sometimes different because they're, you can train, give them more hours of training and they can be with you more throughout the day that they can sometimes pick up on those things.

Dating-Violence and Sexual-Assault Survivors as Prevention Educators

Survivors as presenters have both strengths and possible pitfalls. The engaging qualities and vivid reality of survivors' stories can be potential assets, but a possible problem is that adolescents may hesitate about engaging in true dialogue after a survivor tells an intense or intimidating story:

A lot of people will tell me that survivors are very effective presenters, because they've experienced it. And I tend to differ with them. I do believe that they are . . . that people should hear their story and that, you know, it's reality to them. Like they're seeing the reality. The audience is seeing it in front of them. Like, "Oh, this is a real person and it has happened to them." You know, "She's just not telling me it happens to people." When you see the reality, it's more like a hands-on thing. But on the other side of that, and even being in audiences where the presenter was a survivor, and especially working with kids, even high schoolers, you lose, depending on how the rest of your presentation is. Like if you do tell your story. Depending on how you come off, you will lose that interaction and that openness because . . . I mean, how many times have you ever heard a story and someone was doing a presentation and they told you their story, that you were like, you know, "Should I ask? Should I not say something?"

And that's why volunteers I get, like from the colleges or even that want to do community education, and they're a survivor and everything. And I'll tell them, "You will never do a presentation on your own. If you want to do community education and you want to use your story . . . now if you don't use your story, you can do it on your own, as long as you don't use your story at all. If you use your story, I'm coming with you, and I will do the presentation after you tell your story." Because I don't want them to be like, "Oh, if I say this, I shouldn't say that." You know, especially guys, might react and say something and they're worried about the person's feelings.

A few of our interviewees tell the adolescents in the audience about their own histories of assault or abuse:

I will quickly introduce again that I was in this abusive relationship myself and I don't think it's funny. Then a lot of the kids will snap to attention often.

Also, something else I found that's a good attention grabber for me . . . I was in an abusive marriage myself and I made a flower lei, because I was living with my ex-husband in Hawaii, and I explained to them because they like to hear about Hawaii, just kind of what leis symbolize. And I created this lei to go with the statistic that every nine seconds in America a teenage girl is battered. And that works out to about 440 people in one hour, which is about the average of how long I speak to the students. And while I'm wearing this lei, I explain to them: Number one, it's purple because that's the color for domestic violence awareness. Number two, it's significant to me because of the situation that I came out of and that I've moved on from. Thirdly, it's got the 440 petals that represent each woman that is a sister, friend, cousin that is going to be affected just during our classroom period. And I'll pass that around to the students and they can put it on or look at it. They are very moved by the fact that so many people are being impacted while they're safely sitting in the classroom.

One educator talked about how she refused to answer questions about herself from a particularly challenging group of adolescents:

And he said, "So you were a rape victim, huh?" Just real obnoxious, and I just fired back at him, I said, "That's none of your business, and we're not here to talk about whether I was victimized or not. We're here to talk about, as I said in the beginning, raising your awareness of how you might be victimized or how you can help somebody else who is victimized."

Gender of Facilitators

Schewe (2002) notes the heated debate on the topic of the facilitator's gender, but only one study, which found no effect, focused on the gender of presenters. In reporting on a multi-site evaluation of adolescent sexual assault prevention programs, Schewe (n.d.) found that "a male/female team of prevention educators produces the overall best results for both male and female students."

About 40% of those we interviewed think it is important to have some male prevention educators in order to reach males in the audience, prevent male defensiveness, and act as role models of men who are thoughtful about violence against women:

For men, I think men should do men—I think it should be exclusively male audiences and I think it should be men doing it.

I think it's very important for young people to hear from men as well . . . that it's not okay to be abusive, that that doesn't make you manly by acting in a violent or abusive way.

One of the things [our participants] articulated was that they wanted to see a male voice deliver some of this material. I think some of the boys felt . . . and I think this is verified in other national literature about other teen dating-violence programs that . . . because . . . we continue to do these one-shot deals. We're working on expanding our curriculum, but in the time that we have been given in the schools is short, like 45-, 50-, or 90-minute presentation, they were feeling somewhat "bashed." I hate that word and I hate that kind of notion like we're blaming. Even as clear as we were to talk about the national statistics from the Department of Justice that talk about 85% to 95% of domestic violence crimes are committed by men against women. As much as we talk about that, and this is not about making guys the "bad guy," somehow it was easier for them to hear that when a man was saying that. And they could kind of . . . when they could see and watch us really partnering with a male trainer; somehow our information became more credible.

When women and men co-facilitate a prevention presentation, the adolescents also are exposed to a model of the two genders collaborating:

One of the big things through that model that we hope to achieve is just modeling the respectful behavior and modeling for the kids that two adults, a man and a woman, can relate to each other and can be respectful of each other. And can, you know, model that behavior that a lot of them aren't seeing. That's a really important piece of what we do.

Only one interviewee flatly stated that her program did not need male presenters to increase its effectiveness. Several other educators stressed that gender alone does not qualify a man to be a good educator and that male adolescents were sometimes highly receptive to female facilitators:

But I think it will be not just for the sake of, "Oh, we have to have a guy talk to the guys," I think that's not a good idea unless that man is an effective educator and can make that connection.

When I went to [a local school] just recently and I did all, a group of the girls and a group of the boys; those boys were very attentive. They were more attentive than the girls. They gave me less hassle than the girls. The girls were the ones that gave me a lot of hassle. . . . They weren't nasty, but they were just, you know, doing what kids do. Talking silly and stuff. But the boys were very serious. And I was straight up with them. They said, "We appreciate you being straight up with us."

We learned from our interviews that 10% of the programs were unable to have male educators either because their staffs were too small or they had no qualified, interested males in their communities:

Yes, however impractical and improbable that is. Yeah, I think it's important to not only have a racial match but also a gender match. But I mean that's, that doesn't work 95% of the time. Yeah, I'm limited on the people

I have on staff as well as time commitments. I'm the only male here, so if there's a male group, sometimes I can do it, and sometimes I can't, just depending on whatever the time constraints are. . . . I have two female, three female educators and I've never had a problem with them doing a male group.

Some of our participants appreciate having male volunteers, teachers, or interns available when the program did not have a male on staff:

Yes, I feel it would be beneficial to have a male and female working together and showing that partnership and healthy relationship, modeling that to the students and I think it would benefit all of the students to hear the male perspective. Oftentimes, if there is a male teacher that I am working with, I will utilize his perspective quite frequently. Just to assist the students and any questions that they might have. Sometimes they will think this is "a male bashing class." We don't approach it that way at all, but, because a large percentage of victims are female . . . and I think they want to believe that it is a gender-neutral issue and it really is not.

Ideal Level of Education and Types of Experiences

Most of the programs hire prevention educators who have bachelor's degrees. However, some hire educators with associate of arts degrees, and many hire people with master's degrees:

At the rates that we pay, and nonprofit, it's not always, you don't always get the bachelor's level individual coming in here. I do require an associate's degree. Preferably in Human Services or in Child Care Education. But that's the barest minimum.

We like people who can present and who are a little bit thoughtful, too, of people's feelings. There is a difference between being a marketer and somebody in PR and somebody who can be an educator. So, we look for credentials first. We say, "Has this person ever worked with, doing support groups, are they a counselor, are they . . . a social worker, have they studied social work?" In other words, all of those people have bachelor's degrees in social work, or one has a degree in education psychology.

Most programs want to hire educators who have experience with youths:

I think it helps to have some experience with youth in and of themselves, because we're constantly having to kind of read the crowd and adapt things and if we're not being relevant, then we're not doing much good. So, I think you need to be able to identify with the students and have some experience with them.

A few of the persons we interviewed cited the importance of self-care and the ability to handle the traumatizing effects of frequent contact with victimized people (see chapter 14):

Then when I'm interviewing for someone to be hired, certainly how they interact with children, how they take care of themselves, because we often get a lot of disclosures and some days you'll hear story after story.

Training for Prevention Educators

Three-quarters of the program representatives we spoke with shared information about the training they provide to presenters. (Some programs primarily conduct peer education, so we discuss training for peer educators in the chapter on that subject.) Some interviewees viewed prevention-educator training as a "given" that did not require extensive discussion. Furthermore, some were the only educators in their programs and thus did not have experience training other, new educators.

The most commonly mentioned need for preparing prevention educators was that new educators should "shadow" experienced educators and observe how they conduct their presentations. One-fourth of those we spoke with specifically mentioned this practice:

We're always looking for continuing improvement of our programs and who better to help advise than the people who are out there presenting? So, we're constantly giving each other feedback and giving ideas for ways of improvement and strategy and all of that. But we're very particular about our training process and having people, when they're new in the program, shadow others and an in-depth evaluation of performance.

Often, after new staff members have "shadowed" the experienced educators, the veterans observe new staff members as they begin to give their own presentations. Some programs periodically observe both new and experienced staff.

Most programs have training sessions for their educators on the dynamics of sexual assault and dating violence, often training them along with advocates and shelter staff. Trainings ranged from nineteen to fifty-five hours, forty hours on average, and specialized prevention training was usually conducted after new staff or volunteers completed the general agency training:

> To be honest with you, the majority of us don't come from the background that I have. I started working in college on the issue. The majority of people that come in don't have that background, and we have a pretty extensive staff training model, so we do a lot of professional development and reading of articles and discussing of articles. We're very process-oriented as an organization. So, we have two people in training now. They'll read articles; then we'll sit down and discuss them. So I think, coming in, people just have to be willing to learn . . . I think the most important thing is that people need to understand our curriculum and they need to understand why it works.

A few of those we surveyed indicated that doing prevention work with youths requires the ability to respond to a wide range of questions and comments, which makes in-depth training essential:

> For me it's hard to train someone in a short period of time to truly be prepared on their own to go out and deliver these programs, because you never can predict some of the questions that you are going to get or some of the resistance and some of the attitudes [you encounter]. And even if you think you know the basics of what rape is about or what abuse is about, sometimes people can ask you some really, really tricky questions that almost make you sit there and go, "Well, I know that you're wrong, but I can't exactly explain to you why."

> When we both got here, we had to memorize . . . just straight memorize . . . some of the facts out of the curriculum. I hadn't been involved in any type of prevention program, and . . . there were a lot of things about domestic violence that I didn't know. And you know, you have to be prepared . . . they'll ask you things that are not necessarily in the curriculum and that you know your knowledge is well-rounded enough that you answer things that are a little outside of maybe what we would normally, or at least we know where to go to find the answers, which sometimes I have to do, if I don't know.

Other training elements that frequently turned up in our interviews include classroom management, feminist theory, cultural sensitivity, and adolescent development. A few respondents said that their training also included methods for handling disclosures, crisis management, the aftermath of trauma, group facilitation, and conflict resolution:

> And even if you're just doing presentations and speaking to audiences, it's still helpful to have an understanding of groups and group facilitation training, because so much of it is learning to referee, and field questions, and engage, and have discussion, but not letting it go crazy.

> They should have training in diversity, especially in our community, where we have a very diverse community, even though the population is largely African American and Latino. We also have a large Asian population. They should have training in facilitation. Particularly facilitation of . . . youth groups. They should probably have training in conflict resolution . . . and they should have . . . on-the-job training.

According to a number of interviewees, handling disclosures is a particularly sensitive and important part of the prevention educator's job (see chapter 14). Some programs hire educators who already worked as crisis responders or on hotlines or as advocates, so they have experience working with survivors. Others offer new educators training in handling disclosures:

> They're not trauma counselors. And every one of my community educators is trained in risk assessment and safety planning and trauma management. So that anything that's disclosed during or after a presentation can be handled right then and there.

Often training includes role-plays:

> We will sit in our conference and we will act like "bad kids." Fire a few questions at them that they can't answer. Because kids will do that, you know. We try to give them a real-life situation, things that we have actually experienced ourselves. The most horrifying experience we had when we started and we give it to them. And we say, "Okay, this is going to actually happen to you so what are you going to do?"

Several participants in our study said that they hold weekly supervision or group meetings of prevention educators:

> We do a lot of internal staff development, so we spend a few days in the very beginning going through the curriculum, going over all the program

materials, talking, creating, planning, and when we keep that spirit, we meet, as a group, weekly and continue to develop the program as we go.

We all go through a forty-hour rape crisis training and then we all participate in training throughout the year. And I always require people to research and go look and find and explore to keep them abreast. We have team meetings twice a month where we go over a new curriculum, issues, what's happening, what's hot, what's in the media and make decisions on altering the curriculum.

Three prevention educators we interviewed reported that their training periods for new staff or volunteers were somewhat briefer than the typical time of more than twenty-five hours. Sometimes this was because programs ask presenters to adhere strictly to a script or manual, so they did not need the extensive knowledge that improvising might require. But even some programs that did not extensively use a manual had shorter training period. Clearly, careful screening is required when volunteers are given minimal training and not expected to adhere to a script. In small communities, however, program staff may feel they know the volunteers well enough to trust them. A few states require certification of staff in order to receive state funding for prevention programs, and some states certify volunteers and require a minimum of thirty to forty hours of training for certification.

Summary of Qualities of Ideal Prevention Educators

The participants we interviewed generally agreed that the ideal prevention educator should combine knowledge with passion and the ability to establish rapport with adolescents. These personality traits or experiences should be required at the outset and then refined by training, modeling, and practicing. However, our survey revealed some disagreements about the qualities of ideal educators, and these disagreements might exist in the larger prevention community. The primary points of contention were about the importance of matching the age, gender, and ethnicity of educators to those of the audience. Program representatives also varied in their views of whether and how to use volunteer educators and whether survivors should be educators and whether they should present their own stories. Some believed that ethnic matching is essential to facilitate rapid bonding between adolescents and the presenters with whom they believe they have a lot in common. Others felt that a skilled presenter can reach any audience, and that training in adolescent development and cultural sensitivity can resolve potential problems with cross-cultural communication. Interviewees had mixed opinions about the importance of having male prevention educators, but many favored including male prevention educators if interested men could be found in the community who were willing to work for the salaries that programs offer. In general, lack of funding or the existence of a small pool of potential staff in smaller communities sometimes prevented programs from hiring the "ideal" prevention educator. Most programs provide forty hours of training to educators in order to feel confident that presenters understand the dynamics of dating violence and sexual assault, and are able to answer questions and discuss adolescents' views in a manner consistent with the program's philosophy.

The authors are confident in the view that prevention educators should be well trained, have strong communication skills, and understand and enjoy adolescents. Otherwise, we find no basis in the research literature to enable us to state which characteristics define the ideal prevention educator. We encourage programs and researchers to investigate the characteristics of successful prevention educators, but readers, meanwhile, can make their own decisions in that regard based on their experiences, communities, and some of our interviewees' cogent arguments.

15

Rewarding, Troubling, and Challenging Aspects

The prevention educators we interviewed often brought up the most re-warding and challenging aspects of their work, as well as the potential positive and negative consequences of youth sharing their own victimiza-tion/survivor experiences with the prevention educators or other youth. The ability to connect survivors with needed resources can be rewarding, but it also raises concerns of confidentiality. This chapter focuses on effec-tive methods of handling various situations that arise in group sessions and how to help youth decide what experiences to share during prevention programs.

Evaluative research has rarely focused on prevention educators' reac-tions to the rewarding or troubling aspects of their work, but some lit-erature does shed light on the issues discussed in this chapter. As already mentioned, several studies have suggested that adolescents are often very private about their experiences with dating violence and sexual assault, and the may especially resist telling adults about these experiences (Black et al., 2008; Ocampo, Shelley, and Jaycox 2007). It is not surprising, there-fore, that adolescents often reveal their negative experiences for the first time after meeting charismatic, empathetic, and knowledgeable prevention educators.

Most Rewarding Aspects for Prevention Educators

Although the literature does not discuss the rewarding aspects of preven-tion programming, our interviewees clearly are finding great satisfaction in this work, including the opportunity to help survivors, to provide new perspectives on troubling issues, to make a difference in young people's lives, to work, with peer leaders and other volunteers, and to experience the enjoyment of working with, and being appreciated by, adolescents.

Helping Survivors and Perpetrators

According to 40% of the prevention educators we interviewed, the most rewarding aspect of prevention work was when victims approached them for help or when an adolescent, for the first time, spoke about his or her experiences of victimization. Many of the educators (about 25%) mentioned that simply being able to connect victims with help was itself gratifying. Similarly, presenters felt rewarded when they were approached by adolescents who wanted to help victimized friends. In general, our interviewees expressed satisfaction in being able to make a referral or arrange help for someone who needed it:

> Young people coming up to us after class and confiding in us about something that is, or was, going on with them that they'd never told anybody before, and that they never felt there was a safe person to talk to about it before, but they wanted to talk to our presenter. That's really one of those moments that will keep you going for a while. But we have had some good experiences . . . [we] do a workshop and somebody comes up afterwards and says, "I've never told anyone this before but . . . " and they tell you some horrible thing that happened to them, and you know that you said something that made them feel safe to tell.

> A lot of . . . high school girls . . . will come up to us afterwards and say, "I didn't realize. I didn't realize I was being abused." I think every once in a while you'll read an evaluation or a personal experience where the student says that, because of the presentation, it has helped them to realize that they are in an abusive relationship and that they would like help getting out of that relationship. And so that makes you feel really good, especially when you've helped them get out of a relationship; but just to know that because you have been there, and you did give them all the information that that has helped them to understand that it's not a healthy relationship.

> With older kids, you know, we've certainly had kids that told us that their friend was raped and they didn't know what to do about it. They were afraid to tell. An older girl talked about being afraid to tell because the kid [perpetrator] was in a gang and they knew that kid had already

burned down somebody's house that they were angry with. So it was this heavy situation. So sometimes it's not an easy fix, but getting this child to talk and feel safe and being able to help her out the best you can in her situation. And I think it's just knowing that you were there at a time in their life when maybe they didn't have anybody else to share that with . . . maybe it was a disclosure of something that was going on. That we were there with the message and if we had not been there, how would they have known that they could come forward? Who would they have talked to and would it just kept on, would it have continued because they would have thought that they could never talk about it and because we were there, they knew they could. There was someone they could talk to. Sometimes we get notes that we don't read [aloud] but they are notes to us like "thanks for being here; it was really important that you came. It helped me a lot."

Three program representatives recounted situations where youths who believed they had been abusive in a relationship approached them for help after a presentation:

I remember presenting a program to just a male class of senior students, and after the class, one of the young men came up to me and thanked me for giving him some information that he had never looked at and that he had acted inappropriately with several young women and that he really wanted to have relationships with women from a different standpoint. So that was pretty rewarding. It made me feel pretty powerful in regards to being able to give that information in a way that the kids could hear.

Several interviewees described situations where adolescents went home after a presentation, told their parents who were victims of abuse what they had learned from the program, and the parents sought help or changed their behavior as a result of their children's help:

He said, "Well my son came back and talked to me about what happened in your class, and that's what really made me come to anger management group . . . he said, "My son talked me into going and getting anger management and I am in the process of getting a divorce" and this and that "but you really helped my son and it really gave me the push to come forward and start taking care of some of the stuff."

There have been a lot of rewards, which is why we keep sloggin' along, even though we deal with a lot of dirty stuff. The rewards are when you see, for instance, sometimes what has happened in the programs is that you'll have a family . . . in chaos, and the, say, mom, is the victim of severe domestic violence, and it'll be the kids that will start working on mom and start taking the stuff that they've learned through the programming and educating their mother about it. And the next thing you know, mom pops up out of the blue and starts wanting to talk about it and just didn't realize she had that level of support in the community.

Providing New Information and Perspectives

A third of the prevention professionals stressed the importance, for adolescents, of being given new information and different ways of looking at things. They spoke of the rewards in seeing young people with rigid, victim-blaming attitudes start to consider other ways of looking at these issues:

With the teens, especially when I go to the alternative schools where they are, oh, jaded sometimes or desensitized to any type of violence. I can see that they are maybe start[ing] out very nonchalant about it and then towards the end are very intensive in wanting information. And you know, maybe it's just that the topic interested them and that was it. But maybe it could be that this kind of [thing] happened to them. And they developed this hard exterior because of it. And now having this information and knowing that it's not their fault somehow kind of shifted something inside of them.

Or a student who comes up to us and says they want to volunteer and help out because they believe [in] so much of what we do. Or a young person who comes to us and says, "I think maybe I'm acting in an abusive way and I don't want to be like that." And the sort of "aha!" moments that you see happen with young people . . . it's why a lot of people go into teaching regardless of what the subject matter is . . . people often ask me, "Well, isn't the work you do depressing?" And I say, "No, it's the opposite of that, because we have moments of real inspiration and moments of seeing . . ." That's the whole point of doing prevention work and proactive work. It's to try to reach young people at a place where you really still can make a difference.

This work is always about touching one person at a time. And infiltrating the community's consciousness. I think the small rewards, for me, it's almost looking at our job isn't to change people's beliefs overnight. But moving a student from a belief that they rigidly held to a belief that they now question is a tremendous reward, particularly with attitudes toward gender.

Watching students change, watching them grow, watching them develop, watching them develop skills, become assertive for what they need and want to set down. For myself, I think the most rewarding aspect is when you see one of the students that maybe wasn't quite cluing into what you were saying really make a connection . . . that little "aha" moment, the light bulb going off. You can see it in their body language and in their eyes that this woman is in here talking to us about something, and they can see that I really care.

Four interviewees spoke about the satisfaction they felt when they started a good discussion among the youths:

I always feel good if we have a dialogue back and forth . . . Even sometimes almost as a debate among the students as, "Well, I see girls treating their boyfriends that way." I mean, I guess for me, that is rewarding, that at least they're taking a look at that and talking about it and kind of taking a risk in front of their peers to express their opinion on the subject. It's a good place to start.

Sometimes it is when you have that really, really good dialogue in a class, back and forth between the students, when I'm pretty much just standing up there. And they are just back and forth with each other having a really, really good discussion about their different opinions and different attitudes. That makes you feel good that you have sparked that kind of discussion.

Making a Difference

A rewarding aspect that often closely parallels the gains from providing new information and perspectives is the feeling that one has made a difference. Survey participants mentioned the benefits of making a difference for individual adolescents but also making a difference in a school or community:

I think it's rewarding to have just raised the level of awareness to some degree in this community about interpersonal violence. Just knowing that you are part of the change agent.

I know that [at] the end of my day, whenever that time comes, but at the end of the day we have made an impact on people's lives in an important, positive way. Well, I think with youth, the part where we're able to see visible changes, like, for example, a seating arrangement that was changed [in a classroom]. Even though I'm a big-picture gal, seeing the success in the small changes and having that impact on a small level has been really rewarding.

Working with Adolescent Leaders and Volunteers

One-quarter of those we interviewed mentioned that working with volunteers and peer educators is very satisfying. Some of our interviewees specifically discussed the rewards of working with energetic, committed peer educators:

Their parents say, "I can't believe the difference in this kid, how this opened up lines of communication in our family. My daughter now sits at dinner and tells me about what she has learned, and we talk about some things we never talked about before." And then they go off to college and so many of the girls are involved in the *Vagina Monologues* at college and directing it and acting in it. And we have a guy who started a Men Can Stop Rape group at Yale this year. That is so exciting.

Enjoying the Age Group

Several interviewees mentioned how much they enjoy working with adolescents, because young people they are so open and energetic:

I really enjoy working with this age. I love it. I think they are so open. They are honest and I value that. I usually like doing education, because kids are usually much more honest than adults, and they will say what their real opinion [is,] even if it is not like the socially sanctioned opinion. And they are more kind of flexible and curious. Cause I do training with adults, too, and adults are like . . . there will be a guy sitting there, like "I really hate you." But a kid will be like, they are not so mean about it. It is not like a power thing . . . I feel like I've learned a lot more about what young people think and just who they are as people and I've realized that, even though I'm only twenty-six, that I kind of had a skewed idea of what a fifteen or sixteen year old was like already. You know, that I just realized how capable they are.

Being Appreciated

The educators found it particularly rewarding when young people remembered them and wanted them to return. They mentioned meeting adolescents at the school or in the community who remembered them and what they had talked about and asked when they would be back:

> I have had several times when the big kids have asked their director or whomever is over their program, "When is Miss . . . coming back to talk to us?" Or when I am leaving they say, "We want to learn some more. Can you come back so we can talk about something different?" A lot of times, where I live, it is a small community and you tend to see people all the time. I will see them and they will remember me.

In a similar vein, the presenters felt good when school personnel wanted them to come back. Sometimes encounters in the community were rewarding, because youths would tell them how their presentation made an impact, such as when they related the content to friends or family. Three interviewees specifically mentioned feeling rewarded when youths said they talked about the presentation afterward. As one noted, she felt good knowing that the message had an influence beyond those who actually attended the presentation:

> Sometimes I have gone in and done a presentation in the classroom, I might see this person working at Kmart and she says, "I went home and talked to my boyfriend or my family about what you did in class today and this is what went on." I don't necessarily know who this person is, but she recognized me as coming to her class and talking about these issues. I get some feedback from the teachers and guidance counselors and it is all positive. That is very rewarding.

Negative Aspects

Some interviewees did not recount any troubling events related to their prevention work with youth. A common concern among others, however, was that hearing stories of abuse and assault was upsetting and exhausting. Equally disturbing were the reports of legal and social-service systems often letting victims down.

Hearing Upsetting Stories

Literature on vicarious traumatization (Pearlman and Saakvitne 1995; Schauben and Frazier 1995; Trippany, Kress, and Wilcoxon 2004) and compassion fatigue (Figley 2002) addresses some of the troubling aspects of doing prevention education. Like many counselors and therapists, prevention educators may experience painful emotions after hearing repeated stories of the abuse of young people.

A third of our interviewees mentioned problems related to survivors' disclosures. Several spoke of the combined difficulties of hearing the stories of abuse and then encountering a non-responsive or insensitive response from authorities. Adolescents often view prevention educators as knowledgeable and willing to help, but it is extremely troubling to know that there are so many victims in their communities:

> I've seen too many victims; I've been with too many victims; it is a really painful thing. The stories are sometimes hard to listen to because you just think, "How could somebody do this to a child?" The other thing that always takes our breath away is when a student discloses any kind of trauma that they have had to endure. After sixteen years, with me, it still does take my breath away. So those are always difficult situations to know that kids endure so much pain from abandonment, divorce, drug abuse, sexual violence, to physical violence. It is amazing how they are able to collectively move forward. Making reports is always hard. Doing that whole thing and letting kids know that, you know what, we have a legal responsibility to make these reports. I think honestly, and I think about this a lot, because some days I come home from work and I'm just exhausted emotionally from hearing some of the horrible stories the kids tell me, and some days I feel like I'm hearing one after another, after another, after another. It makes me get angry with parents; it makes me get angry with community people, and I just, I feel like I, some days I feel like I am really angry at a lot of people. Not the people that I should be angry with, and it probably is not an effective emotion to have at the time, but it's how I feel.

Some prevention educators found it difficult to bear when a presentation clearly upset an adolescent who chose not to tell his or her story. Interviewees worried that these victimized individuals might never receive help:

> She was vomiting in the wastebasket because she had such a physical reaction to what we were saying. Another time, um, you know, when

you see a 17-year-old boy who gets so upset because you're talking about the impact of witnessing domestic violence on children, that they get so upset they have to walk out of the room.

Ineffective Systemic Response to Victimization

Prevention educators may find it frustrating when they report an assault or incident of abuse and then never learn the outcome. Equally difficult is when educators learn that no effective legal or social-service intervention occurred:

> Where I have felt really frustrated, is when, mostly girls, will come and tell me they reported the rape. They did everything that I said, that I taught in the class. And nothing happened. The guy is still out there. He didn't get in trouble. He's, in fact, maybe still harassing her. You know, phoning her, having his friends tell her that he's going to kill her, that kind of thing. That's really frustrating when a girl, or someone tells you they've done everything you just told them in class and it didn't make a bit of difference.

> I would say one thing specifically that we deal with is, that, because of the age of the kids that we're working with, a lot of times there's a lot of red tape as far as the services that they can take advantage of. I'm talking to a student specifically now who's been sexually assaulted in the past and her mother doesn't want her to go to any counseling or follow through with anything, because she doesn't want any of their business out. It was her brother who molested her. And the mother doesn't want their business, you know, out and about, and so she refuses to sign the consent for this student to get counseling and she's under 17. So, a lot of times, your hands are tied as far as what kind of services they can receive unless the parents will consent.

While the indifference of the justice system can be a problem, others we interviewed mentioned that it is difficult when survivors just want to tell their story but do not want to take action against the abuser, or when educators suspect that someone may have been abused but the victim is not yet ready to tell anyone.

Because practitioners in smaller agencies might have less support or fewer people to commiserate with about these stresses, the problems may become more acute. For example, one interviewee mentioned how difficult it is being the only one in her position without a colleague to debrief her.

Hostile or Challenging Audience Members

Casey and Nurius (2006b) are in favor of educators reminding classes that a survivor may be in the room and to "gently challenge" (p.513) statements students make blaming the victim. They encourage prevention educators to remind adolescents that they want to create a safe atmosphere for everyone in the room.

The next most frequently mentioned troubling aspect of prevention programming was coping with hostile or challenging audience members. These events may be viewed as problems of discipline or problems related to societal norms that blame the victim or as the result of students' discomfort at hearing about issues that "get a little too close" and thus arouse reactions of denial or defensiveness. One-fourth of our respondents described problems with hostile or challenging audiences:

> It is hard sometimes when you have a group that, either because of their own personal experience or background, or just for whatever reason, they are really, really opposed to the information that I'm sharing with them and really obstinate and stubborn about even trying to look at things from a different perspective and in a different light. . . . For the most part, I tell them that they can express any opinion that they want to. That they can disagree with me, that they can say whatever they want to say, as long as they phrase it in a way that is not disrespectful to either me or to somebody else in the room that has some type of connection to this issue. And sometimes they follow those guidelines and sometimes they don't. Sometimes they just flat out say things that are really offensive. Or laugh. Sometimes the classes where they laugh at stories, like if somebody is sharing a personal story of something that happened to them or a family member, sexual assault, and then other students in the class laugh at it. You are just standing up there thinking, "What is wrong with you?" Those are some hard times.

> This kid stood up on this table and started screaming at me, and I had no knowledge prior of what was going on in their school and in their community at that time. He was challenging me and I was challenging him back, not in a disrespectful way, but I wasn't going to just agree with what he was saying. He actually walked up and got right in my face. I was just extremely calm. He started pointing his finger and touching my chest. I just stayed really calm and I continued to say that he needed to stop touching me and he needed to walk away and leave the room . . . At one point, I

looked over at all of these teachers and finally someone did kind of come up and made a statement to him and he backed off and he started walking out of the room . . . He had a group of 10 guys that followed him out the door . . . while he stood up and was kind of challenging me, there was a girl that stood up and started . . . because he was talking about the way that girls dress and how they are asking for it and they want it and all of this stuff and this one girl stood up and started yelling at him and counteracting what he was saying. No one really had control of these kids. . . .

And I'll be like, "there could be people in this class right now who this has happened to, and you're laughing at them." And that's usually when the guys will stop laughing. The guys will stop laughing, but the girls will keep going. And when I have females that will laugh and joke and kind of be real boisterous about it the whole session, I'll say to the teacher afterwards, "Do you know anything about that student?" And they might say "no" but the majority of the time, they've said, "her sister" [was victimized] or "she has" [been victimized] or, "There have been suspicions that something has happened," or, "She's currently going through it." But I don't try to come down on them like, "Okay, leave the room," or stuff like that, because I still want them to get the material.

I mean if they're wanting to fight you to the death and it's obvious . . . that you're not going to change years of what they've heard within a day, typically what I'll try to do is move on to something else and try to talk to that student privately after class. Sometimes, you can reason with them and say, "Well, how would you [feel] if somebody thought that about your mom? Or your sister?" . . . Sometimes they'll think twice about it, but we're not there to spend our entire 90 minutes arguing with one specific person. You know what I mean? And I spoke with a very hostile male audience once, which was very challenging. They were making it personal. Not about me, but, "Why are you talking to us? Why don't you have numbers on men and how often they are victimized?" And [they were] very defensive and not hearing it as, "This is information that you can use to help the people you care about," but more, "We didn't do anything wrong," kind of defensiveness. I did the best I could. I explained to them why we don't have a lot of information about victimization rates of men. And again reiterated that I was not there because I think they are all rapists, but I think that they are all people who are able to help us prevent sexual violence by getting involved and by learning information that can help them. And that was one of those times when someone in the group spoke up and reiterated what I said. The teachers are really, really really good with them but you will have—because of the either criminal background of some of these kids or the lack of manners that—may be already offenders it's really difficult to do the whole empathy-victim things, because they're calling down girls and they're saying really obnoxious, hateful, nasty things. Now this usually—I have an arrangement with the teachers that those kids are—have to leave.

Not all practitioners view challenging audiences as a big problem:

Sometimes you have particularly a mixed-gender group, somebody who really wants to challenge every [statement we make] to the point where it is hard to progress, and so you have to deal with that in a way that is respectful, but also move on with, "the workshop is important" . . . But I kind of expect that, to some degree, in any group, and usually the host of the group is much more upset about it than I am, because I feel like I have the skills to work around that and to manage those kinds of things that come up, without getting negative and having to yell at kids. . . . But I think often the staff of the host organization feels badly. They often apologize for groups that I think were absolutely delightful.

Deeply Entrenched Myths

A fifth of our interviewees expressed displeasure on encountering deeply entrenched myths in their audiences. As discussed in chapter 12, teachers may also be among those who support myths that contradict the program's message. Typically the upsetting myths relate to attitudes blaming the victim which parents or society, or both, seemed to have taught the adolescents:

It is a real reality check to come in, especially when we talk about rape myths, to see how far we have come and to see how far we have yet to go. One of the bigger changes is that, starting about the middle school or high school level, every kid I know, will say to me "No means no." And I think that is a change from 30 years ago. But then we explore a little bit deeper and for a lot of kids it's "no means no, except when." Then you still find, not exactly the same myths, but a lot of the same myths. So, you get a sense of how we are still fighting a lot of those same issues.

One frustration for me, the amount of time that we spend just dealing with the overall cultural attitude about violence and that, "Violence is okay and a way to get power, and violence is a way to solve problems."

And we are coming in to talk about a specific kind of violence, and it is just frustrating to me with how much time we have to spend on "what is the difference between an aggressive and assertive response?" The kids just dismiss assertiveness as "that doesn't work." Because what they are seeing around them in real life and certainly in the media [is] that aggressiveness is what gets you power. "Aggressiveness is what is cool and anything [else] just isn't going to work." And that has been frustrating, because I feel like we have to spend a lot of time just trying to deal with the cultural attitude around violence before we can even get into the more specific issues that we are trying to cover. I've had people say things that have been very victim-blaming and based in ignorance that have been disappointing to hear, especially when they come from women.

Denial About the Need for Prevention Programs

Slightly more than 10% of the prevention educators we spoke with said they are troubled when they encounter an audience or a school that is in denial about sexual assault and domestic violence:

Working with school administrators can be challenging. And there are some that are wonderful and some that are wonderful about specific things, but I'm not sure that they always understand the importance of the prevention programs. Or always understand how trauma affects young people . . . After there has been a rash of sexual assaults or sexual harassment in the school, then they want us to come in. It's like, that's like closing the barn door after the horse is out, so to speak. This has already occurred, and we are not going in there and be counselors to patch it up. Our idea is prevention and not that this has occurred and "we have never been in your school because you don't want us to come in and now you are going to have us come in and say what?" And they say "well, educate them so this won't happen again." And while we can buy it, we have to know the dangers of doing stuff like that. We are not going to be used. It is like, "oh if we can just show that we had those [program] people out here, that will shut up the media because we have covered our bases." And it is like, you know, I just wish you would have had us out there in the beginning because it would be better for these kids. And for the community so they would just be aware.

One or two interviewees raised additional troubling issues, including schools changing their schedule without warning and a lack of resources. We discuss the scarcity of resources in depth in chapter 16.

Issues Related to Disclosures of Victimization

Hickman, Jaycox, and Aronoff (2004), reporting on a program whose personnel we interviewed, noted that laws requiring the reporting of child abuse can be an obstacle to adolescents' disclosures of victimization in states where any violence against a minor must be reported (except a mutual fight between equals, such as playground fights). At times adolescents may lose trust in program facilitators because of the limits of confidentiality.

Based on their review of dating violence prevention programs, Meyer and Stein (2004) encourage prevention educators to be prepared to help youth decide what experiences to share during programs. Even though youth should be reminded about confidentiality and respect, survivors must be protected from revealing information that may become the source of gossip or ridicule after the sessions are over. Meyer and Stein also recommend that presenters inform youth about professional obligations to report child abuse or threats of violence, and to have a plan and resources in place to respond to disclosures of child abuse or dating violence.

Because disclosures or potential disclosures of victimization are important issues for many prevention programs, we asked the professionals how they help youth decide what experiences to share during prevention programs and how they handle confidentiality issues. Although we originally viewed disclosures in a group setting as an "unintended consequence," this was clearly not the view of many interviewees. Locating victims and being able to connect them with services is a formal or informal goal of many of these programs and not an unintended consequence. However, inviting and responding to disclosures in a sensitive and ethical manner requires forethought and planning.

Why Adolescents Disclose to Prevention Educators

The receiving and handling of disclosures is important, because adolescents often have difficulty trusting others, especially adults, with personal vulnerabilities and information about victimization. Several of those we spoke with who do prevention programs with both elementary school students and adolescents mentioned that adolescents are much more guarded about what they reveal than the younger children are. Our interviewees noted that adolescents often viewed them as the first adults who were willing and able to hear about sexual assault and dating violence victimization:

They [the students] don't have anyone in the schools they can say anything to without triggering some type of parental notification or something. It amazes me how often I do presentations in the classroom where people will disclose that they are survivors of sexual assault. And I think, I think probably, rarely before the interaction of our program, have they had the opportunity to talk about it.

I've been at performances where on several occasions somebody said, "I was a victim of rape and this is the first time I have ever said that to anybody, and I never would have [said anything] except that by seeing this play it makes me feel that I am not so alone."

One of the really good things about my program is that I am at the schools one day a week and I think for students who are looking, who are part of the intervention programs, there is one student who just recently disclosed to me that her father sexually assaulted her when she was 12, but she has known me for two years . . . So, I think having that consistency with all the students and for them to recognize my face and know who I am and know what I do. I think can be really beneficial. So I think that is one of the wonderful things and that there aren't the same barriers of travel and aren't the same barriers of the economic part of it. I go to them and it is free for them.

They [the students] knew that [they were being abused], but they didn't know who to tell . . . I mean, we heard some really pretty awful stuff that these kids are disclosing about what's going on. Like they thought that they deserved it or it was not against the law or something like that.

Aspects of Confidentiality

Two types of confidentiality policies must be considered: whether peers in a group will maintain the confidentiality of disclosures or discuss the victimization with their friends; and whether prevention educators will maintain confidentiality about all the disclosures they receive, because sometimes they must reveal disclosures to school authorities or to parents. However, mandated reporting was the main concern of those we surveyed. Half the interviewees discussed this topic, and most mentioned that they inform their audiences at the start of a presentation that they are mandated to report abuse that is disclosed to them. Others mention mandated reporting only when someone seems about to disclose. One interviewee related that presenters from her program begin with a statement about mandated reporting, but then they remind adolescents about it again if someone seems about reveal a personal story:

> The other thing we say is, "If you tell us something that's about being abused, neglected and those types of things. And we can't keep it a secret, like that kind of stuff, we would have to tell someone." So, the kids know up front where we're coming from.

Warning adolescents in advance about mandated reporting usually alleviates the possibility of adolescents feeling betrayed if the educators are required to make a report:

> I don't really have a problem with people disclosing too much information—information that they didn't want to [reveal] and they are surprised that something has to be done about it. They seem to have that understanding of where that line is. So that the times that I have had students come up and tell me that they themselves are a survivor, that something has happened to them recently, they know and understand that by doing that I'm going to have to take some steps because of that. I can't just turn my eyes from that and pretend like I don't have an obligation to try to help them.

Some interviewees view mandated reporting as an effective tool in achieving their program's goal of stopping sexual assaults or dating violence:

> When we do our presentations we tell them this [report] is gonna happen. So when they already sort of know then when they disclose, and most of the time they want it, they want it to stop and they never, they didn't feel as though they had anybody that they could talk to or they weren't at a place where they recognized this as being abusive behavior . . . we had this happen on a fairly regular basis and, and have had very successful prosecutions as a result of it too. I mean that's not the intent, but . . . to me any day you shut down a child molester, that's a good day . . . We had two, two in one day in court a couple of weeks ago. That was a great day in court.

State laws vary, however, and so those we interviewed had different mandates related to their professional positions. In some states, mandated reporting extends to dating violence, whereas in others it only covers familial abuse:

Part of the reason why our program is taught by attorneys—it's not just because of the legal content, it's also because attorneys can offer the young people attorney-client confidentiality. . . . So, we have a lot of young people who approach us and say, "I've never talked to anybody about this before, but you said that whole confidentiality thing. Can you elaborate on that?" And they will confide in us because they're relying on that confidentiality . . . But they understand that if they tell their teacher or their counselor that they are being abused, that person has to report it. So what they do is, they don't tell. They choose not to tell. While they are still children under the law, they're mature enough to make a conscious choice not to reach out for help. And what could be more dangerous than someone who is experiencing this [and] not reaching out for help? I think if they are in a dating violence relationship, their parents aren't always going to be supportive, or you know it just might not be safe for them to disclose some stuff. I mean for more reasons than just that. I think that is one of the good things about our program is that, because we are a separate entity, because we are not affiliated with the school, we are there but we're a separate agency, it works well for students to be able to come and get services and not have to get their parents involved.

Kids don't have anybody to turn to, really, if they want to disclose. If the teacher was doing the training, they're not a safe person to disclose to. So, we always emphasize that although we are mandated reporters, we're separate from the school system . . . with dating violence, date rape we would never report that, unless somebody was under twelve. You know, because it's up to them to decide whether or not they want to do that.

Prevention presenters often do not know the names of the youths who are attending, and indeed some may prefer that the teens remain anonymous so they do not have to make mandated reports. In some cases, schools want to be responsible for making the reports:

I couldn't even make a PS [protective service] report because I didn't have any information and they wouldn't let me use the child's name. Part of the problem for us is that we almost lost our total [access], and the school wrote back saying, "If a child discloses, then you have to have a staff person present." And so we most commonly do that. We most commonly will say, "Is there someone [from the school who can be present]?" Now, if they said, "no, absolutely not," we wouldn't shut them up, we'd just take it. We would take it however it went. But most of the time, a child's most comfortable having a teacher or somebody there they know. And then we both make hotline calls. The school makes it and we make it.

A few interviewees mentioned that mandated reporting prevents some adolescents from getting help, those who do not want protective service authorities inquiring into their lives:

> What I'm worried about is they've even got their own idea [about mandated reporting]. Like they're keeping things from me that aren't even reportable, you know, because they happened in the past or they don't rise to the level and stuff. So, I'm really concerned that kids are walking around in these bubbles of secrecy that nobody is popping because we're all mandated. So, they can't confide in anyone, which just seems to make it easier for perpetrators in my mind.

Peer Confidentiality

Forty percent of the prevention professionals we interviewed stressed the importance of peer confidentiality, which means that adolescents who hear a disclosure must not discuss it with friends who did not hear it. If peers gossip or bully a survivor after a disclosure, the victim is potentially re-victimized. Several of the interviewees said that they ask youths not to mention names if they tell stories about someone they know who was victimized. Some interviewees also pointed out, however, that, when adolescents tell stories about the victimization of friends or relatives, especially in small communities, everyone knows whom they are talking about:

> Generally, if somebody does bring that up, I will say to the class, "That takes a lot of guts for somebody to share their experiences and say something about their own relationship." I will ask that everybody be respectful of that and that, "It is probably not something that you need to be talking about in the halls or in the cafeteria."

> I don't think we talk about confidentiality in the class, because I don't think we can promise it. There is no way, if somebody says, "I was raped" that somebody in that room is not going to tell someone. Kids are kids and if something is disclosed to them, are they really going to keep it confidential with their friends and stuff like that? And I've told people at the beginning too, but I say it at the beginning, "You know, people aren't always nice to each other. Just be aware of that." And when we talk about

confidentiality, I say, "we are making this agreement not to talk about it in the hallway but no one is going to be held to that. I'm not going to do it. But protect yourself and do what you have to do." I've had people who have come to me and say, "Well I want to tell the group this," or "I want to do that." And I usually say, "No, it is completely your decision, but let me just tell you. I'm not going to be here next week and you are and kids are not always nice to each other. And it depends on how you feel about it."

Another facet of peer confidentiality is the potential benefit that disclosure to friends can bring to survivors. One interviewee noted how her program encourages this:

> We always encourage them that for their own protection and safety that they can talk to their friends about it 'cause they need their peer support. And . . . and we've also had several cases where kids have disclosed to their friends that they've been being victimized, and then their friends will go to teachers and the guidance department and say, "you really need to talk to this kid." And they'll haul them in and then, or they'll have us come in and, and then the kid will spill their guts and, and then we go from there.

Preventing Public Disclosures

Nearly half the prevention professionals who responded raised the question of whether they stop adolescents from disclosing victimization to peers during presentations. Most seemed to try to stop adolescents from revealing details about victimization to a group because of the survivor's potential vulnerability to gossip or bullying. Adolescents might be eager to disclose during a presentation and then regret having broadcast such personal information. One interviewee used the term "protective interrupting," which is defined on an Internet site originating in Australia:

> Protective interrupting was originally developed to stop someone from disclosing in a situation that would increase his or her victimization. When a facilitator recognizes the signs of disclosures, for example, the participant may be looking uncomfortable, leaning forward, and comments like, "That happened . . ." / "Last night . . ." / "Sometimes my . . ." they interrupt the statement immediately. It also involves follow-up, for example, by suggesting an alternative time to discuss the issue about to be disclosed. (http://www.ruralhealth.utas.edu.au/padv-package/guidelines.html)

The following are examples of how presenters phrase an interruption in a supportive way. Commonly many thank the adolescent for sharing and avoid probing or encouraging the youth to expand on his or her personal victimization:

What I will do is try to balance, "I'm glad you told me," and maybe something like "I know this was really hard" and possibly reinforce the lessons that we talked about before. Then saying, "I really want to talk about that with you later." Then either me and/or the counselor talking one-on-one with the student afterwards. I try not to shut it down, because obviously, we want them to tell, but I also give them the privacy that they need so that they don't regret sharing that in front of all of their classmates.

If someone discloses something we say, "Thank you so much for sharing that; that's really great," and that's it; and we do talk to them after. I don't do like, "What do other people think about that situation with their mother and father?" We don't process that. We will process stories that I tell as a group, but we don't process a story [from a student] like that as a group.

I have said, "Can I stop you there?" And we don't entertain them to start talking because this is not a support group, but what we say is "I would be interested in hearing more about that if you would [see me] at break or after we are finished. We need to talk more about that. But when we get through the presentation we certainly want to entertain, hear what you have to say." Because they could go on and on forever about that. And we want to help them, steer them in the right direction, rather than have them go on and on even if it is vital material and kids aren't comfortable around "oh geez, they're going to be talking about that." So, we do acknowledge it and keep moving. We don't just keep talking, "oh, well, that's really serious, well anyway." We acknowledge them. We let them know it is a very serious thing that has occurred, and we don't at all delve into what has happened in that family right then and there.

I try not to stay on that student's personal experience long, but stay on it long enough to respect them and let them know that it was all right to share it because if they feel comfortable sharing it in front of their peers, then that's their choice, but I don't ever dig further in.

Some interviewees talked about "redirecting" rather than stopping or interrupting. However, interrupting with respect can provide a useful model for the audience:

> I think almost any negative thing [disclosure] is a good thing, because the way we handle it, and the way the kids see that we can handle it, and, "we don't want to talk about it; there might be a better place." Or, "we need to be respectful," which again reinforces that we all have to be respectful of each other, regardless of what we might think or what might be going on. So we try to use those opportunities. We try to be very positive about everything.

Some programs are so brief and have so much material to cover that personal disclosures would prevent them from presenting essential material:

> We don't always have time where there is time for questions and answers, depending on interaction through the rest of it. Sometimes it is more that we are in and presenting, and they are involved in and out of it during the presentation, but that there isn't a lot of extra time where disclosure would happen.

Another reason for stopping or cutting disclosures short is to protect other youths from hearing these upsetting stories:

> It depends on the circumstances and we don't discourage [disclosure], but we do discourage spending a lot of time on details. We discourage sharing a lot of information because we don't want to traumatize or trigger others. We always go into presentations in groups knowing that . . . there's going to be at least one survivor in the group. We are sensitive to that in the beginning. It can be helpful, too. Sometimes someone has disclosed and that's actually been kind of a helpful thing. But we always want to make sure that it doesn't turn into everyone asking the survivor questions and having her be in the spotlight.

It is not always possible to interrupt a disclosure:

> So there's not any way of me preventing [disclosure] from happening. I always make it a point to check in with them after the class and talk about what that was like for them, what talking about it was like for them, and I always try to observe the classroom while I'm doing the

presentations to look for the students that are withdrawn or who look like the presentation might be troubling for them. To do some intervention at the end.

Supporting Adolescents' Choices About Disclosing to a Group

A fourth of the experts we spoke with described how they try to support and empower adolescents who choose to reveal personal victimization in a group. This can include praising them for their courage in coming forward. Some may offer this support but still try to prevent the discloser from revealing too much. Others believe it is important for adolescents to make their own choices about how much to tell the group. Still others point out that personal disclosures make the topic seem more realistic and meaningful, because other adolescents see that these types of abuse or assault happen to real people in their own communities:

> If they are telling a story about themselves that is really bad that happened . . . It really isn't the time or place, but I am not going to cut the kid off and say this isn't the time or place, 'cause this is, if they felt the need to share it at that time, then they did that for a reason. But I will always thank the child for sharing that [saying], "that was very courageous to do" and move on from there and maybe later [say], "Okay, we are not going to share any more stories here today" kind of thing.

> I have had a couple of students that have actually shared personal experience in class and they did pretty okay by handling it. I think the most important thing is acknowledging how hard it is to admit something like that. And then we will help connect them with counseling if they want that. Or talk through with them about . . . give them handouts about how to identify abusive behavior in yourself or someone else. And really try to be as positive at reinforcing the step of coming forward.

> I think if it gets too personal . . . usually our experience is that the kids will share a piece of the story and that can be a helpful tool to then make it personal to the kids and it is not just us coming in and talking about dating violence in theory but that somebody real in their class has had an experience with that. I think when we try and stop it, is when it really started to turn more into a full disclosure for the student versus them sharing something that they think might help their classmates understand the issue better.

Rewarding, Troubling, and Challenging Aspects

One can view disclosure as an important aspect of group discussion that engages youth and makes the discussion more realistic and meaningful. Some believe that an appropriate public discussion about sexual assault or dating violence victimization experiences can dispel isolation, secrecy, and the none-of-my-business attitude that often pervades youth culture (MEE Productions, Inc. 1996; Weisz and Black 2008):

> A lot of times they'll say, you know, "Yeah, I have a sister that went through that," and they'll say, "Really?" So, you know, "What was that like?" you know, "How are things going?" We go through ground rules with the audience so that everything that's said during the workshop should be confidential, try not to use names, it's good to share your experiences, but don't single people out where they can be identified . . . But we encourage participation; we encourage people to share their experiences, and then a lot of times if one person says, "Yeah, you know, I know a friend whose boyfriend was abusive to her. He was controlling." And then other audience members, you know, say, "Yeah, me too. I know someone who's like that." You know, even if they might be talking about themselves, it kind of encourages that participation.

Some of the interviewees believed that adolescents who share personal experiences are able to handle it well. One described an example of a surprisingly personal disclosure from a young girl:

> One time a girl blurted out how she had been raped by an older person and actually had a baby, had to give the baby up for adoption. And so she just like threw it out there like it was no big deal and everything. . . . See, we don't know these kids. And maybe this is known by everybody, and she's comfortable saying it.

Other Aspects of Disclosures

Peer-education programs present special challenges in handling disclosures, and our interviewees differ about whether or how peer educators should handle such disclosures:

> There is sometimes a situation where a kid in the classroom starts to reveal something, and I work with my [peer education team] members on what to do if something like that happens, and I am always with them in a presentation, so if ever there is anything that comes up that

they can't handle, I am always there. Usually when a kid starts [disclosing] that we stop them and tell them that if they want to come talk to us after class, but please let's focus on the question that we asked, or, "if you have personal stories that you want to share with us, then come see us afterwards, but let's not do that during class time." If somebody were to disclose during a classroom session, then I will talk with the teacher and guidance counselor, because they are also mandated reporters, so we will have to do something about it.

We try in our training to talk to the peer educators to talk about what to do if that [disclosure] happens. One of the things they say at the beginning of their presentation is, "these are difficult topics for people to talk about and to hear about, if you feel uncomfortable at any time for any reason, feel free to leave the room or let someone know," because they try to set it up at the start that it may be hard for somebody to hear. So then we try . . . if we do have somebody respond that way or leave, we have our staff member go out and check on them and make sure they are okay.

During presentations, it was common for youths to talk at times about their exposure to domestic violence in their families. Some interviewees also mentioned that adolescents sometimes trusted them enough to discuss other types of problems with them as well:

So they will tell us things that have, you know, sometimes they will tell us things that have absolutely nothing to do with dating violence just because I think they think they can trust us and that we'll listen. And so we hear a lot of things that are completely non-related to what we've talked about. Just because there's nobody else, they feel they can tell like us.

One interviewee made the important point that, when adolescents do disclose their experiences or an event that happened in the community, educators should avoid acting shocked or reacting emotionally to the violence. An emotional reaction, she continued, might lead adolescents to think that the educator did not want to hear or could not tolerate hearing what had happened.

Post-presentation Contacts

Roden (1998) describes a prevention program that includes a crisis-intervention period. Presenters are available "at specified times in a location on campus that ensures privacy. Students are advised of these times and locations during the classroom sessions" (270). Roden believes that this intervention period is a critical part of a program, because students may have repressed feelings about some past victimization or may not have identified an event as victimization until participating in the program. The knowledge that prevention educators are available to students helps "alleviate school personnel's anxiety about being left to handle student disclosure crises after the prevention specialists have left the school" (271).

Most presenters who believe in stopping public disclosures have developed other ways for victims (and occasionally perpetrators) to contact them. Two-thirds of those we interviewed arranged private time for youths to ask questions or disclose their concerns about being a victim or a perpetrator. Many of the programs, at the start of a presentation, announce the times and places for adolescents to see representatives privately after the presentation:

> Usually [we say] "We really don't want your personal experience like that. You know, save it and we'll talk to you afterwards." One of the things that I'm trying to do, and sometimes if my educators have time, is they hang around during lunch. They'll go down to the lunchroom or something. Or they'll say, "I'm going to be here after school for half an hour and I'm coming early tomorrow and I'll be in the guidance office." That is really important, because more and more the kids are coming up and disclosing stuff and needing, you know, some kinds of referrals and immediate counseling for whatever their issues are. So, we try to extend our community ed. by being available sometime during that week, for kids who want to talk one-on-one.

Other prevention educators simply allow youth to approach them as a presentation nears completion. A few arrange for all adolescents to submit written questions, and then they follow up with youths who disclose victimization in that way. A program representative may make follow-up calls to those who have provided private contact information. Other prevention educators proactively approach youth who appear to be upset or anxious during a presentation and talk with them privately to see if they are being victimized:

> At the end of the presentation, I'll ask them if they have any questions. And I'll say, "No stories. Just questions. If you have stories for me, I'm here." Like in one school, I'm there on Monday and Tuesday. The other school, I'm there Thursday and Friday. So, I say, "You can find me in the counselor's office on Monday or Tuesday,"

We say it is confidential within the room, and they always get the option to stay after if they want to talk, and that does happen. I was in a school somewhere and there were six girls lined up to talk to me after the presentation. One of them was suicidal.

But we also make the effort that, if by chance, something is happening, we'll schedule a couple days just to come in and do question time and follow-up. Just if it is a comment or they are asking me a question, and I try to respond to whatever the comment is or they are asking me a question specifically about their relationship, I try not to, in the middle of a presentation, give advice without knowing what is going on. So I will tell them they can talk to me after class, I will tell them I have some ideas or a few things that I want to share with them.

One interviewee pointed out that many adolescents will only disclose privately. Another noted that sometimes youths are embarrassed to ask questions in front of a group but may feel more comfortable doing so in a private talk with the presenter. She also said that older adolescents usually need fewer opportunities to ask questions compared to younger children:

When we do a fourth or fifth grade, if we have 30 kids, they'll all come to question time. They absolutely will. We are totally busy. In the middle schools, the girls will come down. The boys, you stop seeing [as they get older]; less and less boys come down.

And then, with high school, unless something is going on, you know, if there was an assault that happened in the school, or if there's something going on that a group of girls might want to come down and talk about . . . It really varies, but generally speaking, we're not really overrun with a lot of question time unless there's been an incident because I think usually kids have a lot of resources by that time and they feel comfortable . . . They might have a teacher or guidance counselor.

Another method for assisting victims to find help is to leave literature that has contact information for reaching the presenters, their agency, or the agency's confidential hotline. Handouts may include, for example, business cards, pamphlets, and ballpoint pens with phone numbers printed on them. The advantages of handouts with phone numbers are that youths can contact the agency for help without being observed, and they can keep the phone number until they are ready to make the call:

We'll stay right in the classroom if we can. Sometimes students don't want to be that conspicuous, so we'll arrange [another meeting place]. Someone might come up and say they'd like to meet somewhere else. We try to hang around between classes and after classes where possible. We also hand out our business cards to every student in the class. In addition to having our contact information, it has a list of warning signs of abuse on it, as sort of a continuing reminder. We've had a lot of people contact us six months or a year later saying, "You came to my classroom six months or a year ago and I held onto your business card."

Connecting Survivors with Resources

Whether adolescents disclose in the group setting or privately, prevention educators usually have plans to connect them with further help. We did not ask a specific question about these plans, but a fourth of those we interviewed volunteered the information:

The problem is, they don't reach out for help very readily. There's a window at that moment after class, and if you are dismissive of them or you hand them a phone number without getting engaged with them, the chances of them ever calling anyone are slim.

It's about helping to connect young people to help. And once they've reached out to us, we talk to them about, "Okay, who in your life needs to know about this? We'll help you explain it in a way that is comfortable to you, that is effective in getting you the results that you need." We won't go ahead and talk to one of our client's parents without their permission.

We do follow-up with all the kids and we refer anything that we have concerns about, whether we think they're small or large. We don't know the kids that well. We'll refer them . . . we usually have a contact person at the school that will take any of the referrals or concerns that we have.

Survivors Who Do Not Disclose

Even though some victims do not approach presenters for help, they may find the presentation upsetting. A fifth of respondents to our survey warn the audience in advance that the presentation might be upsetting. Several will tell youths at the outset that they are free to leave the room if they become upset. Others tell youths that there is no requirement to participate in discussions. Most indicated that if an individual appears upset or leave the room during a presentation, they will follow up and offer help, or arrange for a school counselor to follow up with the youth.

Summary of Rewarding, Troubling, and Challenging Aspects

The potential presence of dating violence and sexual assault survivors in prevention program audiences presents the most rewards but also the greatest challenges for educators. Those we interviewed said that their greatest satisfaction comes from being the first to learn of the victimization and being able to connect survivors with much-needed help. Others spoke of the rewards of raising awareness or getting information to the victimized friends or family of audience members. These practitioners also valued the opportunity to work with volunteers, peer educators, and lively young people in general. A few mentioned the reward of reaching men who had been abusive in relationships and wanted to change those relationships.

The interviews revealed differences in the ways that prevention educators handle the disclosures that survivors make. Some respondents emphasized the wish to empower youth, respect adolescents' judgment, and avoid exercising power and control over them. Others were acutely aware of the need to protect young survivors from further victimization that could result from public disclosures. The authors are concerned that allowing public disclosure of victimization could be harmful to adolescents, who might be carried away by the excitement of finally meeting adults who are willing to discuss dating violence and sexual assault. It might be unethical to encourage such disclosures without a strong plan to protect and support survivors. We believe that prevention educators need thorough training in the handling of disclosures. We favor the idea of "protective interrupting" of public disclosures, while encouraging adolescents to seek the prevention educators' help privately. Prevention programs and the communities in which they operate should strongly commit to follow-up for a sufficient period after a disclosure. We encourage educators who do allow public disclosures to be well prepared to respond in ways that protect survivors.

Some prevention educators find it emotionally difficult to hear so many stories of victimization and realize how widespread it is. We encourage prevention educators to learn more about vicarious traumatization and compassion fatigue, including self-care. Those we interviewed discussed other major challenges they faced, such as audiences or communities that seemed closed to new ideas.

16

Wish Lists, Strengths, and Trends

Our interviews demonstrated the existence of a vibrant community of dating violence and sexual assault prevention educators in the United States. This chapter discusses the prevention educators' expressed needs for their programs and their views about the next steps they see for them. We then summarize what we learned about the strengths, challenges, and trends in the field, and discuss our own "wish list" of future developments.

Wish Lists

Increased funding, as one might expect, was the primary wish of many program staff members. When those we contacted discussed other needs, such as a larger staff or more curricular materials, money was usually needed to meet those needs.

Financial Support or Funding

Two-thirds of the programs represented by our interviewees needed more money. Some programs were struggling to stay open, and others had to operate with inadequate funding for materials:

> Funding. I'm sure that's the first thing for everybody. Definitely funding . . . It has been, it is very, very difficult to even find the funding to support and to staff my position, and it's not even funded at 100%, as far as parts of my full-time position are paid for from other sources, really for me to do other types of roles.

Well, prevention is the first area to be cut. . . . We did forced ranking of our programs internally and my program was eighteenth or nineteenth with the staff. Because they couldn't put victim services below prevention. I think there are endless opportunities for us to do prevention. There are schools that are begging us to do peer-ed. programs.

If we had like an unlimited budget, and unlimited amount of money and [could] get it whenever you want, it would be great. Like videotapes. . . . Like pens or things we can put our numbers on, that aren't so easy to throw away. We had pens at one point. They were great. The kids loved them and they hold onto them for a while. And some things like that. Or even curriculum material is good, too. Because when a good curriculum comes out and you've seen it, it's, "Oh wow!" You know. And videotapes would be awesome and supplies really. We like supplies for the kids because you're dealing with—a lot of times the kids I see don't have any school supplies.

[Our state] suffered some cuts this year and you know, for us what we've tried to do is to compensate with some volunteers and some interns to help make up the difference, but we've lost the equivalent of one full-time staff person and one part-time staff person. And any time you lose a full-time staff person, that is a lot, when you are covering the territory that we do. We have three counties that we cover and, while we have a medium-sized city, that contains our biggest school district that we're contracted with, we also have a lot of rural area around us which means a lot of traveling time. So, we have some real limits on what we can do . . . Given our staff limitations, and the amount of territory and schools, we do a pretty phenomenal job. It is just amazing to me when I sit down and look at it.

We just need more funds and then on top of the more funds, for staff, money for incentives, because middle and high school kids love incentives. You know, the whistles on the little bracelets and you know . . . And food, they love food. Families love food. So if you're really going to get these families in there, you've got to have money for food, and so those are real things that help you to get your message out.

We've got the know-how and we've got the desire and we've got a ready community. That's really, we don't have the money to fund educators to actually do the work. If we had more money, we could do a lot more.

We need a raise. We did a school last week where the kids wrote on the evaluation that we needed a raise, so we gave it to our executive director. That felt pretty good.

In many programs, money issues were clearly related to staffing issues:

And then getting good people to do the work and to stick around . . . and we don't have a lot of room for advancement or adequate compensation. There just tends to be turnover in the work that we do.

More Staff Members or Different Responsibilities

Almost as many programs need more staff or staff time as need money. Nearly two-thirds of the interviewees brought up the need for more adult staff or more peer educators. In some cases, programs seeking more peer educators also needed more adult staff to work with them:

Our biggest thing is we just need to have more staff, which means we need more money and better salaries to attract the people who are going to stay. Because that's the other big problem in this work is that I [as the one who does the hiring] tend to attract younger people just out of college and this is their first stepping stone in their career. And I understand that, but you don't really feel comfortable with the material, and you don't get to a point where you can say, "Oh, I get this. And now let me see what I can do." When you get to that point, that's when they leave. That's the end of your second year of doing community ed., that you get to that point where you can start doing something new and creative. And that's when they are ready to leave because they want more money.

I need more staff . . . Everybody says "money," and I am one of those people that says the problem isn't always the money or lack of money. Sometimes we aren't using our money well and sometimes we need to think more creatively and work with other agencies more. I think it is easy to say "money." It is harder to say what you would spend the money on, but my major challenge is I need support staff, and there is not a grant out there that will pay for support staff. My salary itself is a challenge to fill because I don't do 100% direct work with clients, because I am managing people and also trying to be collaborating in the community and attend, at the bigger level, the major commission meetings and that kind of thing, and programs don't want to fund that kind of work, but we have to do that in order to have the system coordination.

I think it would be really great if we could have, say, another coordinator just so we can—it would just be easier to maybe attend—well, not even attend more workshops, because I think it's really good that they [peer educators] go on their own after a while. But just for development and—because it really does take up a lot of time, coordinating the teens and a lot of the teens, they have problems also, you know, just other teen problems. And so it's kind of hard to balance some of the issues that they may be going through and then also the job itself. And so I think that's a big challenge and so I think it would be helpful to have maybe two coordinators. And it would be great if we could have a male and female coordinator.

It is tough to get males working, especially being not an extremely high-paying type of job.

Working in rural areas can present special challenges when there are few staff members:

We need another staff member. The problem is now because [colleague] and I are both based in [a small city] and we're serving four counties. There are some schools that are an hour and a half from here. So the problem is that we're so, time is such an issue anyway, that, say that if we do one of those high schools, that's the only thing we can do that whole day.

One program has an innovative Web site but has difficulty providing adequate staffing for it:

I would love to have one staff person who is completely devoted to the website, because I think it could position itself in a larger way than it has so far. Especially because it is the only website that has 24/7 advocacy, so people can post anonymously and be responded [to] by an advocate who will research in their area how to hook them up and provide support and information. We are the only website out there for kids that does that.

Several of the interviewees said that they wanted to change the description of their own jobs or those of other prevention educators in their agencies. They wanted more opportunities to work on system-level change, advocacy for social change, or program administration:

> My only job should be like program development and never actually running anything. Because when you actually have to develop and run, you know what happens is, you're just doing the programs. You're never fixing them or developing anything new.

Material Resources

Twenty percent of those we interviewed mentioned a need for material resources, such as prizes, and videos:

> Some of the videos that we show, the content is still really good, but you really have to close your eyes, because they don't look like kids today . . . We always give our little disclaimer before, and it doesn't matter if the video is only four years old, it will still seem a little bit different to them. So I think that just having updated and current videos, books and pamphlets and that kind of thing.

> Lots of stuff that we need, the posters and these give-aways and things that we get. So that we can distribute those kind of things. Give-aways that we are thinking of giving to the kids in the schools. Things like pencils, with our name on them. And the crisis line so people know where to call and we are trying to get the word out everywhere. And the kids that go home and say "There was this lady that came out from this place" . . . they put a pencil down or they have something from us, and mom may be being abused, for example. And they will say "oh" if they have that number around at home, it is just another way we try to reach out. All those things cost money.

Collaboration with Other Agencies

Twenty percent of the educators mentioned a desire to improve or increase their collaboration with other agencies:

> If we really want to do the work of community development, we have to establish relationships; we have to kind of hang in there with some projects. Things are not going to be of a short turn-around time. And it takes a while for communities or schools or whatnot to be ready to kind of look at social change.

Recognition of the Need for This Work

Nearly twenty percent of the interviewees talked about a wish to see increased recognition of the importance of dating violence and sexual assault prevention work and "for prevention to become more mainstream":

> The other thing that I believe our prevention program needs is visibility . . . And as far as the laws are concerned, that the legislature really starts pushing for more prevention but not excluding our agencies. And not putting it, "Okay, put it in the curriculum and leave it to the teachers."

Evaluation of Practice

Fifteen percent of the prevention educators mentioned that they would like to improve the evaluations of their programs. Clearly resources needed for evaluation relate to funding issues:

> I could probably utilize someone who is just responsible for the evaluation piece. Obviously, the facilitators implement . . . They administer the surveys, but as far as collecting it, organizing it and inputting it and analyzing, it is very time-consuming.

> Well, it has to be formally developed in terms of the whole foundation of it with the research and the whole program capacity. Being able to track things and count things and get current feedback, and information and things. Really, we don't get feedback at this point. Very little. So that has to, in order for us to survive, we have to make that happen. Really by this summer is our feeling. We've got to develop that quickly and then implement it at this summer's conference so we can start to track some things. Because we really have missed a huge opportunity. National networks send over huge grants [Requests for Proposals] and "Hey, are you all ready for this?" We don't even have the basic numbers to apply. So, it has been frustrating.

Education or Training for Staff

Fourteen percent of the prevention educators want to increase opportunities for staff education and training. This often requires money to attend conferences or purchase materials:

Not feeling like we always have to reinvent the wheel and that we know what resources are out there, that they're affordable or retainable so that there's more of a collaborative going on, so that we're not always starting from scratch.

Volunteers

More than 10 percent of the interviewees want to expand the number of volunteers that work with their prevention program:

Community support we always need and volunteers. Volunteers we really struggle with . . . The volunteers typically will come on board for about a year, as with any agency I think . . . We understand that we want to have a regeneration, so to speak, of people to either return to volunteer or do an outreach to, more preferably to outreach [to] the people who may have an interest in getting involved, or trying to energize people to get involved and we hope to do that through partnering with different community programs.

And really just being able to, realistically being able to, pull in more trained volunteers, because that is really what we rely on a great deal. Trained volunteers to come help us out in the schools and with our programs.

Access to, and Collaboration with, Schools

A third of the people we surveyed wanted to increase their access to schools or improve their collaboration with them. One prevention educator expressed a wish to "have those type of interagency agreements or collateral agreements with the schools to have a more structured and consistent delivery of the programs. Just to have that stronger partnership."

Most programs needed more money, but one program that had enough money needed more access to schools so that their well-funded program could reach more adolescents. Apparently some prevention educators would appreciate more ideas about how to increase this access:

There are still schools in our area that we hardly do anything in and that is a challenge. What else can I do to convince them that this is needed?

We wish we could be a part of every health class, be a more institutionalized part of the curriculum, and that's something that we felt like if we could reach every seventh grader in their health class, every tenth or eleventh, whatever year they take health in high school, that we'd be able to have much more impact, and they could be more aware of our services and all of those things.

Interviewees' comments about wanting to increase collaboration are related to expanding existing programs, a topic discussed in detail in the next section.

Next Steps for Programs

Almost all the program representatives had ideas about how they wanted to proceed. Two-thirds of those we spoke with wanted to expand existing programs, and about 10 percent preferred keeping things as they are. Half the prevention educators wanted to create a new program within their agency or reach new communities, and a third wished to expand an existing program. By expanding existing programs, the interviewees meant adding more topics to presentations, as well as increasing the number of presentations to reach more groups of adolescents:

> Where I want to go next: a parent advisory group is very important to me, from the community at large, as well as a youth group. Having special community events in our new facility, really being able to have lock-ins for kids, to really work with them in understanding all these issues more in depth, in kind of a fun way, in our own environment. That's really exciting to me . . . We would be partnering with other people in the community to really come in and talk to them. Again, here is our healthy relationships again. And gender issues, and all the things that we really want to talk about . . . in an interactive kind of way, with games and music and art and all kinds of things like that. So, we think we can really do this in a very fun environment that helps them to internalize these messages better than just going into the schools.

> The kids want more sexuality education and want more just informal discussion groups. Not support groups but just kind of psycho-educational, a girls' group and a boys' group, or a LGBT [Lesbian, Gay, Bisexual, Transgender] group, or whatever.

> We have started collecting information and research about Internet safety to try and develop some programming with regards to that. I was at

a meeting with some police officers, and they asked if we had any programming, and I told them no. But just developing more programming, working more on our evaluation stuff.

I think I would like to continue building a stronger relationship with the school system and get to a point where I have the ability to do multi-session programs where we go in for maybe three days, as opposed to just one day, and go into more detail or allow time for more interaction and activities. I would like to get to a point where there is some sort of collateral agreement between us and the schools that says, "Yes, every ninth grade health class is going to have this information."

I would like to be able to have more time in the schools; I would like to be able to go back to the classroom, at least four times, on a quarterly basis about the school year. And I would like to be able to bring more programs into them.

I just want to include more out-rightly prevention-based material, because they make such a huge distinction between that and risk reduction and that seems just to be where all the funding is, in the changing of belief systems.

Keep Things the Same

Some programs that do not want to make any changes may be far from stagnating. One coordinator spoke of keeping the program the same for the time being, because it had recently experienced a growth spurt:

Right now I am feeling in maintenance mode. I am really not expanding anything to it. It was just two years ago that we added all of the community parts. In a lot of ways, I had done a lot of that community stuff before, but it is a lot more formalized and evaluated now, whereas before it wasn't. So I feel like over the past two years we have grown to the point where it is barely manageable as it is.

Until the schools have more time, it's like silly to develop any more specialized programs because they don't have the time to have us come in to do them.

Ideas for New Programs

The most common new direction, mentioned by about 20% of those we spoke with, was to add a peer leadership or educational component:

> I think the peer education piece and the mentoring piece is a big piece for me, to have schools more involved in those sorts of things.

> We would like to start the student support group. We'd also like to start a teen panel, you know, of students, just to help.

> A peer theater. I would really love to see that. . . . and a strong peer theater, so that if they're looking for something, and to me that's a good . . . you could have the whole school in like the auditorium or something, you know, and do it or something. And they get the message. Then have something afterwards, something more visual. And that the school systems be more accepting to the material.

> I'd like to see them [peer advisory board] doing more with peer education presentation stuff. Like I said, you know, finding ways to be a more regular part of their schools, their classes, that kind of thing.

Fifteen percent of our participants wanted to expand their program to reach more adults in general and more teachers or parents in particular. Ten percent of the interviewees talked about wanting to expand their programming for males. Several viewed this change as more clearly addressing primary prevention, with a focus on potential perpetrators rather than potential victims:

> I would like to see a really strengthened primary prevention program, which for me means a full-time, hired male trainer who can kind of . . . who can take leadership on running a boys-to-men campaign in tandem with the [other program].

> We're doing more of that redefinition of masculinity. I think that's very exciting work to awaken the silent majority of males who are being held hostage by this minority who are the abusers and the rapists. And so to do that redefinition work that women did 30 years ago; well, that's what guys are doing right now.

We would like to find a man, even part time, to work with our men, be-cause we feel like they need that type of attention and connection.

Three programs specifically mentioned wanting to add technology-based prevention components, such as developing CDs or Internet sites.

I would really like to do some distance learning kinds of things. I would really like to have something that's on the Internet. A little bit more interactive, that's not only, for example, a place where adults can go and maybe go through a curriculum and that kind of stuff. I mean we do have a website that just has handouts and things like that they can get. But also something that, for example, for students who are doing a speech about sexual assault and those kinds of things. That here's some ideas of how you could talk about it. Here might be some interesting ways to get the audience involved in the topic. So it's a little bit more interactive. And I think a lot more youth come to the Internet for infor-mation than, for example, them using the sexual assault resource line, even though we tell them you can call anonymously, you can call just for resources or ideas.

We are developing a technology-driven program that we can distribute much more widely; we have a proposal for an interactive CD so that we can reach many youth even in states where we don't have offices; it has choice points; it is a "blended learning" approach, using technol-ogy in the classroom, an interactive program meant to be presented by a teacher, who guides students in where to start, where to go next, etc.

Two educators we spoke with wanted to work toward having dating vio-lence and sexual assault materials integrated into school curricula:

I would love to see domestic violence prevention integrated comprehen-sively into the health curriculum throughout the state, in all the schools. Not just this one school, or those health teachers who are really passion-ate about the issue, but a really comprehensive, integrated piece.

My long-term goal is to get dating violence information integrated as a standard part of the health curriculum for ninth graders. All ninth grad-ers have to go through Health, and that would be my goal, to get dating violence stuff implemented in terms of like small groups.

Two other educators wanted to develop programs to reach particularly vulnerable adolescents, such as those in juvenile detention centers or with serious school problems:

> Since our focus is going to be so much with people coming out of incarceration or in incarceration or transitional housing, that is definitely the areas that I am going to be wanting to target.

> We would like to go in to the juvenile justice system, for sure. We are actually working on a grant. If we get the grant, then we are going in. There is a real need there. We would like to provide, we would like to have a legal component to our program. You know, young people, at least in [our state], can get restraining orders if they are 12 years old or older. So we would like to have a legal component that more fully and adequately addresses their legal rights. . . . We have the capability, we have lawyers.

Summary of What We Learned and Trends

It was a very rewarding experience for us to talk with so many energetic and thoughtful prevention practitioners. Despite the challenges they face in most of their communities, these professionals seem to be forging ahead with exciting, continuously developing programming ideas, and they continue to engage adolescents and their communities in discussions of topics too often avoided in our culture.

In reviewing our interviews, the major trends that strike us are the recognition that there is so much to do and the desire to do much more. Those who participated in our interviews want to be involved in primary prevention—reaching adolescents before dating violence and sexual assault occur—and also to respond effectively to youth who have already been victimized. To be effective in primary prevention, most programs must focus on changing knowledge and attitudes, because they do not have enough contact with teens to be able to work on skills. Some programs would like to direct their efforts to males as much as possible, because males are the primary aggressors in sexual assault and in severe dating violence. We learned that many practitioners find it important and rewarding to alert survivors to the availability of help and to connect them with these resources. We also learned that prevention educators need to be well prepared to respond to survivors who approach them for help, because they need a plan to respond to issues of confidentiality and (often) mandated reporting.

The controversy over the use of the word "prevention," and the reluctance of some to use the word, reinforced the need to continue to think about our own use of that term. We are cautious in our use of the term and acknowledge that only perpetrators can prevent acts of violence. We do not want to imply in any way that victims/survivors of violence could, in some way, prevent their victimization. It is essential to avoid practices that blame the victim, no matter how a program labels itself.

In examining the logistics of prevention programming, a few issues stand out. One is the dependence of most programs on schools as a venue for reaching the maximum number of adolescents. This dependence brings programs to a large number of teens but also confronts programs with educational controversies, such as content restrictions. Because standardized test scores are the top priority for most schools, another issue to consider is the widespread question of how much time should be devoted to improving the adjustment of youth. Prevention educators are keenly aware of time limitations and are often forced to present programs that are much briefer than they ideally should be.

Other important logistical issues relate to whether males and females should be addressed together or separately and how much prevention programs should focus on discussion, as opposed to the presentation of information. Among those we interviewed, no clear consensus was found on whether to combine or separate males and females. Although many saw value in having both girls and boys hearing from each other, they also recognized the importance of having participants feel safe in speaking, without the posturing that adolescents so often do in front of the opposite gender. If they had no time constraints, many would likely advocate for multiple sessions, where genders were sometimes separate and sometimes combined. We discuss our thoughts about this issue in our wish-list section, below.

Educators seemed to agree on the importance of allowing adolescents ample time for interaction and discussion. Most recognized the importance of hiring lively, engaging adult educators who enjoy adolescents, and they strongly endorsed programming that allows teens to discuss their views and to participate actively, rather than passively absorbing information. We concur with educators' general practice of basing programs on standardized curricula but modifying and adapting it to best meet the needs of each audience.

Although most programs endorse the importance of cultural sensitivity, many communities are too diverse to offer culturally specific programming. Many programs are careful to include gay and lesbian youth in their discussions and case examples, whereas some communities prohibit such discussions. The most common view of the educators we interviewed was that it is important to remind youth that anyone can become a victim of dating violence and sexual assault, regardless of gender, ethnicity, or sexual orientation.

Peer education and peer leadership seemed to be "cutting edge" components of many programs. It makes sense that adolescents can reach other adolescents successfully, and that teens can lend meaningful direction and leadership to programs designed to address their own communities, and to be sensitive to "adolescent culture." We also learned, however, that peer leadership is not a miracle solution, because ingenuity is often required to maintain a consistent group of peer leaders when potential adolescent leaders and educators are busy with school and many other competing activities.

Another essential goal, according to many prevention educators, is reaching the entire community, not just adolescents. These programs seek to change the beliefs and practices of communities, families, and schools, so that dating violence and sexual assault prevention are not just topics adolescents learn about for a few hours each year. Program developers and presenters strive to collaborate with one another to reach as many youth as possible and to continually reinforce the message in every possible setting. Involving parents in prevention programming is also critical. If the messages delivered during programs are not reinforced in the home and schools, educators fear that the programs will have little long-term impact. We learned that reaching busy parents and community leaders can be challenging, and some communities and families continue to maintain that such prevention programs are not needed within their social and educational systems.

It came as no surprise that most programs need additional funding. Access to money from government sources or foundations increasingly requires that program successes be thoroughly documented, and so many programs value evaluation. Despite the many challenges involved, often including the lack of time and expertise, most prevention educators conduct some form of program evaluation.

The Authors' Wish List for Sexual Assault and Dating Violence Programming for Youth

We remind our readers that we did not evaluate the programs we surveyed and, in our work, we do like to apply advanced critical thinking (Kasschau 1986), which, at its highest level, is "multiplistic, tentative, and contingent" (Kasschau 1986, 13). We therefore keep in mind that many of the unresolved controversies in the field may be viewed in different ways. Often the controversies continue for good reason. We respect the multiple views of our interviewees and the literature, and we do not recommend a single model that will be right for all prevention educators or communities.

Nonetheless, we will share our thoughts on the ideal program and our reasons for taking this view. We will not repeat earlier citations from the literature or our synthesis of practice wisdom to support these thoughts.

- Programs can be successful whether they combine or separate sexual assault and dating violence, but in this era of scarce resources and scarce opportunities to make presentations to youth, many advantages accrue to combining the content about both topics . It may also be effective to integrate sexual assault and dating violence prevention into general violence prevention programs.
- The ideal program has multiple sessions. The literature primarily expresses this view, but it is also logical that it takes time to learn new behaviors and change attitudes widely supported in our society.
- Programs should include both single- and mixed-gender sessions, with careful attention to constructing messages that do not blame either gender. Programs directed to girls should not blame the victim by implying that girls can take precautions that would stop perpetrators; not only is this hurtful, but it is not true. Girls or any victims/survivors may sometimes reduce their risk by avoiding high-risk situations, but they are never responsible for the behavior of perpetrators. Programs for males should also avoid blame, as that "turns them off" from absorbing the messages. In addition, it is not the fault of individual males that they are growing up in a sexist, violent culture. It is important, however, to recognize that males perpetrate most sexual assaults and acts of severe dating violence.
- Programs should be based on a theoretical framework; that is, they should articulate their views on the causes of dating violence and sexual assault in society. A program's views on the causes of violence should guide program development.
- Programs should include peer education or youth leadership components. Doing so is empowering, respectful of youth, and makes programs more relevant to the adolescents. However, programs need sufficient resources to conduct peer education and provide adequate assistance and support for youth who are involved in any aspect of youth leadership.
- Programs should be sensitive to cultural differences and sexual orientation, but educators should not assume that an exact cultural match between educators and youth is the only way to achieve this sensitivity.
- Interactive programs that include discussion and experiential exercises or role-plays are more likely to engage youth, as students are

exposed to a great deal of lecturing and may likely ignore anyone who lectures to them.

- Programs should use a manual to guide educators and enhance evaluation efforts, but, whenever possible, opportunities should be provided for adolescent participants to direct the conversation, according to their own questions and interests.

- Most programs should not encourage public disclosures of victimization either by peer educators or adolescents in the audience. Teens need guidance and protection from revelations that can never be retrieved, and programs should offer opportunities for youth to talk to the presenters privately, because, unfortunately, other qualified, helpful resources are often scarce. It is our hope that we will all continue to lobby for increased funding for resources that reach victimized youth so that prevention educators are not the only available persons to whom teens feel comfortable disclosing their experiences.

- Programs should regularly address teachers and parents because of their essential, long-lasting roles in adolescents' lives. .

- Communities should pay sufficient salaries to prevention educators to enable them to work in the field long past the apprenticeship stage. Experience enables educators to improvise skillfully in order to address teens' interests and respond effectively to survivors in the audience.

- Finally, the ideal program will evaluate itself and try new interventions based on other well-evaluated programs or practice wisdom. Our interviews show that educators are eager to be sure they are doing the most effective work possible. Some are convinced that they are effective because of enthusiastic individual and group responses from youth, but others seek research to support their confidence in the program. We encourage practitioners to value responses from youth and the community, and to gather these responses methodically as well as anecdotally. We also encourage them to partner with university personnel or professional evaluators to assist them in their program evaluation efforts.

Last Words for Now

We are excited to see that dating violence and sexual assault prevention programs for adolescents are vibrant, growing, and here to stay. We hope for a world where such programs are not needed, but, meanwhile, we salute the adults and adolescents who address these important needs.

Programs Interviewed

Alabama

- Women's Resource Center, Tuscaloosa

California

- Break the Cycle, Los Angeles
- Family Violence Law Center's Oakland Relationship Abuse Prevention (RAP) Project, Oakland
- Los Angeles Commission on Assaults Against Women, Los Angeles
- Shasta Women's Refuge, Redding
- STAND! Against Domestic Violence, Concord

Connecticut

- Women's Center of Greater Danbury, Danbury
- Women's and Families Center of Meriden/Middletown, Meriden

Delaware

- Project P.R.I.D.E., Wilmington

Florida

- Children's Crisis Center, Jacksonville
- Hubbard House, Jacksonville
- Women's Center of Jacksonville, Jacksonville

Georgia

- Gwinnett Sexual Assault Center, Duluth
- SAFE, Blairsville

Hawaii

- Domestic Violence Clearinghouse and Legal Hotline, Honolulu

Illinois

- Chicago Metropolitan YWCA, Chicago
- Community Crisis Center, Elgin
- Inner Strength, Peoria
- Lake County Council Against Sexual Assault, Gurnee
- Mujeres Latinas En Acción, Chicago
- YWCA Sexual Assault Crisis Services, Danville

Louisiana

- YWCA, New Orleans [two programs in two locations: one for sexual assault and one for dating violence]
- YWCA, New Orleans

Maine

- Sexual Assault Victims Emergency Services, Farmington

Massachusetts

- Mentors in Violence Prevention, Boston
- Portal to Hope, Salisbury
- STAR, Casa Myrna Vazquez, Boston

Michigan

- First Step, Plymouth
- Haven, Pontiac
- Kent County Health Department, Grand Rapids
- Safe House, Ann Arbor
- Turning Point, Mount Clemens
- WISE, Big Rapids

Programs Interviewed

Missouri

- MOCSA, Kansas City
- YWCA, St. Louis Regional Sexual Assault Center, St. Louis

Nebraska

- Center for Sexual Assault and Domestic Violence Survivors, Columbus
- Rape/Spouse Abuse Crisis Center, Lincoln

New Hampshire

- Support Center, Littleton
- Women's Supportive Services, Claremont

New Jersey

- HITOPS Inc., Princeton

Rhode Island

- Sexual Assault & Trauma Resource Center, Providence

South Carolina

- The Megan Project, Safe Harbor Project, Greenville
- Pee Dee Coalition Against Domestic Violence and Sexual Assault, Florence

Texas

- Safe Place, Austin
- Texas Association Against Sexual Assault, Austin

Vermont

- AWARE, Hardwick
- Community Paradigm Project, University of Vermont, Burlington

Washington

- King County Sexual Assault Resource Center (KCSARC), Renton

Programs Interviewed

Washington, D.C.

- WEAVE

Wisconsin

- AVAIL, Antigo
- DAIS, Madison
- New Horizons Shelter and Women's Center, La Crosse

Interview Guide

Practitioner Interviews

How long have you been working in the field of youth dating violence and sexual assault prevention?

How long have you been working with your current agency in youth dating violence and sexual assault prevention/community education/awareness?

Do you lead/facilitate the prevention/community education/awareness groups? If so, do you facilitate the groups alone?

How old are you?

With what ethnic group do you identify?

What is your gender?

What is your educational background?

Tell Us about Your Program

Recruitment of Youth

How are youth recruited to participate in your program?

Do you believe programs should be required or voluntary?

What are the advantages of your approach to youth dating violence and sexual assault prevention?

How does your program address the recruitment of ethnic and racial minorities and sexual minorities?

Do you recruit youth from specific populations based on age, grade, or gender?

Do you recruit youth in specific schools, religious settings, or agencies?

Where is the best location to offer programs?

Do you prefer school settings, churches, social service agencies, or community centers? Why?

Do you specifically recruit youth who are already engaged in violent dating relationships?

How do you handle issues related to parental consent to participate in the program or in program evaluation?

Do you think prevention content can or should be incorporated into pre-existing programming in these settings, such as health curriculum?

Cultural Specificity

What is the primary cultural group of the youth who participate in your program?

Do the youth in your program differ by geographical location?

How does your program include ethnic and racial minorities and sexual minorities?

How does your program address gay and lesbian dating?

Do you believe it is important to have a cultural match between the group leaders/trainers and the youth in prevention groups? Gender match?

Group Membership

Does your programs separate or combine girls and boys?

How did you make the decision to separate or combine girls and boys?

What is the group size?

Why do you feel that size works well for your program?

What is the age range of participants?

How did you make that decision?

What are the advantages and disadvantages of your current approach to group composition?

Program Structure

How long is your prevention program? How many sessions are included?

How are the sessions spaced?

How much time is devoted to role-plays and skill development?

How much time is devoted to discussion versus educational lessons?

Do youth complete homework assignments or exercises between sessions?

Program Content

How does your program attend to larger, societal violence issues?

If your program is on dating violence prevention, how much emphasis on sexual violence is included?

Is content on dating violence and sexual violence prevention combined or separated?

Is peer education incorporated into your program?

Is mentoring incorporated into your program?

How much content is devoted to increasing knowledge versus changing attitudes versus building skills?

Is your program based on a manual developed by others or by your program staff?

How much do group leaders adhere to the manual or expand on impromptu issues raised by youth?

What type of training do you feel group leaders/trainers should have?

Goals

What are your program's goals?

Are there any other specific goals?

[If not covered before, ask how these goals were selected.]

How do you know your program is effective?

How do you measure goal achievement?

Are you finding that funding sources are placing increasing importance on program evaluation? What are your challenges and successes in evaluation?

Theoretical Perspective

Is your program theory based? [If no, skip to next section]

On what theoretical perspective is your program based?

How do theoretical perspectives influence program content?

Parental Involvement

How much involvement do parents have in your program?

How do you encourage parental involvement?

Community Involvement

Do you encourage community involvement? How?

Do you involve other agencies? How?

Do you involve the media? How?

Programs' Unintended Consequences

What were some of the most rewarding events regarding the responses of the youths to your program?

How have your group leaders handled troubling events during a presentation? Please provide examples.

How do you help youth decide what to share during programs?

How do you handle issues about confidentiality and its limits?

Wish Lists

Where do you want to go next with your youth prevention programs?

What are your program's major needs?

General Comments

What are the important lessons you have learned that we have not touched upon?

What else do you think we should know about your program?

What are your comments or suggestions about this interview and how to improve our interviews with prevention practitioners?

Does your agency wish to be identified by name and location in our publications?

Would you like us to send you a transcript of the interview for your review and additional comments or corrections?

If yes, please indicate your e-mail address.

If no, a copy of the book will be sent to your program after publication.

Do you know of any other excellent prevention/awareness programs that you think we should contact for an interview?

Name

Contact information

Thank you so much for your time.

References

Abbey, A. 2005. Lessons learned and unanswered questions about sexual assault perpetration. *Journal of Interpersonal Violence* 20 (1): 39–42.

Ackard, D. M., and D. Neumark-Sztainer. 2002. Date violence and date rape among adolescents: Associations with disordered eating behaviors and psychological health. *Child Abuse Neglect* 26 (5): 455–473.

Ackard, D. M., D. Neumark-Sztainer, and P. Hannan. 2003. Dating violence among a nationally representative sample of adolescent girls and boys: Associations with behavioral and mental health. *Journal of Gender Specific Medicine* 6 (3): 39–48.

Acosta, O. M., K. E. Albus, M. W. Reynolds, D. Spriggs, and M. D. Weist. 2001. Assessing the status of research on violence-related problems among youth. *Journal of Clinical Child Psychology* 30 (1): 152–160.

Ajzen, I., and M. Fishbein. 2005. The influence of attitudes on behavior. In D. Albarracin, B. T. Johnson, and M. P. Zanna, eds., *Handbook of Attitudes*, pp. 173–221. Mahwah, N.J.: Erlbaum.

Ajzen, I., and T. J. Madden. 1986. Prediction of goal-directed behavior: Attitudes, intentions, and perceived behavioral control. *Journal of Experimental Social Psychology* 22:453–473.

Albee, G. W., and T. P. Gullotta, eds. 1997. *Primary Prevention Works*. Thousand Oaks, Calif.: Sage.

Anderson, L. A., and, S. C. Whiston. 2005. Sexual assault education programs: A meta-analytic examination of their effectiveness. *Psychology of Women Quarterly* 29 (4): 374–388.

Arriaga, X. B., V. A. and Foshee. 2004. Adolescent dating violence: Do adolescents follow in their friends', or their parents', footsteps? *Journal of Interpersonal Violence* 19 (2): 162–184.

References

Ashley, O. S., and V. A. Foshee. 2005. Adolescent help-seeking for dating violence: Prevalence, sociodemographic correlates, and sources of help. *Journal of Adolescent Health* 36:25–31.

Astor, R. A., and H. A. Meyer. 1999. Where girls and women won't go: Female students', teachers', and social workers' views of school safety. *Social Work in Education* 21 (4): 201–219.

Avery-Leaf, S., and M. Cascardi. 2002. Dating violence education in schools: Prevention and early intervention strategies. In P. A. Schewe, ed., *Preventing Violence in Relationships: Interventions across the Life Span*, pp. 79–106. Washington, D.C.: American Psychological Association.

Avery-Leaf, S., M. Cascardi, and M. K. O'Brien. 1995. *Baseline Findings and Program Evaluation Design of the Philadelphia Dating Violence Prevention Project.* Paper presented at the Fourth International Family Violence Research Conference, Durham, N.H., July.

Avery-Leaf, S., M. Cascardi, D. O'Leary, and A. Cano. 1997. Efficacy of a dating violence prevention program on attitudes justifying aggression. *Journal of Adolescent Health* 21 (1): 11–17.

Bachar, K., and M. P. Koss. 2001. From prevalence to prevention: Closing the gap between what we know about rape and what we do. In C. M. Renzetti, J. L. Edleson, and R. K. Bergen, eds., *Sourcebook on Violence against Women*, pp. 115–142. Thousand Oaks, Calif.: Sage.

Bandura, A. 1977. *Social Learning Theory.* Englewood Cliffs, N.J.: Prentice Hall.

Banyard, V. L., E. G. Plante, and M. M. Moynihan. 2004. Bystander education: Bringing a broader community perspective to sexual violence prevention. *Journal of Community Psychology* 32 (1): 61–79.

Barth, R. P., D. S. Derezotes, and H. E. Danforth. 1991. Preventing adolescent abuse. *Journal of Primary Prevention* 11:193–205.

Begun, A. 2003. Intimate partner violence, adulthood. In T. P. Gullotta, and M. Bloom, eds., *Encyclopedia of Primary Prevention and Health Promotion*, pp. 640–647. New York: Kluwer/Plenum.

Bennett, L., and S. Fineran. 1998. Sexual and severe physical violence among high school students: Power beliefs, gender, and relationship. *American Journal of Orthopsychiatry* 68 (4): 645–652.

Berg, D. R., K. A. Lonsway, and L. F. Fitzgerald. 1999. Rape prevention education for men: The effectiveness of empathy-induction techniques. *Journal of College Student Development* 40 (3): 219–234.

Bergman, L. 1992. Dating violence among high school students. *Social Work* 37 (1): 21–27.

Berkowitz, A. D. 2002. Fostering men's responsibility for preventing sexual assault. In P. A. Schewe, ed., *Preventing Violence in Relationships: Intervention across the Life Span*, pp. 163–196. Washington, D.C.: American Psychological Association.

Bernard, M. L., and J. L. Bernard. 1983. Violent intimacy: The family as a model for love relationships. *Family Relations* 32: 283–286.

Biglan, A., P. J. Mrazek, D. Carnine, and B. Flay. 2003. The integration of research and practice in the prevention of youth problem behaviors. *American Psychologist* 58 (6–7): 433–440.

Binder, R. L., and D. E. McNiel. 1987. Evaluation of a school-based sexual abuse prevention program: Cognitive and emotional effects. *Child Abuse and Neglect* 11:497–506.

Black, B. M. 2005. *Mixed or Single-Gender: Does It Matter for Prevention Programming?* Poster presented at the Ninth International Family Violence Research Conference, Portsmouth, N.H., July.

Black, B. M., R. M. Tolman, M. Callahan, D. G. Saunders, and A. N. Weisz. 2008. When will adolescents tell someone about dating violence victimization? *Violence Against Women* 14 (7): 741-758.

Black, B. M., and A. N. Weisz. 2003. Dating violence: Help-seeking behaviors of African American middle schoolers. *Violence Against Women* 9 (2): 187–206.

———. 2004. Dating violence: A qualitative analysis of Mexican-American youths' views. *Journal of Ethnic and Cultural Diversity in Social Work* 13 (3): 69–90.

———. 2006. Effective interventions with dating violence and domestic violence. In C. Franklin, M. B. Harris, and P. Allen-Meares, eds., *The School Services Sourcebook: A Guide for School-based Professionals*, pp. 519–528. New York: Oxford University Press.

Bloom, M., and T. P. Gullotta. 2003. Evolving definitions of primary prevention. In T. P. Gullotta, and M. Bloom, eds., *Encyclopedia of Primary Prevention and Health Promotion*, pp. 9–14. New London, Conn.: Child and Family Agency of Southeastern Connecticut.

Bohmer, C., and A. Parrot. 1993. *Sexual Assault on Campus: The Problem and the Solution.* New York: Lexington Books.

Botvin, G. J, K. W. Griffin, and T. D. Nichols. 2006. Preventing youth violence and delinquency through a universal school-based prevention approach. *Prevention Science* 7:403–408.

Bowlby, J. 1982 [1969]. *Attachment and Loss*, Vol. 1, *Attachment.* 2nd ed. New York: Basic Books.

Brecklin, L. R., and D. R. Forde. 2001. A meta-analysis of rape education programs. *Violence and Victims* 16:303–321.

Breitenbecher, K. H. 2000. Sexual assault on college campuses: Is an ounce of prevention enough? *Applied and Preventive Psychology* 9 (1): 23–52.

Breitenbecher, K. H., and C. A. Gidycz. 1998. An empirical evaluation of a program designed to reduce the risk of multiple sexual victimization. *Journal of Interpersonal Violence* 13 (4): 472–488.

Briere, J., and N. M. Malamuth. 1983. Self-reported likelihood of sexually aggressive behavior: Attitudinal versus sexual explanations. *Journal of Research in Personality* 17:315–323.

Bronfenbrenner, U. 1977. Toward an experimental ecology of human development. *American Psychologist* 32:523–531.

Burt, M. 1980. Cultural myths and supports for rape. *Journal of Personality and Social Psychology* 38 (2): 217–230.

Callahan, M. R., R. M. Tolman, and D. G. Saunders. 2003. Adolescent dating violence victimization and psychological well-being. *Journal of Adolescent Research* 18 (6): 664–681.

Cappella, E., and R. Weinstein. 2006) The prevention of social aggression among girls. *Social Development* 15 (3): 434–462.

Capuzzi, D., D. R. Groiss, and M. D. Shafuffer. 2006. *Introduction to Group Work.* 4th ed. Denver, Colo.: Love.

Carlson, B. E. 1999. Student judgments about dating violence: A factorial vignette analysis. *Research in Higher Education* 40 (2): 201–220.

Carmody, M., and K. Carrington. 2000. Preventing sexual violence? *Australian and New Zealand Journal of Criminology* 33 (3): 341–361.

Cascardi, M., S. Avery-Leaf, K. D. O'Leary, and A. M. S. Slep. 1999. Factor structure and convergent validity of the conflicts tactics scale in high school students. *Psychological Assessment* 11 (4): 546–555.

Cascardi, M., M. K. O'Brien, and S. Avery-Leaf. 1997. Can dating violence be prevented? Effect of a dating violence prevention program on attitudes and behavior. Paper presented at the Fifth International Conference on Family Violence Research, Durham, N.H.

Casey, E. A., and. P. S. Nurius. 2006a. Acquaintance sexual assault and sexual harassment among teens: School-based interventions. In C. Franklin, M. B. Harris, and P. Allen-Meares, eds., *The School Services Sourcebook: A Guide for School-based Professionals*, pp. 497–504. New York: Oxford University Press.

——. 2006b. Engaging adolescents in prevention of sexual assault and harassment. In C. Franklin, M. B. Harris, and P. Allen-Meares, eds., *The School Services Sourcebook: A Guide for School-based Professionals*, pp. 511–518. New York: Oxford University Press.

Center for Disease Control. 2004. Youth risk behavior. Retrieved December 10, 2005, from http://www.cdc.gov/yrbss.

——. 2005. *Measuring Violence-Related Attitudes, Behaviors, and Influences among Youths: A Compendium of Assessment Tools.* Atlanta: Centers for Disease Control and Prevention.

Chaplin, T. M., J. E. Gillham, K. Reivich, A. G. L. Elkon, B. Samuels, D. R. Freres, B. Winder, and M. E. P. Seligman. 2006. Depression prevention for early adolescent girls: A pilot study of all girls versus co-ed groups. *The Journal of Early Adolescence* 26 (1): 110–126.

Chen, H.-T. (2004). *Practical program evaluation: Assessing and improving, planning implementation and effectiveness.* Thousand Oaks, CA: Sage.

Close, S. M. 2005. Dating violence prevention in middle school and high school youth. *Journal of Child and Adolescent Psychiatric Nursing* 18 (1): 2–9.

Coben, J. H., H. B. Weiss, E. P. Mulvey, and S. R. Dearwater. 1994. A primer on school violence. *Journal of School Health* 42:309–313.

Conduct Problems Prevention Research Group. 2002. Predictor variables associated with positive Fast Track outcomes at the end of third grade. *Journal of Abnormal Child Psychology* 30 (1): 37–2002.

References

Corcoran, K., and V. L. Vandiver. 2004. Implementing best practice and expert consensus procedures. In A. R. Roberts and. K. R. Yeager, eds., *Evidence-based Practice Manual: Research and Outcome Measures in Health and Human Services*, pp. 15–19. New York: Oxford University Press.

Corey, G. 2004. *Theory and Practice of Group Counseling*. Belmont, Calif.: Brooks/Cole- Thompson Learning.

Cornelius, T. L., and N. Resseguie. 2007. Primary and secondary prevention programs for dating violence: A review of the literature. *Aggression and Violent Behavior* 12 (3): 364–375.

de Anda, D. 1999. Project Peace: The evaluation of a skill-based violence prevention program for high school adolescents. *Social Work in Education* 2 (3): 137–149.

de Beauvior, S. 1957. *The Second Sex*. New York: Vintage.

DiGiovanni, L. 2006. Substance abuse prevention: Effective school-based programs. In C. Franklin, M. B. Harris, and P. Allen-Meares, eds., *The School Services Sourcebook: A Guide for School-based Professionals*, pp. 245–257. New York: Oxford University Press.

Dryfoos, J. D. 1990. *Adolescents at Risk: Prevalence and Prevention*. New York: Oxford University Press.

Durlak, J. A. 1997. *Successful Prevention Programs for Children and Adolescents*. New York: Plenum.

Dutton, D. G. 1995. Trauma symptoms and PTSD-like profiles in perpetrators of intimate abuse. *Journal of Traumatic Stress* 8 (2): 299–315.

Dybicz, P. 2004. An inquiry into practice wisdom. *Families in Society* 2:197–203.

Eaton, D. K., K. S. Davis, L. Barrios, N. D. Brener, and R. K. Noonan. 2007. Associations of dating violence victimization with lifetime participation, co-occurrence, and early initiation of risk behaviors among U.S. high school students. *Journal of Interpersonal Violence* 22 (5): 585–602.

Eckhardt, C., and T. R. Jamison. 2002. Articulated thoughts of male dating violence perpetrators during anger arousal. *Cognitive Therapy and Research* 26 (3): 289–308.

Edelstein, M. E., and P. G. Gonyer. 1993. Planning for the future of peer education. *Journal of American College Health* 41:255–257.

Edleson, J. L. 1996. Controversy and change in batterers' programs. In J. L. Edleson and Z. C. Eisikovits, eds., *Future Interventions with Battered Women and Their Families*, pp. 154–169. Thousand Oaks, Calif.: Sage.

——. 2000. Primary prevention and adult domestic violence. Paper presented at the meeting of the Collaborative Violence Prevention Initiative. Retrieved September 6, 2006, from http://endabuse.org/programs/children/files/ prevention/PrimaryPrevention.pdf.

Farrell, A. D., and A. L. Meyer. 1997. The effectiveness of a school-based curriculum for reducing violence among urban sixth-grade students. *American Journal of Public Health* 87 (6): 979–984.

Farrell, A. D., A. L. Meyer, and L. L. Dahlberg. 1996. Richmond youth against violence: A school-based program for urban adolescents. *American Journal of Preventive Medicine* 12 (5): 13–21.

References

Fay, K., and F. J. Medway. 2006. An acquaintance rape education program for students transitioning to high school. *Sex Education* 6 (3): 223–236.

Feltey, K. M., J. J. Ainslie, and A. Geib. 1991. Sexual coercion attitudes among high school students. *Youth and Society* 23 (2): 229–250.

Fennell, R. 1993. A review of evaluations of peer education programs. *Journal of American College Health* 41 (251–253).

Figley, C. R. 2002. *Treating Compassion Fatigue*. New York: Brunner-Routledge.

Fineran, S., and L. Bennett. 1999. Gender and power issues of peer sexual harassment among teenagers. *Journal of Interpersonal Violence* 14:626–641.

Finkelhor, D., and N. L. Asidigian. 1996. Risks factors for youth victimization: Beyond a lifestyles theoretical approach. *Violence and Victims* 11 (1): 3–20.

Fook, J. 2001. Identifying expert social work: Qualitative practitioner research. In I. F. Shaw and N. G. Gould, eds., *Qualitative Research in Social Work*, pp. 116–132. London: Sage.

Foshee, V. A., K. E. Bauman, X. B. Arriaga, R. W. Helms, G. G. Koch, and G. F. Linder. 1998. An evaluation of Safe Dates, an adolescent dating violence prevention program. *American Journal of Public Health* 88 (1): 45–50.

Foshee, V.A., K. E. Bauman, S. T. Ennett, G. F. Linder, T. Benefield, and C. Suchindran. 2004. Assessing the long-term effects of the Safe Dates program and a booster in preventing and reducing adolescent dating violence victimization and perpetration. *American Journal of Public Health* 94 (4): 619–624.

Foshee, V.A., K. E. Bauman, S. T. Ennett, C. Suchindran, T. Benefield, and G. F. Linder. 2005. Assessing the effects of the dating violence prevention program "Safe Dates" using random coefficient regression modeling. *Prevention Science* 6 (3): 245–258.

Foshee, V. A., K. E. Bauman, and W. F. Greene. 2000. The Safe Dates program: 1-year follow-up results. *American Journal of Public Health* 90 (10): 1619–1622.

Foshee, V. A., K. E. Bauman, F. Linder, J. Rice, and R. Wilcher. 2007. Typologies of adolescent dating violence. *Journal of Interpersonal Violence* 22 (5): 498–519.

Foshee, V. A., T. S. Benefield, S. T. Ennett, K. E. Bauman, and C. Suchindran. 2004. Longitudinal predictors of serious physical and sexual dating violence victimization during adolescence. *Preventive Medicine* 39:1007–1016.

Foshee, V., and S. Langwick. 2004. *Safe Dates: An Adolescent Dating Abuse Prevention Curriculum*. Center City, Minn.: Hazelden.

Foshee, V. A., G. F. Linder, K. E. Bauman, S. A. Langwick, B. A. Ximena, J. L. Heath, et al. 1996. The Safe Date project: Theoretical basis, evaluation design, and selected baseline findings. *American Journal of Preventive Medicine* 12 (5): 39–47.

Foshee, V. A., F. Linder, J. E. MacDougall, and S. Bangdiwala. 2001. Gender differences in the longitudinal predictors of adolescent dating violence. *Prevention Medicine* 32:128–141.

Foubert, J. D., and B. C. Perry. 2007. Creating lasting attitude and behavior change in fraternity members and male student athletes: The qualitative impact of an empathy-based rape prevention program. *Violence Against Women* 13 (1): 70–86.

Foubert, J. D., J. L. Tatum, and G. A. Donahue. 2006. Reactions of first-year men to a rape prevention program: Attitude and predicted behavior changes. *NASPA Journal* 43 (3): 578–598.

Foulis, D., and M. P. McCabe. 1997. Sexual harassment: Factors affecting attitudes and perception. *Sex Roles* 37 (9/10): 773–798.

Fredland, N. M., I. B. Ricardo, J. C. Campbell, P. W. Sharps, J. K. Kub, and M. Yonas. 2005. The meaning of dating violence in the lives of middle school adolescents: A report of a focus group study. *Journal of School Violence* 4 (2): 95–114.

Galinsky, M. J., M. A. Terzian, and M. W. Fraser. 2006. The art of group work practice with manualized curricula. *Social Work with Groups* 29:11–16.

Gamache, D., and S. Snapp. 1995. Teach your children well: Elementary schools and violence prevention. In E. Peled, P. G. Jaffe, and J. L. Edleson, eds., *Ending the Cycle of Violence: Community Responses to Children of Battered Women*, pp. 209–231. Thousand Oaks, Calif.: Sage.

Gambrill, E. 1999. Evidence-based practice: An alternative to authority based practice. *Families in Society* 80:341–350.

Gidycz, C. A., M. J. Layman, C. L. Rich, M. Crothers, J. Gylys, and A. Matorin. 2001. An evaluation of an acquaintance rape prevention program: Impact on attitudes, sexual aggression, and sexual victimization. *Journal of Interpersonal Violence* 16 (11): 1120–1138.

Gidycz, C. A., C. L. Rich, L. Orchowski, C. King, and A. K. Miller. 2006. The evaluation of a sexual assault self-defense and risk-reduction program for college women: A prospective study. *Psychology of Women Quarterly* 30 (2): 173–186.

Glass, N., N. Fredland, K. Cambell, M. Yonas, P. Sharps, and J. Kub. 2003. Adolescent dating violence: Prevalence, risk factors, health outcomes, and implications for clinical practice. *JOGNN: Clinical Issues* 32 (2): 227–238.

Gondolf, E. W. 2002. *Batterer Intervention Systems Issues, Outcomes, and Recommendations*. Thousand Oaks, Calif.: Sage.

Gordon, J. A., and L. J. Moriarty. 2003. The effects of domestic violence batterer treatment on domestic violence recidivism: The Chesterfield County experience. *Criminal Justice and Behavior* 30 (1): 118–134.

Gottfredson, D. C., and G. D. Gottfredson. 2002. Quality of school-based prevention programs: Results from a national survey. *Journal of Research in Crime and Delinquency* 39 (1): 3–35.

Gottfredson, D. C., D. B. Wilson, and S. S. Najaka. 2002. School-based crime prevention. In D. P. Farrington, L. W. Sherman, B. Welsh, and D. L. Mackenzie, eds., *Evidence-based Crime Prevention*. London: Routledge.

Gould, J. M., and A. R. Lomax. 1993. The evolution of peer education: Where do we go from here? *Journal of American College Health* 41:235–240.

Grasley, C., D. A. Wolfe, and C. Wekerle. 1999. Empowering youth to end relationship violence. *Children's Services: Social Policy, Research, and Practice* 2 (4): 209–223.

Gregory, M., M. Lohr, and L. Gilchrist. 1992. Methods for tracking pregnant and parenting adolescents. *Evaluation Review* 16:69–81.

Gutierrez, L. M. 1990. Working with women of color: An empowerment perspective. *Social Work* 35 (2): 149–153.

References

Halpern, C. T., S. G. Oslak, M. L. Young, S. L. Martin, and L. L. Kupper. 2001. Partner violence among adolescents in opposite-sex romantic relationships: Findings from the national longitudinal study of adolescent health. *American Journal of Public Health* 91 (10): 1679–1685.

Hammond, W. R., and B. R. Yung. 1991. Preventing violence in at-risk African American youth. *Journal of Health Care for the Poor and Underserved* 2 (3): 359–373.

Hanson, K. A., and C. A. Gidycz. 1993. Evaluation of a sexual assault prevention program. *Journal of Consulting and Clinical Psychology* 61 (6): 1046–1052.

Harned, M. S. 2002. A mulivariate analysis of risk markers for dating violence victimization. *Journal of Interpersonal Violence* 17 (11): 1179–1197.

Heppner, M. J., G. E. Good, T. L. Hilenbrand-Gunn, A. K. Hawkins, L. L. Hacquard, R. K. Nichols, et al. 1995a. Examining sex differences in altering attitudes about rape: A test of the Elaboration Likelihood Model. *Journal of Counseling and Development* 73 (6): 640–647.

Heppner, M. J., C. F. Humphrey, T. L. Hilenbrand-Gunn, and K. A. DeBord. 1995b. The differential effects of rape prevention programming on attitudes, behavior, and knowledge *Journal of Counseling Psychology* 42:508–518.

Heppner, M. J., H. A. Neville, K. Smith, D. M. Kivlighan Jr., and B. S. Gershuny. 1999. Examining immediate and long-term efficacy of rape prevention programming with racially diverse college men. *Journal of Counseling Psychology* 46 (1): 16–26.

Hickman, L. J., L. H. Jaycox, and J. Aronoff. 2004. Dating violence among adolescents: Prevalence, gender distribution, and prevention program effectiveness. *Trauma, Violence, and Abuse* 5 (2): 123–142.

Hilton, N. Z., G. T. Harris, M. E. Rice, T. S. Krans, and S. E. Lavigne. 1998. Antiviolence education in high schools: Implementation and evaluation. *Journal of Interpersonal Violence* 13:726–742.

Holcomb, D. R., P. D. Sarvela, A. K. Sondag, and L. C. Hatton Holcomb. 1993. An evaluation of a mixed-gender date rape prevention workshop. *Journal of American College Health* 41:159–164.

Holder, H. D., A. J. Treno, R. F. Saltz, and J. W. Grube. 1997. Summing up: Recommendations and experiences for evaluation of community-level prevention programs. *Evaluation Review* 21 (2): 268–278.

hooks, b. 1984. *Feminist Theory: From Margin to Center*. Boston: South End Press.

Hopson, L. 2006. Effective HIV prevention in schools. In C. Franklin, M. B. Harris, and P. Allen-Meares, eds., *The School Services Sourcebook: A Guide for School-based Professionals*, pp. 289–297. New York: Oxford University Press.

Hovland, C. I., I. L. Janis, and H. H. Kelley. 1953. *Communication and Persuasion*. New Haven, Conn.: Yale University Press.

Howard, D. E., and M. Q. Wang. 2003. Risk profiles of adolescent girls who were victims of dating violence. *Adolescence* 38 (149): 1–14.

Imre, R. W. 1982. *Knowing and Caring: Philosophical Issues in Social Work*. Washington, D.C.: University Press of America.

References

Irby, M., T. Ferber, K. Pittman, with J. Tolman and N. Yohalem. 2001. *Youth Action: Youth Contributing to Communities, Communities Supporting Youth.* Community and Youth Development series 6. Takoma Park, Md.: Forum for Youth Investment, International Youth Foundation.

Jackson, S. M. 1999. Issues in the dating violence research: A review of the literature. *Aggression and Violent Behavior* 4 (2): 233–247.

——. 2002. Abuse in dating relationships: Young people's accounts of disclosure, non-disclosure, help-seeking, and prevention education. *New Zealand Journal of Psychology* 31 (2): 79–86.

Jacobson, N. S., J. M. Gottman, J. Waltz, R. Rushe, J. Babcock, and A. Holtzworth-Munroe. 1994. Affect, verbal content, and psychophysiology in the arguments of couples with a violent husband. *Journal of Consulting and Clinical Psychology* 62:982–988.

Jaffe, P. G., L. L. Baker, and A. J. Cunningham. 2004. Group intervention with abusive male adolescents. In P. G. Jaffe, L. L. Baker, and A. J. Cunningham, eds., *Protecting Children from Domestic Violence: Strategies for Community Intervention,* pp. 49–67. New York: Guilford.

Jaffe, P. G., M. Sudermann, D. Reitzel, and S. M. Killip. 1992. An evaluation of a secondary school primary prevention program on violence in intimate relationships. *Violence and Victims* 7 (2): 129–146.

Jaffe, P. G., D. Wolfe, C. Crooks, R. Hughes, and L. L. Baker, (2004. The fourth R: Developing healthy relationships through school-based interventions. In P. G. Jaffe, L. L. Baker, and A. J. Cunningham, eds., *Protecting Children from Domestic Violence: Strategies for Community Intervention,* pp. 200–218. New York: Guilford.

Jaffe, P. G., D. A. Wolfe, and S. K. Wilson. 1990. *Children of Battered Women.* Newbury Park, Calif.: Sage.

Jankowski, M., H. Rosenberg, A. Sengupta, S. Rosenberg, and G. Wolford. 2007. Development of a screening tool to identify adolescents engaged in multiple problem behaviors: The adolescent risk behavior screen (ARBS). *Journal of Adolescent Health* 40 (2): 19–180.

Jansen, M. A., T. Glynn, and J. Howard. 1996. Prevention of alcohol, tobacco, and other drug abuse: Federal efforts to stimulate prevention research. *American Behavioral Scientist* 39 (7): 790–807.

Jaycox, L. H., D. McCaffrey, B. Eiseman, J. Aronoff, G. A. Shelley, R. L. Collins, and G. N. Marshall. 2006. Impact of a school-based dating violence prevention program among Latino teens: Randomized controlled effectiveness trial. *Journal of Adolescent Health* 39 (5): 694–704.

Jezl, D. R., C. E. Molidor, and T. L. Wright. 1996. Physical, sexual, and psychological abuse in high school dating relationships: Prevalence rates and self-esteem issues. *Child and Adolescent Social Work Journal* 13 (1): 69–87.

Johansson-Love, J., and J. H. Geer. 2003. Investigation of attitude change in a rape prevention program. *Journal of Interpersonal Violence* 18 (1): 84–99.

Johnson, C. A., J. W. Farquhar, and S. Sussman. 1996. Methodological and substantive issues in substance abuse prevention research. *American Behavioral Scientist*, 39(7): 935–942.

Johnson-Reid, M., and L. Bivens. 1999. Foster youth and dating violence. *Journal of Interpersonal Violence* 14 (12): 1249–1262.

Jones, L. E. 1998. The Minnesota School Curriculum Project: A statewide domestic violence prevention project in secondary schools. In B. Levy, ed., *Dating Violence: Young Women in Danger*, 2nd ed., pp. 258–266. Seattle, Wash.: Seal Press.

Kasschau, R. 1986. A model for teaching critical thinking in psychology. In H. S. Halonen, ed., *Teaching Critical Thinking in Psychology*. Milwaukee, Wis.: Alverno Productions.

Kivel, P. 1998. *Men's Work: How to Stop the Violence That Tears Our Lives Apart*. Center City, Minn.: Hazeldon.

Klein, W. C., and M. Bloom. 1995. Practice wisdom. *Social Work* 40 (6): 799–807.

Knox, L. M., C. Lomonaco, and A. Elster. 2005. American Medical Association's youth violence prevention training and outreach guide. *American Journal of Preventive Medicine* 29 (5): 226–229.

Krajewski, S. S., M. F. Rybarik, M. F. Dosch, and G. D. Gilmore. 1996. Results of a curriculum intervention with seventh graders regarding violence in relationships. *Journal of Family Violence* 11 (2): 93–113.

Kraus, S. J. 1995. Attitudes and the prediction of behavior: A meta-analysis of the empirical literature. *Personality and Social Psychology Bulletin* 21:58–75.

Kreiter, S. R., D. P. Krowchuk, C. R. Woods, S. H. Sinal, et al. 1999. Gender differences in risk behaviors among adolescents who experience date fighting. *Pediatrics* 104 (6): 1286–1292.

Lanier, C. A, M. N. Elliot, D. W. Martin, and A. Kapadia. 1998. Evaluation of an intervention to change attitudes toward date rape. *Journal of American College Health* 46:177–180.

Latane, B., and J. M. Darley. 1968. Group inhibition of bystander intervention in emergencies. *Journal of Experimental Social Psychology* 10:215–221.

Lavoie, F., M. Hebert, and F. Dufort. 1995. Predictive variables identifying dating violence victims and aggressors among grade ten students. Paper presented at the Fourth International Family Violence Research Conference, Durham, N.H.

Lavoie, F., L. L. Vezina, C. Piche, and M. Boivin. 1995. Evaluation of a prevention program for violence in teen dating relationships. *Journal of Interpersonal Violence* 10 (4): 516–524.

Lee, Y., S. Takaku, V. Ottati, and G. Yan. 2004. Perception and interpretation of terrorism, justice, and conflict: Three cultures and two sides of one coin. In Y. Lee, C. McCauley, F. Moghaddam, and S. Worchel, eds., *The Psychology of Ethnic and Cultural Conflict (Psychological Dimensions to War and Peace)*, pp. 217–345. Oxford: Praegar.

Levy, B. 1998. Project NATEEN: Building a bicultural program. In B. Levy, ed., *Dating Violence: Young Women in Danger*, 2nd ed., pp. 196–202. Seattle, Wash.: Seal Press.

References

Levy, B. L., and K. Lobel (1998. Lesbian teens in abusive relationships. In B. Levy (Ed.): *Dating Violence: Young Women in Danger,* 2nd ed., pp. 203–208. Seattle, Wash.: Seal Press.

Lewis, S. F., and W. Fremouw (2001. Dating violence: A critical review of the literature. *Clinical Psychology Review* 21 (1): 105–127.

Loh, C., C. A. Gidycz, T. R. Lobo, and L. Rohini. 2005. A prospective analysis of sexual assault perpetration risk factors related to perpetrator characteristics. *Journal of Interpersonal Violence* 20 (10): 1325–1348.

Lonsway, K. A. 1996. Preventing acquaintance rape through education. *Psychology of Women Quarterly* 20:229–265.

Lonsway, K. A., E. K. Klaw, D. R. Berg, C. R. Waldo, C. Kothari, C. J. Mazurek, et al. 1998. Beyond "No Means No": Outcomes of an intensive program to train peer facilitators for campus acquaintance rape education. *Journal of Interpersonal Violence* 13 (1): 73–92.

Macgowan, M. J. 1997. An evaluation of a dating violence prevention program for middle school students. *Violence and Victims* 12 (3): 223–235.

Malik, S., S. B. Sorenson, and C. S. Aneshensel. 1997. Community and dating violence among adolescents: Perpetration and victimization. *Journal of Adolescent Health* 21:291–302.

Marx, B. P., K. S. Calhoun, A. E. Wilson, and L. A. Meyerson. 2001. Sexual revictimization prevention: An outcome evaluation. *Journal of Consulting and Clinical Psychology* 69:25–32.

McCall, G. J. 1993. Risk factors and sexual assault prevention. *Journal of Interpersonal Violence* 8 (2): 277–295.

McKay, M. M., and W. M. Bannon. 2004. Engaging families in child mental health services. *Child and Adolescent Psychiatric Clinics of North America* 13:905–921.

MEE Productions (1996. *In Search of Love: Dating Violence among Urban Youth.* Philadelphia, Pa.: Center for Human Advancement.

Meyer, H., and N. Stein. 2004. Relationship violence prevention education in schools: What's working, what's getting in the way, and what are some future directions. *American Journal of Health Education* 35 (4): 198–204.

Mihalic, S., A. Fagan, K. Irwin, D. Ballard, and D. Elliot. 2004. *Blue Prints for Violence Prevention.* Washington D.C.: Center for the Study and Prevention of Violence, University of Colorado, Boulder.

Mitchell, K. J., D. Finkelhor, and J. Wolak. 2007. Online requests for sexual pictures from youth: Risk factors and incident characteristics. *Journal of Adolescent Health* 41:196–203.

Molidor, C., and R. M. Tolman. 1998. Gender and contextual factors in adolescent dating violence. *Violence Against Women* 4 (2): 180–194.

Mouradian, V. E., M. B. Mechanic, and L. M. Williams. 2001. *Recommendations for Establishing and Maintaining Successful Researcher-Practitioner Collaborations.* Wellesley, Mass.: National Violence Against Women Prevention Research Center, Wellesley College.

Mullen, E. J., and W. Bacon. 2004. Implementation of practice guidelines and evidence-based treatment: A survey of psychiatrists, psychologists, and social workers. In A. R. Roberts and. K. R. Yeager, eds., *Evidence-based Practice Manual: Research and Outcome Measures in Health and Human Services*, pp. 210–218. New York: Oxford University Press.

Myers-Walls, J. A. 2000. An odd couple with promise: Researchers and practitioners in evaluation settings. *Family Relations* 49(3): 341–347.

Nadel, H., M. Spellmann, T. Alvarez-Canino, L. Lausell-Bryant, and G. Landsberg. 1996. The cycle of violence and victimization: A study of the school-based intervention of a multidisciplinary youth violence-prevention program. *American Journal of Preventive Medicine* 12:109–119.

Nagayama, H., and C. Barongan. 1997. Prevention of sexual aggression: Sociocultural risk and protective factors. *American Psychologist* 52 (1): 5–14.

Nation, M., C. Crusto, A. Wandersman, K. L. Kumpfer, D. Seybolt, E. Morrissey-Kane, et al. 2003. What works in prevention: Principles of effective prevention programs. *American Psychologist* 58 (6–7): 449–456.

National Center for Health Statistics. 1995. *Healthy People 2000, 1994*. Hyattsville, Md.: Public Health Services.

National Institute of Justice (2004. *Violence Against Women: Identifying Risk Factors*. Washington, D.C.: U.S. Department of Justice, Office of Justice Programs.

National Violence Against Women Prevention Research Center. 2003. *Violence Against Women Prevention Programming: Report of What Is in Use*. Charleston, S.C.: National Violence Against Women Prevention Research Center.

O'Brien, M. K. 2001. School-based education and prevention programs. In C. M. Renzetti, J. L. Edleson, and R. K. Bergen, eds., *Sourcebook on Violence against Women*, pp. 387–416. Thousand Oaks, Calif.: Sage.

Ocampo, B. W., G. A. Shelley, and L. H. Jaycox. 2007. Latino teens talk about help seeking and help giving in relation to dating violence. *Violence Against Women*, 13(2): 172–189.

O'Keefe, M. 1997. Predictors of dating violence among high school students. *Journal of Interpersonal Violence* 12 (4): 546–568.

O'Keefe, M., and L. Treister. 1998. Victims of dating violence among high school students: Are the predictors different for males and females? *Violence Against Women* 4 (2): 195–223.

O'Leary, K., E. M. Woodin, and P. A. T. Fritz. 2006. Can we prevent the hitting? Recommendations for preventing intimate partner violence between young adults. *Journal of Aggression, Maltreatment and Trauma* 13 (3–4): 121–178.

Orlando, M., L. H. Jaycox, D. F. McCaffrey, and G. N. Marshall. 2006. Improving the measurement of socially unacceptable attitudes and behaviors with item response theory. Santa Monica, Calif.: RAND Health, RAND Corporation.

Pacifici, C., M. Stoolmiller, and C. Nelson. 2001. Evaluating a prevention program for teenagers on sexual coercion: A differential effectiveness approach. *Journal of Consulting and Clinical Psychology* 69:552–559.

Paciorek, L. B., A. Hokoda, and M. T. Herbst. 2003. A peer education intervention addressing teen dating violence: The perspectives of the adolescent peer educators. *FVSAB* 19 (4): 11–19.

Padgett, D. K. 2004. Introduction. Finding a middle ground in qualitative research. In D. K. Padgett, eds., *The Qualitative Research Experience*, pp. 1–18. Belmont, Calif.: Wadsworth/Thomson.

Patton, M. Q. 1990. *Qualitative Evaluation and Research Methods.* 2nd ed. Newbury Park, Calif.: Sage.

Pearlman, L. A., and K. W. Saakvitne. 1995. *Trauma and the Therapist: Countertransference and Vicarious Traumatization in Psychotherapy with Incest Survivors.* New York: W. W. Norton.

Petty, R. E., and J. T. Cacioppo. 1986. *The Elaboration Likelihood Model of Persuasion.* New York: Academic Press.

Pitner, R. O., R. A. Astor, R. Benbenishty, M. M. Haj-Yahia, and A. Zeira. 2003. Adolescents' approval of peer and spousal retribution in their culture vs. other cultures: The role of group stereotypes. *British Journal of Developmental Psychology* 21:221–242.

Pittman, A. L., D. A. Wolfe, and C. Wekerle. 2000. Strategies for evaluating dating violence prevention programs. In S. Ward and D. Finkelhor, eds., *Program Evaluation and Family Violence Research,* pp. 217-238. New York: Haworth.

Pohl, J. D. 1990. Adolescent sexual abuse: An evaluation of a perpetrator and victim prevention program. Ph.D. diss., Georgia State University, Atlanta.

Proto-Campise, L., J. Belknap, and J. Wooldredge. 1998. High school students' adherence to rape myths and the effectiveness of high school rape-awareness programs. *Violence Against Women* 4 (3): 308–328.

Rehr, H., G. Rosenberg, N. Showers, and S. Blumenfield. 1998. Social work in health care: Do practitioners' writings suggest an applied social science? *Social Work in Health Care* 28 (2): 63–81.

Reid, W. J. 1994. Reframing the epistemological debate. In E. Sherman and W. J. Reid, eds., *Qualitative Research in Social Work,* pp. 464–481. New York: Columbia University Press.

Reis, J., M. Trockel, and S. S. Williams. 2003. Considerations for more effective social norms based alcohol education on campus: An analysis of different theoretical conceptualizations in predicting drinking among fraternity men. *Journal of Studies on Alcohol* 64:50–60.

Repucci, N. D., J. L. Woolard, and C. S. Fried. 1999. Social community and preventive interventions. *Annual Review of Psychology* 50:387–418.

Robbins, S. P., P. Chatterjee, E. R. Canda. 2006. *Contemporary Human Behavior Theory: A Critical Perspective for Social Work.* Boston: Pearson, Allyn, and Bacon.

Roden, M. 1998. A model secondary school date rape prevention program. In B. Levy, ed., *Dating Violence: Young Women in Danger,* 2nd ed., pp. 267–278. Seattle, Wash.: Seal Press.

Rones, M., and K. Hoagwood. 2000. School-based mental health services: A research review. *Clinical Child and Family Psychology Review* 3 (4): 223–241.

References

Rosenbluth, B., and R. B. Garcia. (n.d.. *Expect Respect: A Support Group Curriculum for Safe and Healthy Relationships*. Austin, Tex.: Safe Place.

Salazar, L. F., and S. L. Cook. 2006. Preliminary findings from an outcome evaluation of an intimate partner violence prevention program for adjudicated, African American, adolescent males. *Youth Violence and Juvenile Justice* 4 (4): 368–385.

Salazar, L. F., G. M. Wingood, R. J. DiClemente, D. L. Lang, and K. Harrington. 2004. The role of social support in the psychological well-being of African American adolescent girls who experience dating violence. *Violence and Victims* 19 (2): 171–188.

Sanders, S. M. 2003. *Teen Dating Violence: The Invisible Peril*. New York: Peter Lang.

Schaefer, A.M., and E. S. Nelson. 1993. Rape-supportive attitudes: Effects of on-campus residence and education. *Journal of College Student Development* 34:175–179

Schauben, L. J., and P. A. Frazier. 1995) Vicarious trauma: The effects on female counselors of working with sexual violence survivors. *Psychology of Women Quarterly* 19 (1): 49–64.

Schewe, P. A. n.d. The ICASA Project: Best practices for school-based sexual assault prevention programming. Retrieved August 18, 2008, from http://tigger.uic.edu/~schewepa/web-content/newpages/evaluations.html.

——. 2000. Southside Teens About Respect: Summary report of outcomes. Retrieved August 18, 2008, from http://tigger.uic.edu/~schewepa/web-content/newpages/Results02.html.

——. 2002. *Preventing Violence in Relationships: Interventions across the Life Span*. Washington D.C.: American Psychological Association.

——. 2003a. Re: Men mentoring boys. Retrieved August 18, 2008, from http://mapnp.geeks.org/pipermail/pemv-net/2003/000298.html.

——. 2003b. Sexual assault, Adolescence. In T. P. Gullota and. M. Bloom, eds., *Encyclopedia of Primary Prevention and Health Promotion*, pp. 961–969. New London, Conn.: Child and Family Agency of Southeastern Connecticut.

Schewe, P. A., and L. W. Bennett. 2002. Evaluating prevention programs: Challenges and benefits of measuring outcomes. In P. A. Schewe, ed., *Preventing Violence in Relationships: Interventions across the Life Span*, pp. 247–262. Washington D.C.: American Psychological Association.

Schewe, P. A., and W. O'Donohue. 1993. Rape prevention: Methodological problems and new directions. *Clinical Psychology Review* 13:667–682.

Schissel, B. 2000. Boys against girls: The structural and interpersonal dimensions of violent patriarchal culture in the lives of young men. *Violence Against Women* 6 (9): 960–986.

Sege, R., V. Licenziato, and S. Webb. 2005. Bringing violence prevention into the clinic: The Massachusetts Medical Society Violence Prevention Project. *American Journal of Preventive Medicine* 29 (5): 230–232.

Seimer, B. S. 2004. Intimate violence in adolescent relationships recognizing and intervening. *American Journal of Maternal/Child Nursing* 29 (2): 117–121.

References

Shapiro, D. L. 1999. *A Review of VAW Prevention Programs and Recommendations for Future Program Design.* Lansing: Michigan Department of Community Health.

Sheehan, M., C. Schonfeld, F. Schofield, J. Najman, V. Siskind, and R. Ballard. 1996. A three-year outcome evaluation of a theory-based drunk driving education program. *Journal of Drug Education* 26 (3): 295–312.

Shiner, M. 1999. Defining peer education. *Journal of Adolescence* 22:555–566.

Silverman, J., A. Raj, L. A. Mucci, and J. E. Hathaway. 2001. Dating violence against adolescent girls and associated substance use, unhealthy weight control, sexual risk behavior, pregnancy, and suicidality. *Journal of the American Medical Association* 286 (5): 572–579.

Silverman, M. M. 2003. Theories of primary prevention and health promotion: The spectrum of intervention and the place of prevention. In T. P. Gullota and. M. Bloom, eds., *Encyclopedia of Primary Prevention and Health Promotion*, pp. 27–41. New London, Conn.: Child and Family Agency of Southeastern Connecticut.

Simon, T. 1993. Complex issues for sexual assault peer education programs. *Clinical and Program Notes* 41:289–291.

Skuja, K., and W. K. Halford. 2004. Repeating the errors of our parents? Parental violence in men's family of origin and conflict management in dating couples. *Journal of Interpersonal Violence* 19 (6): 623–638.

Sloane, B. C., and C. G. Zimmer. 1993. The power of peer health education. *Journal of American College Health* 41:241–245.

Smith, P., and S. Welchans. 2000. Peer education: Does focusing on male responsibility change sexual assault attitudes? *Violence Against Women* 6 (11): 1255–1268.

Smith, P. H., J. W. White, and L. J. Holland. 2003. A longitudinal perspective on dating violence among adolescent and college-age women. *American Journal of Public Health* 93 (7): 1104–1109.

Sochting, I., N. Fairbrother, and W. J. Koch. 2004. Sexual assault of women: Prevention efforts and risk factors. *Violence Against Women* 10 (1): 73–93.

Solomon, B. 1987. Empowerment: Social work in oppressed communities. *Journal of Social Work Practice* 2 (4): 79–91.

Stephan, C. W., and W. G. Stephan. 1990. *Two Social Psychologies.* 2nd ed. Belmont, Calif.: Wadsworth.

Strauss, A., and J. Corbin. 1990. *Basics of Qualitative Research: Grounded Theory, Procedures, and Techniques.* Newbury Park, Calif.: Sage.

Sudermann, M., P. G. Jaffe, and E. Hastings. 1995. Violence prevention programs in secondary (high) schools. In E. Peled, P. G. Jaffe, and J. L. Edleson, eds., *Ending the Cycle of Violence: Community Responses to Children of Battered Women*, pp. 232–254. Thousand Oaks, Calif.: Sage.

Tebes, J. K., J. S. Kaufman, and C. M. Connell. 2003. The evaluation of prevention and health promotion programs. In T. P. Gullotta and M. Bloom, eds., *Encyclopedia of Primary Prevention and Health Promotion*, pp. 42–60. New London, Conn.: Child and Family Agency of Southeastern Connecticut.

Terry, D. J., M. A. Hogg, and K. M. White. 2000. Attitude-behavior relations: Social identity and group membership. In D. J. Terry and M. A. Hogg, eds., *Attitudes, Behavior, and Social Context: The Role of Norms and Group Membership*, pp. 67–93. Mahwah, N.J.: Erlbaum.

Thyer, B. 2001. *The Handbook of Social Work Research Methods*. Thousand Oaks, Calif.: Sage.

Tishby, O., M. Turel, O. Gumble, U. Pinus, S. B. Lavy, M. Winokour, and S. Sznajderman. 2001. Help-seeking attitudes among Israeli adolescents. *Adolescence* 36 (142): 249–264.

Tolan, P. 2000. Youth violence prevention. Retrieved September 17, 2006, from www.endabuse.org/programs/children/files/prevention/YouthViolencePrevention.pdf.

Trippany, R. L., V. E. W. Kress, and S. A. Wilcoxon. 2004. Preventing vicarious trauma: What counselors should know when working with trauma survivors. *Journal of Counseling and Development* 82 (1): 31–37.

Tutty, L. 2002. Evaluating school-based prevention programs: The basics. In *School-based Violence Prevention Programs: A Resource Manual*. Retrieved August 27, 2008, from http://www.ucalgary.ca/resolve/violenceprevention/English/evaluate.htm.

Walker, S. A., and M. Avis. 1999. Common reasons why peer education fails. *Journal of Adolescence* 22:573–577.

Walsh, J. F., and V. Foshee. 1998. Short communication: Self-efficacy, self-determination, and victim blaming as predictors of adolescent sexual victimization. *Health Education Research: Theory and Practice* 13 (1): 139–144.

Wandersman, A., and P. Florin. 2003. Community interventions and effective prevention. *American Psychologist* 58 (6–7): 441–8.

Ward, K. J. 2001. Evaluation 1999/2000. Retrieved December 30, 2005, from http://dev.csss.neu.edu/mvp/mvp-evaluation2.htm.

Watson, J. M., M. Cascardi, S. Avery-Leaf, and K. D. O'Leary. 2001. High school students' responses to dating aggression. *Violence and Victims* 16 (3): 339–348.

Webber, J. 1997. Comprehending youth violence: A practicable perspective. *Remedial and Special Education* 18(2): 94–104.

Weick, A. 1999. Guilty knowledge. *Families in Society* 80 (4): 327–332.

Weiler, J. 1999. *Girls and Violence*. New York: ERIC Clearinghouse on Urban Education.

Weissberg, R. P., K. L. Kumpfer, and M. E. P. Seligman. 2003. Prevention that works for children and youth: An introduction. *American Psychologist* 58 (6–7): 425–432.

Weist, M. D., and M. Cooley-Quille. 2001. Advancing efforts to address youth violence involvement. *Journal of Clinical Child Psychology* 30 (1): 147–151.

Weisz, A. N., and B. M. Black. 2001. Evaluating a sexual assault and dating violence prevention program for urban youths. *Social Work Research* 25 (2): 89–100.

——. 2008. Peer intervention in dating violence: Beliefs of African American middle school adolescents. *Journal of Ethnic and Cultural Diversity in Social Work* 17 (2): 177–196.

References

Weisz, A. N., B. M. Black, S. Coats, and D. Patterson. 2001. Understanding the effectiveness of sexual assault prevention programming: A qualitative analysis of audience responses. *Journal of Applied Social Sciences* 25 (2): 131–142.

Wekerle, C., and D. A. Wolfe. 1999. Dating violence in mid-adolescence: Theory, significance, and emerging prevention initiatives. *Clinical Psychology Review* 19 (4): 435–456.

Whitaker, D. J., S. Morrison, C. Lindquist, S. R. Hawkins, J. A. O'Neil, A. M. Nesius, et al. 2006. A critical review of interventions for the primary prevention of perpetration of partner violence. *Aggression and Violent Behavior* 11:151–166.

White, R. T. 1997. In the name of love and survival: Interpretations of sexual violence among young Black American women. In T. D. Sharpley-Whiting and R. T. White, eds., *Spoils of War: Women of Color, Culture, and Revolutions*, pp. 27–45. Lanham, Md.: Rowman and Littlefield.

Wilson, S. J., M. W. Lipsey, and J. H. Derzon. 2003. The effects of school-based intervention programs on aggressive behavior: A meta-analysis. *Journal of Consulting and Clinical Psychology* 71 (1): 136–149.

Wolfe, D. A., C. Crooks, D. Chiodo, R. Hughes, and P. Jaffe. 2006. Strategies for Healthy Youth Relationships RCT Evaluation of Core Program Fourth R: Comprehensive school-based prevention. Retrieved August 27, 2008, from http://youthrelationships.org/html/projects_4th_schoolCurric.html.

Wolfe, D. A., and P. Jaffe. 2003. Prevention of domestic violence and sexual assault. Retrieved August 26, 2006, from http://www.vawnet.org/DomesticViolence/Research/VAWnetDocs/AR_Prevention.php.

Wolfe, D. A., K. Scott, C. Wekerle, and A. L. Pittman. 2001. Child Maltreatment: Risk of Adjustment Problems and Dating Violence in Adolescence. *Journal of the American Academy of Child and Adolescent Psychiatry* 40 (3): 282–289.

Wolfe, D. A., and C. Wekerle. 2003. Dating violence prevention with at-risk youth: A controlled outcome evaluation. *Journal of Consulting and Clinical Psychology* 71:279–291.

Wolfe, D. A., C. Wekerle, R. Gough, D. Reitzel-Jaffe, C. Grasleu, A. Pittman, L. Lefebvre, and J. Stumpf. 1996. *The Youth Relationships Manual: A Group Approach with Adolescents for the Prevention of Women Abuse and the Promotion of Healthy Relationships*. Thousand Oaks: Calif.: Sage.

Wolfe, D. A., C. Wekerle, K. Scott, A. L. Straatman, C. Grasley, and D. Reitzel-Jaffe. 2003. Dating violence prevention with at-risk youth: A controlled outcome evaluation. *Journal of Consulting and Clinical Psychology* 71 (2): 279–291.

Yeater, E. A., and W. O'Donohue. 2002. Sexual revictimization: The relationship among knowledge, risk perception, and ability to respond to high-risk situations. *Journal of Interpersonal Violence* 17 (11): 1135–1144.

Yoshihama, M., A. L. Parekh, and D. Boyington. 1998. Dating violence in Asain/Pacific communities. In B. Levy, ed., *Dating Violence: Young Women in Danger*, 2nd ed., pp. 184–195. Seattle, Wash.: Seal Press.

Yung, B. R., W. R. Hammond. 1998. Breaking the cycle: A culturally sensitive violence prevention program for African-American children and adolescents. In

References

J. R. Lutzker, ed., *Handbook of Child Abuse Research and Treatment*, pp. 319–340. New York: Plenum.

Zastrow, C. 1993. *Social Work with Groups*. 3rd ed. Chicago: Nelson-Hall.

Zeldin, S. (2004). Preventing youth violence through the promotion of community engagement and membership. *Journal of Community Psychology 32*: 623-641.

Zimbardo, P. and E. Ebbeson. 1970. *Influencing Attitudes and Changing Behavior*. Reading, Mass.: Addison-Wesley.

Index

Abbey, A., 26
ABC News Magazine, 192
abortion, 130
abuse, 98, 100, 101, 102, 134, 173, 235, 247;
  child, 37, 187, 246; dating,
  68; definitions of, 101; emotional, 53,
  101; familial, 248; of high school girls,
  234; "non-touching," 122; physical, 53;
  psychological, 200;
  reporting of, 246; sexual, 37, 63,
  153, 187; socialization of, 106; stories
  of, 239. *See also* domestic violence;
  mandated reporting, after disclosure;
  survivors; victims; violence
access: to adolescents and youths, 39,
  46, 249; to resources, 20, 33, 274; to
  schools, 39–43, 59, 267–68
Ackard, D. M., D. Neumark-Sztainer, and
  P. Hannan, 136
Acosta, O. M., et al., 7
adjudicated adolescents, 52, 200
adolescent development, 7, 17, 69, 113, 161,
  214, 230
advertising: analysis of, 93; campaigns,
  190–91, 194; of programs, 168
advisory boards, youth, 133, 143, 160–62, 171
African Americans, 166, 185; adolescent
  male, 19, 52, 200; girls, 209; in high

school, 132; incest and, 132; as interviewees, 14; in middle school, 130, 131;
  as parents, 132; as peer educators, 167;
  as prevention educators, 215, 216, 217,
  218, 219; in prevention programs, 18,
  80, 215, 218; role models for, 131–32, 218;
  victimization rates of, 131; in videos,
  81, 131
age: of consent, 108, 109; of interviewees,
  13; of prevention educators, 221–22; of
  prevention program participants, 61,
  68–70, 196
aggression, 105; adolescents' view of, 98;
  bidirectional, 119; in families, 17; partner,
  196; prevention of, 33. *See also* violence
AIDS and HIV, 124, 140
Ajzen, I., and T. J. Madden, 209
Alabama, programs in, 277
alcohol, 64, 159; alcoholism and, 137; prevention, 111; sexual assault and, 26, 121, 179.
  See also substance abuse
Anderson, L. A., and S. C. Whiston, 32, 62,
  64, 76, 152, 206
anecdotal evidence of program evaluation,
  203–4, 276
Aronoff, J., L. J. Hickman, and L. H. Jaycox,
  246
assembly presentations, 56, 70, 71, 72, 73

References

Index